P9-CIV-286

FUTURE
PERFECT

How *Star Trek* Conquered Planet Earth

JEFF GREENWALD

PENGUIN BOOKS

PENGUIN BOOKS

Published by the Penguin Group
Penguin Putnam Inc., 375 Hudson Street,
New York, New York 10014, U.S.A.
Penguin Books Ltd, 27 Wrights Lane,
London W8 5TZ, England
Penguin Books Australia Ltd, Ringwood,
Victoria, Australia
Penguin Books Canada Ltd, 10 Alcorn Avenue,
Toronto, Ontario, Canada M4V 3B2
Penguin Books (N.Z.) Ltd, 182–190 Wairau Road,
Auckland 10, New Zealand

Penguin Books Ltd, Registered Offices:
Harmondsworth, Middlesex, England

First published in the United States of America by Viking Penguin,
a member of Penguin Putnam Inc. 1998
Published in Penguin Books 1999

1   3   5   7   9   10   8   6   4   2

Copyright © Jeff Greenwald, 1998
All rights reserved

This book was not prepared, approved, licensed, or endorsed by any entity
involved in the creating or producing of the *Star Trek* television series or films.

Pages 265–266 constitutes an extension of this copyright page.

CIP data available
ISBN 0 14 02.7798 6

Printed in the United States of America
Set in Minion
Designed by Jessica Shatan

Except in the United States of America, this book is sold subject
to the condition that it shall not, by way of trade or otherwise, be lent,
re-sold, hired out, or otherwise circulated without the publisher's prior
consent in any form of binding or cover other than that in which it
is published and without a similar condition including this
condition being imposed on the subsequent purchaser.

PENGUIN BOOKS

FUTURE PERFECT

Jeff Greenwald is the author of three previous books, including *The Size of the World* and *Shopping for Buddhas*. His travel and science articles appear in *Wired, Discover,* and a variety of print and online magazines. A resident of Oakland, he divides his time between California and Kathmandu.

For
Celia Lesh
and Jack Betterly-Kohn

"Perhaps I am not the one to make a prediction, Sungo,
but I think the noble will have its turn in the world."
—Saul Bellow, *Henderson the Rain King*

CONTENTS

FUTURE PERFECT

"THIS MEANS SOMETHING!"

Several years ago, during an interview with science fiction writer and futurist Arthur C. Clarke at his home in Sri Lanka, I'd asked if there was anything about the present age that he could never have predicted, say, four decades ago.

Clarke rocked back in his chair. "I was sure we'd go into space," he replied thoughtfully. "Sure we'd go to the Moon and planets. But I didn't think I'd live to see it. *Or live to see it finished!* That's one thing I never would have dreamed of: that we would go to the Moon, and abandon it after five years!"

Clarke's comment struck me like a blow. I hadn't realized, until that moment, how deeply I shared his disappointment. Back in the mid-sixties—when Ed White made the first space walk and Clarke was completing the screenplay for *2001: A Space Odyssey* at the Chelsea Hotel—the United States was poised on a springboard to the stars. The most powerful spaceship on Earth was being assembled at Cape Kennedy, while the delicate choreography of our planned lunar landing was splashed across foldout pages in *Life* magazine.

I remember those days vividly. Just into my teens, I followed every mission with breathless anticipation. For myself and millions of others, America's blossoming space program was spiritual adrenaline: a first step toward the fulfillment of a thrilling destiny. The colonization of the

Moon no longer seemed impossible, but inevitable. In thirty years—forty at most—I could reasonably expect to hop around on Mars.

⸻

After I'd written the first few chapters of this book, I gave them to a friend to read. She returned them to me a few days later and made her pronouncement. "This book," she declared, "is about *longing.*"

Longing? "No way," I replied testily. "It's about the global appeal of *Star Trek,* and the human drive to explore the unknown. It's about the making of *First Contact,* and the team of people who put *Star Trek* together. Most of all," I argued, "it's about a generation that grew up believing in humanity's destiny in outer space, and our . . . uh . . ."

"Yes?"

". . . our, um, *desire* to get back out there."

She offered a superior smile.

Longing, I've since discovered, is a common thread in many of the interviews and encounters described in this book. It shouldn't have surprised me; it's what I feel every time I watch the space shuttle lift off, or see footage of space walks in orbit. I grew up wanting more than anything else to be part of that adventure. Nothing could be more fantastic than to see Earth in perspective—as an iridescent blue ball, lost in the vastness of space—or to press the sole of my hiking boots onto the surface of an unexplored world. "My life's goal," I often tell my friends, "is to ride in the space shuttle. Then I'll be ready to give Jack Kevorkian a call."

When I began this book, I naively imagined that everyone I spoke to would echo my own intuition: that *Star Trek* has become successful because it awakens a collective human yearning to get out into space and explore the "final frontier" in earnest. A number of people on my list did indeed feel this way—but they were in the minority. *Star Trek,* I learned, inspires longings of many kinds. It's a mirror that people tune like a radio, focusing on the aspects that attract them most.

Star Trek invokes an almost primal wanderlust—a hardwired compulsion to break away from the familiar, and plumb the depths of outer and inner space. It inspires a desire to build a society where technology is partnered with conscience. It evokes a yearning for family and friendship, which is played out in a thousand different fan clubs and Web sites around the world. And it fulfills a deep and eternal need for something to believe in: something vast and powerful, yet rational and contemporary. Something that makes *sense.*

But unlike organized religion or spiritual cults, the *Star Trek* fold does not demand blind faith, poverty, or even simplicity. The show dares to imagine a human future both materialistic *and* evolved. It's an attractive idea. Our love of toys is not going to disappear—not as long as we have opposable thumbs—but our relationship to our toys may change dramatically. Take the *Enterprise* itself, a faster-than-light starship representing the zenith of twenty-fourth-century technology. Built by the United Federation of Planets, it is owned by Starfleet yet in service to all. Its mandate is to expand the collective wisdom, keep the peace, and provide compassionate aid to all who need it; qualities which, by the lights of Buddhism (probably the most rational of all religions), are the practices of an enlightened—and *sensible*—soul.

My very first writing assignment (for my college newspaper, in 1972) was the launch of *Apollo 17*, last of the Moon shots. I was eighteen at the time—a sheltered, nerdy kind of guy—and that mind-blowing visit to the Cape Kennedy launchpads sparked a wanderlust that has not abated since. During the past twenty-five years, my assignments have gotten ever more far-flung and exotic. But Hollywood is as bizarre a destination as any. *Star Trek*'s soundstages may be just an hour's flight from Oakland—but they're as romantic as Khmer temples, and as frantic as the souks of Fez.

I won't lie to you—I'm a fan of the show. Not a rabid fan, never one to call myself a "Trekker" or squeeze my gut into a spandex uniform, but a fan nonetheless. I've watched *Star Trek* on and off for the past thirty-two years. This doesn't make me an expert; just about anyone at a *Star Trek* convention can destroy me at trivia. There are episodes of all four series that I still haven't seen. I may *never* see them. To be frank, I'm astonished by the show's global popularity. If someone had told me in 1966 (the year before my Bar Mitzvah) that this Western-in-tights would eventually be shown in over one hundred countries, with followers from La Crosse to Lahore, I'd have backed away from them real slow.

Star Trek is often called a phenomenon, but the nature of that phenomenon is ill-defined. Like everyone else, I've got my own theories. One of them is this: The saga endures because it is the first great story cycle to celebrate our own epoch, "the neosilicate age." Created in real time, broadcast week after week to a worldwide audience, it is the nearest we have to a new global mythology.

Which means exactly what? Well, a myth is defined as "a traditional story of ostensibly historical events that serves to unfold part of a worldview of a people or a practice, belief, or natural phenomenon." (This mealy mouthful is from *Merriam-Webster's Encyclopedia of Literature*.) Myths describe spectacular deeds performed by gods or superhuman beings; actions that are beyond the ken of ordinary human life, yet central to it. "These extraordinary events," our source concludes, "are set in a time altogether different from historical time."

When I talk about *Star Trek* as a contemporary myth, a global myth, I realize that it doesn't strictly fit the definition above. After more than three decades, one might quietly call Gene Roddenberry's portrayal of the future "traditional"; but there's no getting around the fact that we're talking about human beings here. Captains James T. Kirk, Jean-Luc Picard, Benjamin Sisko, and Kathryn Janeway are neither superhuman nor godlike. They're our great-great-grandchildren, with far better health-care plans.

But there are other, stronger parallels to traditional myth. *Star Trek*, we'll discover, definitely unfolds a worldview: a vision of the future that took root during the can-do years of the Kennedy administration and the cold war. Its setting is light-years removed from ordinary human life, yet is an unavoidable reflection of it. Timewise, the era in which the show's adventures take place is as distant from our own as Shakespearean England.

And extraordinary deeds are the very foundation of *Star Trek*'s story line. A home planet that is truly a global village; a captain and crew assigned to "boldly go where no one has gone before"; and the ability to create starships like the *Enterprise*, a magnificent vehicle that rivals the celestial chariots of the great Hindu epics.

Most important for any global myth, *Star Trek* is absolutely inclusive. The show's heroes may be archetypes, but the attributes they share —confidence, intelligence, and compassion—are implicitly granted to us all. There is no one, of any age, creed, or class, who is denied a part. Ireland, Zanzibar, and Guinea Bissau; Muslims, Taoists, and Jews— nations and religions no longer exist, at least as divisive entities. In a cosmos teeming with inhabited worlds, we are united in the only way that makes sense: as citizens of Earth.

It is a vision so compelling that *Star Trek* is watched, season after season, by members of nearly every race, religion, and nationality in the world. The exploits of Kirk and Picard are at least as famous as the labors of Hercules; Mr. Spock and Mr. Data are familiar to millions of people who have never heard of the Australian Aborigine Yingarna or of Gucumatz of the *Popol Vuh*. The *Enterprise* itself may be the most famous vehicle ever created—how many Americans can as easily identify the *Eagle*, the *Beagle*, or the *Enola Gay*?

My second theory about the show's global appeal is deceptively simple. *Star Trek* has entered popular culture at a crucial juncture, a time when our relationship to science and technology can take any number of paths. Societies everywhere are developing a casual acceptance of the tools and pace of scientific progress. We don't hear so much about the dehumanizing effects of technology these days. To the contrary, tools like satellite television and the Internet are broadening our sphere of social contact (even if the Web isn't an ideal social environment). Our biggest worry, perhaps, is that science is *homogenizing* the world; that it's answering too many questions and parking in the spaces reserved for mystery and nobility. Science and technology are losing their ability to dazzle us. If we are destined to exist within a wired world, we need to reclaim that sense of awe.

"Any sufficiently advanced technology," Arthur Clarke once commented, "will be indistinguishable from magic." *Star Trek* is a place where science and magic meet: in the Parisian nightclubs of the holodeck, on the glowing pads of the transporter room, in the casual ability to hurl the *Enterprise* through a streaking corridor of stars.

But if previous myths have taught us one thing, it's that magic without conscience can be deadly. Dazzling as 24th-century science may be, the deeper message of the series is that we've learned how to control it. Here, again, is a longing: We long for the day when our rush toward progress is tempered with wisdom, and informed by a sense of universal responsibility.

There is both magic and honor in the *Star Trek* world. The protagonists of Roddenberry's universe have found their Grail. Like the Arthurian knights, they have earned their earthly paradise through courage, perseverance, and an unwavering loyalty to the highest ideals.

Yet, even these explanations do not completely satisfy. There is something more, some ineffable quality shared by all great epics and mythologies. What do Italians and Hungarians see in this American-made fantasy? Why do people study the Klingon language? Why have the Japanese embraced these ships and these captains? Is it because *Star Trek* is simply, as Michael (Worf) Dorn insists, "good television"?

Is it because the show provides entertaining role models for living with nobility in our accelerated age? Or did Gene Roddenberry tap into something deeper still, smacking his chisel into some vast strata of the collective unconscious?

My own opinion: all of the above. Time after time, witnessing the hold that this singular vision has on its fans, I've recalled the crazed character played by Richard Dreyfuss in *Close Encounters of the Third Kind.* As his wife and children flee in alarm, the obsessed Dreyfuss fills his suburban living room with dirt and mud, sculpting a butte-topped mountain. He has no idea that it is a replica of Devil's Tower—the precise spot where an alien spaceship is preparing to land.

Longing for something he can neither understand nor express, Dreyfuss continues his mad enterprise. His eyes are wide, his energy boundless. He has lost his wife, his children, even his job. The only thing left is his utter conviction: *"This means something!"*

During the past few years I have tracked *Star Trek* across two oceans, tracing its warp signature from the pubs of London to the *sentos* of Japan. I've interviewed its actors and producers and discussed its import with Kurt Vonnegut in New York, His Holiness the Dalai Lama in India, and Arthur C. Clarke. I have gulped bloodwine at a Klingon wedding in Germany, seen the captain of *Voyager* with her hair down, and paid homage to Leonard Nimoy's ears. I have journeyed far and wide through this fictitious universe, following some mysterious longing of my own.

I can now tell you, with absolute certainty, that *Star Trek* means something. In a few centuries, we might all agree on what.

MASTERS OF THE UNIVERSE

Outside the window, global warming bakes the L.A. asphalt into a sneaker-sucking stew. The air smells of burgers and exhaust. Airplanes are exploding, the ozone layer is disappearing, and drivers settle their differences with handguns and machetes. Humanity, in short, is in serious trouble.

In room 406 of Paramount's Hart Building, however, an ideal world is in the making. The blinds are drawn, and the air conditioner churns like a fetal heartbeat. Within this hermetic oasis, surrounded by spiked fences, security guards, and a moat of soundstages, Brannon Braga and Ron Moore—the writer-producers of *Star Trek: Voyager* and *Deep Space Nine*—labor like midwives over their script for the new *Star Trek* film.

We're in Moore's office. Pictures of the Captain and the King (i.e. James T. Kirk and Elvis) line the walls, interspersed with bits of Klingon, Romulan, and Federation chic. Braga is hunched over Moore's terminal, the *First Contact* screenplay reflected in his glasses. His fingers hover above the keys. Moore paces the carpet slowly, with the script in his hands. Unlike Braga—who seems as if he might spontaneously combust at any moment—Moore appears dead calm.

It is mid-April, seven months before *First Contact*'s scheduled release. Location shooting has already started, high in the hills east of Los Angeles. But some last-minute tweaks to the screenplay—from

Patrick Stewart, director Jonathan Frakes, *Star Trek* executive producer Rick Berman, and the Paramount brass—are needed. Brannon and Ron have agreed to let me sit in on this final script meeting, as long as I remain "unobtrusive."

The Hart Building is a blockish, four-story structure on the southwest corner of the Paramount lot. Anonymous and beige, it's about as 20th-century as a building can be. Nonetheless, it has been the *Star Trek* nerve center for at least ten years. It was here, in March 1995, that Rick Berman (whose posh offices are across the alley in the Cooper Building) approached Brannon Braga and Ron Moore with an offer to co-author the eighth *Star Trek* movie.

Braga and Moore hammered out the basic story line during a month of two-hour lunches, then started working knee-to-knee on the screenplay. They had a first draft eight months later. Today—after another half year of rewrites and revisions—they're just an hour or two away from locking the script.

The *First Contact* story, if you haven't seen the movie, goes roughly like this:

It's April 2063, a few years after World War III. Humanity has descended into a dark age. Amid the ramshackle huts of a Montana refuge, a drunken and abrasive rocket scientist named Zefram Cochrane (James Cromwell) has developed "warp drive": the key to interstellar travel. Cochrane and his assistant Lily (Alfre Woodard) are preparing to test the *Phoenix*, the first warp-powered rocket. The flight will have earthshaking consequences: a ship of aliens passing through our solar system on a survey mission will observe the rocket's warp signature and drop by to visit, providing humanity's "first contact" with extraterrestrials (I guess they didn't count the Martian bacterium).

Enter the Borg: a powerful and ruthless race of skinhead alien drones. Half human, half machine, the Borg dwell in a vast, cubic hive that bears an uncanny resemblance to the Georges Pompidou Center. Resistance to the Borg is futile; they "assimilate" their victims in a messy and invasive cyber-ritual.

Bent on destroying Cochrane's rocket before it can change history, the Borg time travel back to 21st-century Earth. Their mission: prevent first contact and turn Earth's citizens into cyborg slaves. When the *Enterprise* attempts to stop them, the Borg and their queen (Alice Krige) commandeer the starship. It's an ugly business, further complicated by the fact that Captain Jean-Luc Picard (Patrick Stewart) has some unhappy history with these creatures. Having once been captured and assimilated himself (in a two-part *Star Trek: The Next Generation* episode called "The Best of Both Worlds"), he despises the Borg with an Ahab-like fervor.

"I think both Ron and Rick Berman would agree," says Braga, "that *First Contact* is definitely the most 'adult' of the *Star Trek* movies. It's also the most violent—and certainly the most sexual. There's one scene in particular, where the Borg Queen basically gives Data a blow job . . ."

Before I morph into a fly on the wall, I have a quick question for the wunderkind. Quite simply, how do they do it? Between them, I count two brains, two mouths, and two writer-sized egos. How do they churn out a 131-page script without coming to blows?

"We're close enough friends that we're not afraid to tell each other when something doesn't work." Animated and impish, Braga looks like Quentin Tarantino—minus the Dudley Do-Right jaw. "As a result, we're very fast. We don't fight about shit. If we ever come close to arguing it's because Ron tends to resist changes, whereas my instinct is to change everything."

"Brannon's into hard, darker stuff," adds Moore. "He's very strong at bringing in a weird idea that I never would have thought of, a different approach to a scene. I'm good at taking that and guiding it into the narrative. I can't really say that one of us is stronger at dialogue than the other, or that one of us knows the characters better; we just bring different instincts to the table."

"On a story this complex, you can't split it up." Brannon's hand snakes into a bag of Milano cookies. "I have weirder, more sci-fi sensibilities, very action-oriented. Certainly there's some perversion in the film, some dark eroticism, that has me written all over it."

Offhanded answers, maybe, but if there's a deeper secret to their alchemy they're keeping it to themselves. I perch my microphone on Ron's desk, between a hand phaser and a Klingon Attack Cruiser. Moore flips through his copy of the script—a rainbow collage of color-coded pages—and finds the first Post-it note.

It's stuck to Scene 243. Lily, a techno-scrap scavenger from a ravaged encampment in 21st-century Montana, finds herself transported aboard the *Enterprise*. Confused and frightened, she bolts down one of the starship's corridors and runs smack into Captain Picard. He drops his phaser—and Lily snatches it up.

Braga winces. "This is the section where I didn't take any fucking notes . . ."

Moore nods patiently. "Lily wants to get back home, to Montana, and Picard has to tell her that they're in a spaceship. They stop in front of a wall panel, a control panel, and he tries to make her understand."

Brannon rotates his shoulder blades, and a rapid exchange ensues:

BB: *This will be hard for you to grasp . . .*

RM: *but you're not on Earth anymore. You're in a spaceship. Orbiting at an altitude of 250 kilometers.* Do we need to say "altitude"?

BB: I like "altitude." It has that airplane feeling that people can relate to.

RM: So now she needs a really deprecating line. She's got to say, *Stop fucking with me,* basically.

BB: She's got to give him an ultimatum.

RM: She's got the phaser; maybe she lifts it and points it at his face. *I think I'll press the red one.*

BB: She looks at him a long moment, then calmly raises the phaser a little higher and points it directly at his face. She says, *I think I'll press the red one.*

RM: Picard then realizes he has no choice but to shock her into accepting what he's saying: *All right. You want the way out? Here it is.* He hits a button on the wall panel; The air lock opens.

BB: Lily gasps, *What is this?* and Picard says, *That's Australia, New Guinea, and the Solomons. Montana should be coming into view in a few minutes. But you may want to hold your breath; it's a long drop.*

They ham up the dialogue, sounding out each line before committing it to paper. They relate like brothers—both are in their early thirties—but their chemistry is completely noncompetitive. They *listen* to each other; there's no sibling shakedown at all. Everything drives the story or develops the characters. It's industrial writing, free from ego or attachment. They know their job: keep the dialogue sharp and see that the action never lets up.

BB: Okay. So Lily's with Picard. She's looking around in wonder at this fucking big-ass ship. She could ask something about the engines . . .

RM: The natural thing would be the size.

BB: Yeah. She could ask how big it is: *How big is this, uh, spaceship of yours?*

Braga spins in his chair, picks up the phone, and calls Karen, his secretary. "Hey, babe. Could you do me a favor right away? Get [technical adviser] Mike Okuda, and ask him how big this goddamned ship is. The new *Enterprise*, the 1701-E. If he's not in his office, try him at home. Get back to me with a few different measurements: length, size . . . Thanks."

First Contact, Moore tells me while they wait for tech support, will trot out the sixth incarnation of the *Enterprise*. He and Brannon destroyed the last one—NCC-1701-D—in *Star Trek: Generations*, running it aground in a crash landing that one critic described as "the noisiest scene in all of cinema." They also bumped off Kirk, a ploy that sparked an endless stream of furious letters, insults, and death threats. Braga woke up one morning to find his house wrapped in toilet paper; Moore got repeated calls from a guy who would whisper, "Ron Moore: You know what you did. And now I'm going to come blow your fucking head off." It's an occupational hazard; both guys change their phone numbers routinely.

Moore turns to Brannon. "We've got to ask what the fans want to know: How big is it, how many people does it hold . . ."

Braga nods. "She could ask, '*How many people can it hold?*" And Picard says, '*Five hundred*,' or whatever . . ." The telephone rings. Brannon snatches the receiver. "Karen?" He listens for a second and turns incredulously to Moore. "Okuda doesn't know."

"What!?"

Braga's face prunes with irritation. "How the *fuck*," he barks into the phone, "could Okuda not know?"

"He *has* to know," insists Moore. "Call him again."

Braga pushes another button and awaits a response. There's a charged, giddy atmosphere in the room. "Hi, Denise. Brannon. Is your illustrious husband around?" A beat. "Mike, Brannon. Hi, how are you? What do you mean you don't know how big the fucking new *Enterprise* is?" Another pause. He motions quickly to Moore for a pencil. "Tell me

U.S.S. *ENTERPRISE*

(sung to the tune of "American Pie")

A long, long time ago
I can still remember how that starship
   used to make me smile
And I knew if I had my way
That I could make those people stay
And maybe we'd be happy for a while

But Paramount filled me with woe
They canceled my favorite TV show
Bad news on the *Enterprise*
Jean-Luc said his last "Energize"

I can't remember if I cried when I
Read about their final ride
But something touched me deep inside
The day that *Star Trek* died. So . . .

Bye, bye U.S.S. *Enterprise*
Our starship was a great ship, but it no
   longer flies
And that starship crew was drinking
   synthetic rye
Singing "This will be the day that I die,
This will be the day that I die . . ."

[Numerous versions of this parody have cropped up on Internet. The version used here seems to be by one John Martz, whose home page was unavailable when we tried to contact him.   —JG]

again? Twenty-four decks. Twenty-six hundred feet. Okay. Well . . . how many meters is that? How do they measure stuff in the future? Someone asks Captain Picard, *'How big is your ship?'* So what does he say—*'Mighty big'*?"

" *'Mighty big,'* " Moore chuckles slyly, parroting Patrick Stewart's smooth Shakespearean elocution. " *'I'm glad you asked.'* "

" *'How big is it?'* " Braga joins in with glee. He clamps his hand over the receiver, mimicking Britspeak as well. " *'Counting the foreskin?'* "

Listening to this, it's hard to believe that these guys have the weight of the cosmos on their shoulders. Yet it's true. When *First Contact* hits the theaters, millions of obsessive Trekkers—from Bangkok to the Bronx—will scrutinize the story taking shape in this office today. Online chat rooms will analyze each scene; glossy fanzines in the United States, Europe, and Japan will dissect every character. At *Star Trek* conventions, now held in nearly every world capital, Braga and Moore will be celebrated, scoffed at, or burned in effigy. Everything from Academy Award nominations to death threats will come their way.

Blockbuster or turkey, *First Contact* will enter the *Star Trek* canon—and they'll have to answer for it the rest of their lives.

The reason for this, of course, is that *Star Trek* is more than the century's most enduring television show. It's a global empire, a prime example of what people mean when they talk about American culture taking over the world. The *Enterprise* warps into light speed in Berlin, Tehran, and Tel Aviv. Indians in New Delhi cafés know what "Beam me up, Scotty!"

means, and pedestrians in Belfast shout "Red Alert!" when British troops grind down the streets. From *The Weekly World News* to Salman Rushdie, from textbooks on theoretical physics to reports of the Heaven's Gate suicides, you can't open a newspaper or magazine without tripping over some reference to the show, its lingo, its credo.

No media fantasy of the '60s—except maybe James Bond—has weathered as well as *Star Trek*. Created in 1965 by a former airline pilot and motorcycle cop named Gene Roddenberry, the show and its spin-offs cling to a wildly optimistic view of humanity's future. Poverty has been eradicated, racism is dead, and nobody breathes secondhand smoke. Money no longer exists, and Earthlings don't squabble or bicker; even organized religion is a thing of the past. Starfleet officers—the best and the brightest—comb the cosmos with a smile and a shoeshine, seeking out "new life and new civilizations."

> ## To Boldly Go—Away
>
> JENNIFER WEBER
> *Sacramento Bee*, March 15, 1996
>
> Oh, boy. An alternate juror who wore a "Star Trek" uniform to the Whitewater trial every day was beamed off the panel Thursday for talking to the media. U.S. District Judge George Howard, Jr. removed Barbara Adams for giving a TV interview about the maroon-and-black costume complete with phaser, tricorder and communicator badge.
>
> In the interview Wednesday with "American Journal," Adams, a 31-year-old print shop supervisor, said she is a devotee of the series because it is an alternative to "mindless television" and promotes inclusion, tolerance, peace, and faith in mankind.
>
> She wore the Starfleet uniform on Thursday for the ninth time in nine court sessions. The judge never had admonished her for her wardrobe.

Roddenberry's blend of Ben Cartwright morality and Flash Gordon physics (a mix that Trekkers and staff alike revere as "Gene's Vision") has turned out to be the most robust formula in television history. Some sixty-three million *Star Trek* books are in print, translated into more than fifteen languages. Thirteen of these books are sold every *minute* in the United States alone. A mint condition 1968 lunch box, featuring the *Enterprise* on one side and Kirk and Spock on the other, will fetch more than a thousand dollars at auction. The television show itself is syndicated to 108 countries, while *Star Trek* movies have grossed around a billion dollars in theater receipts, overseas rights, and video rentals.

Was Roddenberry a genius? Lots of people think so. But the word *genius* has a hollow ring in Hollywood, a town that owes more to Machiavelli than Einstein. Roddenberry, basically, was a survivor. The original *Star Trek* series, known by fans as TOS, was a flop the first time

WHEN STAR TREK GOES GLOBAL

- In Hong Kong, *The Next Generation* is called *Space Adventures*, and airs on the English-language station.

- In Israel, the series is titled *Masa beyn haKokhavim, haDor haBa*, which literally translates to "Trek among the stars, the generation the next."

- In Lebanon the show is called *alrhlt byn alkwakb aljyl alqadm*. It is broadcast on Middle East Television (METV) in English with Arabic subtitles.

- In Mexico and Puerto Rico, *The Next Generation* is known as *Viaje a las Estrellas: La Nueva Generacion.*

- Iranians know *Star Trek* as *Persh taxan e' faza* (Space, the final frontier).

- The original *Star Trek* has not aired in Quebec since 1985, when it was called *Le Patrouille du Cosmos* (Cosmos patrol)

around—thanks as much to studio politics as to anything else—and was axed by NBC in 1969, within weeks of Neil Armstrong's stroll on the Moon.

That odd bit of timing may hold a clue as to why TOS withered. In the late 1960s, after all, we had the real thing: from those awesome Saturn rockets to ESP experiments on the Moon. But the Apollo project ended in 1972, and America's manned space program was put on hold. This was when *Star Trek* really took off. Reruns of the show became immensely popular, and the first four feature films were produced. NASA, it seems, had fumbled—and Gene's vision ran with the ball.

In spring 1981, America's long-delayed space shuttle program finally began. Granted, trips into Earth's orbit aren't quite as riveting as expeditions to the Moon. But NASA planned to sweeten the pot by sending ordinary people—starting with a popular schoolteacher—into space. Journalists would come next. And after them . . . who knew? Here, once again, was an opportunity for reality to vie with fantasy.

But that era, and all it promised, was stillborn. It ended on January 28, 1986, when *Challenger* wrote its obituary across the Florida sky.

One year later, *Star Trek: The Next Generation*—with its sexy new ship, enlightened crew, and Congress-proof mission—stepped in as America's surrogate manned space program.

There's been no stopping it since. There have now been a total of twenty *Star Trek* seasons: three with Kirk and Spock, seven featuring *The Next Generation* crew, six aboard *Deep Space Nine* (DS9), and another four on the starship *Voyager**. This unflagging output is generated by a crack team of writers and producers, toiling under the able

---

* The animated *Star Trek* series, a morning cartoon which aired from 1973 to 1975, adds another twenty-two episodes to the mix.

hand of Rick Berman (who took the reins when Roddenberry died in 1991). A vast amount of the inspiration and grunt work, though, comes from Braga and Moore, both of whom were in diapers when Kirk fired his first phaser.

Braga, born in 1965, grew up under a cloud of pot smoke near L.A.'s Venice canals. He's the dark prince of *Star Trek*, a feverish workaholic as notorious for his sexual escapades as his macabre story lines. Moore, a year older, is the son of a former marine combat officer. He kicks back by taking his wife to Disneyland and devouring books on military history.

Braga always wanted to work in Hollywood. Though he never saw an episode of TOS until 1993, he's been writing sci-fi and horror since he was a kid. Moore, a *Star Trek* fan from the day he could reach the television dials, never dreamed he'd end up in showbiz. Had he fulfilled his adolescent wish—to become a Navy pilot—he and Braga would never have met. But fate conspired to beam them both into Roddenberry's universe where, together and individually, they've penned scores of *Star Trek* episodes—as well as the movie *Star Trek: Generations.* They've shared two Hugo Awards (one for "All Good Things . . . ," the *Next Generation* finale) and an Emmy nomination for Best Dramatic Series.

Do they make a lot of money? You bet they do. Are they worth it? They'd better be; the fate of the galaxy rests in their hands.

RM: Here's the next problem. We've lost all our references to the fact that Lily's a scrounger; that she steals things, gets things for Cochrane. We're trying to work in a line that will imply that. So we need something like,

How much copper is in the ship?

Oh, there's fifty thousand metric tons.

Wow, it's taken me three months just to get two pounds of copper . . .

BB: What do the *Enterprise*'s engines use? Antimatter.

RM: I don't think the *Phoenix* uses antimatter.

BB: (Puzzled) Then how do they go to warp speed?

RM: Well, we've implied that they're using a nuclear warhead in some way. We've been careful not to say *how*, because we haven't a fucking clue. No, it has to be something else. Something she's had trouble finding on Earth. What would be *really* scarce after the Third World War?

BB: Everything.

At half past six the script is locked. An assistant producer runs in, snaps up the newly revised pages and races them over to Berman's office. That's it: the screenplay is done. Any future changes will be made on the sets themselves, or in the editing room.

I watch the writers for signs of elation, but the closing moments of their fifteen-month collaboration are subdued. Braga slumps in his chair, staring vacantly at the screen saver. Finally he stands up, yawns loudly, and stretches toward the ceiling. Moore walks over to where I'm sitting, hefts the hand phaser from his desk—an awkward new design that they'll be using in *First Contact*—and aims it at Braga's crotch.

"Do you like this phaser?"

"No. It looks like a fucking Dustbuster."

"They should look like *guns*," Moore agrees.

Braga stoops over the desk, muttering under his breath, "That was Gene's Vision . . ."

Moore sets the weapon down. "Roddenberry," he pronounces. There's genuine reverence in his voice. "That guy sat down with a piece of paper, and created something that's going to outlast us all."

A DECENT HAIRCUT

Half an hour's drive northwest of Paramount's Hart Building, on the tightly guarded campus of the Jet Propulsion Laboratory (JPL), a very different space opera is being scripted. The deadlines are just as inflexible, the pressure equally intense, and the energy level of the players every bit as amped. But the cost of this production is somewhat higher—and a hell of a lot more is at stake.

Six days after *First Contact*'s premiere—on Thanksgiving Day 1996—a Delta II rocket will launch the *Mars Pathfinder* on a seven-month journey to the Red Planet. By the time you read this, *Pathfinder* will have accomplished what no other spacecraft had done since 1976: alighted on the surface of another world, and radioed back live images of an alien landscape.

A model of the *Mars Sojourner* at JPL.

Probes like *Pathfinder*, boldly going where no transistor has gone before, are about as close as we come these days to the *Enterprise*. Each mission evokes great distances and the suspense of confronting the unknown. Every landing has the potential for mind-blowing discoveries. And while such missions may lack the breathless panache of a manned mission, there's something wonderfully *expansive* about them. With no human proxy to influence our perceptions, the lander's eyes and ears (i.e., its cameras and sensors) become extensions of our own.

Mars Pathfinder, like most of NASA's planetary missions, is managed by JPL. The laboratory (whose checks are signed by the California Institute of Technology) consists of a few dozen institutional-looking buildings, arranged on a tree-lined mall just a few miles west of Pasadena.

Aside from a few weathered spacecraft models and a fenced-in, tennis court–sized "Mars Yard" (a rocky sandbox used to test-drive the *Sojourner*), there's no indication that the people inside this compound are doing anything the least bit otherworldly—much less designing vehicles that will roam the Martian terrain, explore the moons of Saturn, or travel five billion miles to reach Pluto. They could just as easily be auditing your tax returns, or developing a radically new form of cat litter.

A couple of days before my visit to JPL, I went to a salon and had most of my hair chopped off.

It was just one of those things. I wanted to fit in, to be one of the guys. My head was filled with images of crew cut nerds wearing horn-rimmed glasses and white shirts with pen holders, standing around big computers. You know the scene: "Mission Control." It's funny how our memory clings to these clichés. Never mind that I was fifteen during those first Moon landings, or that Nixon was still president. I somehow maintained the idea that NASA's little corner of the universe had remained frozen in time, like a Pennsylvania Dutch village where tourists ride hay carts driven by guys in stovepipe hats.

Luckily, it's a decent haircut. Because the people I actually meet at JPL—the project managers and engineers who are designing our upcoming flights to the Moon, Mars, and other planets—are very cool neogeeks in their twenties and thirties. They ride mountain bikes to work, listen to Blues Traveler, and play hackey-sack during their lunch breaks. They wear T-shirts and jeans, and there's not a buzz cut among them.

Best of all, an amazing number of JPL's employees are die-hard *Star Trek* fans. Some know the show backward and forward, and unabashedly credit the series with launching their own careers in space exploration.

It makes perfect sense that Gene's Vision has been embraced by the vast population of Baby Boomers and Gen-Xers who make their livings in aerospace and computer technology. In the 1950s and '60s, such jobs were the antithesis of cool; they were bedfellows of the defense industry and often shrouded in secrecy. Even space exploration—first popularized by Disney's *Man in Space* television show*—was dominated by the military. NASA itself was a civilian organization, but becoming an astronaut meant years of Air Force or Navy training—and who among us yearned to join the ranks of slide rule–toting engineers, laboring behind the scenes? There was another obstacle as well. For the socially conscious, America's space-faring achievements were tempered by daily exposure to technology's other face: the war in Vietnam.

During the fourteen-year period between Nixon's resignation (1973) and *Star Trek: The Next Generation* (1987), the demographics of the aerotech industry began to shift. The cold war ended, computers moved into the mainstream, and NASA, ending a long tradition of jet-jockey astronauts, began scheduling scientists and technicians for shuttle flights. Planetary exploration was consigned to satellites and robotic probes, but hacking such missions was more fun than Flight Simulator (and the quarters came to you). A new generation of whiz kid students—weaned on *Star Trek*, David Byrne, and Tetris—moved into territory once dominated by the likes of Dr. Strangelove.

———

My visit to JPL has been organized by Steve Matousek, a player in this new string of aerospace engineers. Matousek—a 33-year-old Mars mission designer—leads me to his office in Building 301. It's a no-nonsense niche dominated by a computer, stacks of printouts, and voluminous texts of fuel-to-weight ratios. There are two maps on his wall: one of the Earth, the other of local mountain bike trails.

"I started watching *Star Trek* before I was in kindergarten," Matousek says, dropping into his swivel chair, "when I was about four.

---

* Inspired by a series of articles that ran in *Collier's* from 1952 to 1954, the shows premiered in March 1955. Hosted by Walt Disney himself, each show featured rocket scientists such as Willey Ley and Werner von Braun extolling the virtues and challenges of space exploration. Combining animation and live-action, they were essentially "infomercials" for another nascent American enterprise: Tomorrowland.

From junior high on, I wanted to be an aerospace engineer. I wanted to be an astronaut, but I also wanted to be an aerospace engineer, because I knew that they were the ones who designed the things that went out into space. That just drove me. Studying in high school, taking the tough classes, I knew I'd have something fun to work on in the end."

Matousek and I had met on the Web, in a chat room about round-the-world travel. Somewhat shy, with a round face and widely spaced eyes, Matousek has been at JPL since 1984. He's worked on half-a-dozen orbital and interplanetary missions, including the *Solar Mesosphere Explorer* (built to study Earth's ozone layer), *Voyager* (the *real* one, during its 1986 and 1989 encounters with Uranus and Neptune) and the nascent *Pluto Express/Europa Orbiter*. He's now steeped in the planning phase of an ambitious mission that will depend upon *Pathfinder*'s success: the Mars Sample Return project. Scheduled for launch in 2004, this robotic spacecraft will land upon the Martian surface, scoop up rocks and soil, and bring them back to Earth.

If there's one thing the JPL engineers and *Star Trek*'s producers have in common, it's the huge gulf between their workaday jobs and the glamorous result. Brannon Braga and Ron Moore pound away at their keyboards, weaving together scenes that will serve as the framework for a fictional universe; Steve Matousek hacks strings of algorithms, creating a series of instructions that will guide a landing craft to Mars. In both cases, the work can be pure drudgery. But the common result will be a drama of cosmic proportions: space-age entertainment devoured by viewers in every part of the world.

What mainly inspires Matousek—and, in his estimation, a good 75 percent of the six thousand men and women working at JPL—is the conviction that NASA's new generation is actually germinating the future that *Star Trek* has seeded in their minds. The mythical epoch of Starfleet and the United Federation of Planets is a kinder, gentler El Dorado: the conceptual carrot, crunchy and golden, that spurs their imagination onward.

"*Star Trek* gives you a way to see ahead; to look into the future. If your mind projects that you can do something, you go do it," Matousek says. "*Star Trek* and the first moon landing were two very important things for me. That whole period of the late 1960s was when everything came together to say, 'Yeah! We can do this!' It proved that our civilization could do things in space—and now we're outdoing 'em."

"If you'd never watched *Star Trek*," I ask Matousek, "do you think you'd have the same kind of life you have now?"

"I can't imagine what my world would be like without it." He scoots his mouse across its mottled pad. "It's a very big influence. People here talk about it all the time. We'll discuss it over lunch, and go see the movies together. Even our engineering teams interact like the characters on the show. You have people who are the thinkers, like Spock, and people who are kind of flashy, like Kirk. When George Takei—Sulu from the original series—visited JPL a couple of years ago, the mall was just packed. So there's definitely a connection there. And it seems to go both ways."

What Roddenberry's vision offers the aerotech industry, really, is redemption. *Star Trek*—along with more ambiguous visions like *2001*, *Contact*, and *Close Encounters of the Third Kind*—belongs to a renegade class of stories that dare suggest that science and technology may sow the seeds of our salvation.

For, despite the evolving attitudes of the post-Nixon years, nearly every sci-fi yarn produced since the 1970s has cast science as the villain. Our machines whip around to bite us, or grab us by the balls. From *Alien* to *Mad Max*, sci-fi writers dine out on our fears of technology run amok. Nuclear weapons (*Planet of the Apes*, *The Day the Earth Caught Fire*, *A Boy and His Dog*), robotics and cloning (*Blade Runner*, *The Terminator*, *Robocop*, *Westworld*, *Jurassic Park*), medical science and the food industry (*A Clockwork Orange*, *Outbreak*, *Soylent Green*), even the James Bond and Batman movies contribute to the image of science as a seductive but all-too-easily corrupted path. All such plots share a simple subtext: Our tools are beyond our intelligence, and the potential for evil in these devices may ultimately destroy us.

Star Trek disagrees. In *First Contact*, even our shit smells sweet. It's the warp-drive signature of Zefram Cochrane's experimental rocket —a future form of space pollution!—that attracts a Vulcan starship's sensors, leading to Earth's initiation into the family of planets. Cochrane's rocket may be named the *Phoenix*, but it's not a metaphor for humanity. Technology itself has risen from the ashes, redeeming the race it had all but consigned to destruction.

It's lunchtime. Steve Matousek and I leave his office. We navigate a maze of cubicles, strolling past photocopied Dilbert cartoons and clipped *Weekly World News* headlines ("Halt All Space Probes or We'll Destroy Your Planet!"). We carry our sandwiches to the shaded patio of the building's second floor, where two paddle-swinging engineers are

Steve Matousek on Mars.

locked in a furious game of Ping-Pong. Matousek greets them, and gives me the rundown.

The tall, lanky guy on the left—the one who's playing defensively—is John Smith. Thirty-six years old, Smith is a mission designer for Cassini: a controversial project to send a plutonium-powered, robotic spacecraft careening around Saturn and its moons. Cassini will then use the gravity of Titan—Saturn's biggest moon—as a slingshot, sending itself on a variety of missions. Smith's job is to listen to what the planetologists want, size it up against Cassini's hardware and the laws of physics, and work out a compromise.

Smith has a deadly serve, but my money's on the other guy. Matousek introduces him as Ralph Roncoli, a fourteen-year veteran of JPL. By my lights, the thirty-seven-year-old Roncoli has the most intriguing job of the bunch: He's a systems architect for NASA's "New Millennium" program. Roncoli explains this in staccato bursts, darting after the slams and slices served up by his long-limbed opponent.

"It's a program," he grunts, "designed to flight-test technologies considered too new or too risky for current science missions. The idea is to help future missions do their jobs better, faster, and cheaper. Our first project is called Deep Space One. It's an asteroid and comet flyby mission. We're testing out about a dozen different technologies that haven't flown before." He slams an ace into Smith's right corner.

"Such as?"

"Such as solar electric propulsion. That's not a chemical rocket. It's a solar-powered electrical engine that shoots out ions at high speed." Smith's serve arrives at a comparable velocity, but Roncoli parries it effortlessly. "This'll be the first time we use solar electricity as a spacecraft's main propulsion system. We're also testing a new navigation system. Instead of receiving instructions from Earth every day—*Ha!*—a spacecraft uses the stars and relative motion of nearby asteroids to steer itself."

Risky business, all right, but Roncoli knows about risks—he was the mission design manager for the *Mars Observer*. A few days before the probe was scheduled to move into orbit around the planet, it disappeared. Years of effort and passion simply blipped off the screen, without so much as a fare-thee-well. To this day, no one has the faintest clue why.

Roncoli doesn't dwell on it. Deep Space One, he informs me, is already out of his lap. He's well into Deep Space Three and Deep Space Four. "Of course," he says, "when we get to Deep Space Nine, it's going to be just like the *Star Trek* show. We won't have a project manager and an engineer—we'll have a captain and first officer." He spies my pen poised above the page. "It's a joke," he adds hastily.

The game has escalated to the final frantic points, so I sit down at a nearby table with Matousek. After Roncoli nails Smith to the wall, the two grab their water bottles and join us.

"I'm a die-hard *Star Trek* fan," Smith says, "and I'm not ashamed to admit it. I've watched every episode close to a dozen times. I was in the fifth grade when I really started watching the show. I thought it was totally cool; I couldn't believe that anyone actually got paid to do space stuff for a living. I *didn't* believe it, in fact, until my first year in college, when I saw what aerospace engineering was like: NASA people get paid money! From then on," he laughs, "my life was set."

Matousek nudges Roncoli. "Tell him about the Gorn."

A few years ago, Roncoli recounts, he and his friends learned that "Arena"—a classic original-series episode in which Kirk battles the reptilian captain of a Gorn starship—was filmed at Vasquez Rocks. The park is only forty minutes from Pasadena.

"One of the guys who had a videotape of the episode copied it onto his camcorder," says Roncoli, "and we all drove up there. Sure enough, there were the rocks, and there was the place where Kirk ran up the cliff. By keeping one eye on the viewfinder and one on the scenery, we could tell within five feet where everything had been shot. So we filmed the same scene, each of us taking different parts. Then we edited it all together with the sounds and dialogue from the original show."

"Did you sew up your own Gorn costumes?"

"No . . . This was just a quick jaunt up there."

I ask the engineers if they like the new shows as much as the old ones.

"*Voyager* has its moments," Smith says thoughtfully. "*Deep Space Nine* has a lot more moments. *Next Generation* I kind of miss now. We ragged on it while it was on, but now we're all, 'Gee, that was a really good show.'"

Roncoli nods. "I think most of us, with all due respect to the other *Star Trek* shows, prefer the original. Maybe that's because it's what we grew up with."

"We've all got the lines memorized," adds Smith. "You just have to kick into a conversation at the lunch table and we all pipe in. Or you listen the day after a good *Star Trek* episode is on, and you'll hear people talking about it. When a new *Star Trek* movie comes out, it's the big topic for the week. Everyone cuts out early to see it at the best theater in town."

"I'm sure you've heard the joke that 'Everything I know about life I learned from *Star Trek*.' " Roncoli laughs. "My friends and I often come up with quotes or recall incidents from a *Star Trek* show that relate to the situation at hand. In a fraction of a second, everybody knows what we're talking about. There's no lag time, or need to explain it."

The idea that sound bites from *Star Trek* could become a shorthand language among NASA engineers intrigues me, and I ask for examples. Instant brain-freeze, of course, results, but Roncoli finally dredges one up. It's from "Mirror, Mirror," first aired in 1967. In the episode, Kirk is accidentally transported to a parallel universe. The version of Mr. Spock he encounters on the alternate *Enterprise* is ruthless and diabolical. At the show's conclusion, before returning to his own ship, Kirk tries to persuade the "evil" Spock to reform.

"So Kirk makes his impassioned speech and steps onto the transporter pad." Roncoli speaks solemnly. "The alternate Spock looks directly at Kirk and says, *'I shall consider it.'* " There's a beat of silence. Steve Matousek and John Smith bob their heads like rabbinical scholars. "Lines like that carry an awful lot of weight and meaning around here. If someone on a project makes a suggestion and one of us replies, 'I shall consider it,' you know the import behind it.

"That's where *Star Trek* has had the most impact on our lives," Roncoli continues. "It's part of our personalities. Not so much that it made me go into the space program, but it's clearly been part of my development—and my relationship to a lot of things that go on."

I weigh his words. The synergy of the *Star Trek* phenomenon, I reflect, may be unique in human civilization. I wonder if any previous vision of humanity's destiny—in any religion or mythology—ever had a more compelling influence on the secular workforce charged with bringing that future to life.

"JPL is the closest thing to Starfleet that there is," John Smith declares, "because we're actually going out and exploring the planets.

We're not earthbound. We do astronomy and Earth-orbiting missions, but our basic missions are to other planets: Mars, Jupiter, Saturn, Uranus, Neptune. We're even considering Pluto and Europa orbiters."

"They do a good job in *Star Trek*, in terms of realism and how things might work," Matousek breaks in. "We sometimes poke fun at it, but when you get down to the nitty-gritty of, say, warp drive or the transporter, it's conceivable we could do that kind of thing." I note the collective pronoun *we*.

"We're pretty grounded in reality," Smith appends. "But *Star Trek* really is an inspiration to us."

"And not just to us." Steve picks up a paddle and gives Ralph the evil eye. They stand up, and walk toward the Ping-Pong table. "It's also opened up the public's ability to understand what we're doing. When I give a talk in a grade school, I tell the kids that what I do here is sort of like being the navigator aboard the *Enterprise*. But if I tell them that I sit in an office and crank out numbers for a trajectory . . . ," he

> ### THE SCIENCE OF *STAR TREK*
> —DR. DAVID ALLEN BATCHELOR, NASA PHYSICIST
> dbatchelor@leaf.gsfc.nasa.gov
>
> "I'm a physicist, and many of my colleagues watch *Star Trek*. A few of them imagine some hypothetical, perfectly accurate science fiction TV series, and discredit *Star Trek* because of some list of science errors or impossible events in particular episodes. This is unfair. They will watch Shakespeare without a complaint, and his plays wouldn't pass the same rigorous test."

grimaces as Ralph's serve curls past him, "they just don't relate to that."

Twenty minutes later, the defeated Matousek escorts me across the JPL compound. We walk in the shade past missile casings varnished by the sun. A pyramid of giant inflated air bags—the ingenious padding designed to cushion *Pathfinder*'s landing on the rocky Martian surface—stands by the entrance like a Claus Oldenburg sculpture.

Before passing the guard, I turn around and fix the site in my memory. Again, the sheer *unremarkableness* of the place assails me. It's nothing like Florida's Kennedy Space Center, with its stupendous Vehicle Assembly Building, or the marvelously understated facade of the Manned Spaceflight Center in Houston. The JPL is grunt-work central: Hackerstan.

But it's Starfleet as well. The engineers at work in the generic structures around me are among the only people on Earth doing the nuts-and-bolts work of interplanetary travel. And they're doing it, I realize, because it's *fun*.

TRANSPORTER TECHNOLOGY 101

AP Online, December 10, 1997
Malcolm Ritter, AP Science Writer

NEW YORK (AP) Scientists have pulled off a startling trick that looks like the "Beam-me-up-Scotty" technology of science fiction. In a laboratory in the University of Innsbruck in Austria, scientist Anton Zeilinger and his colleagues destroyed bits of light in one place and made perfect replicas appear about three feet away.

The phenomenon that made it happen is so bizarre that even Albert Einstein didn't believe in it. He called it spooky.

In addition to raising the rather fantastic notion of a new means of transportation, the trick could lead to ultra-fast computers.

The work is the first to demonstrate "quantum teleportation," a bizarre shifting of physical characteristics between nature's tiniest particles, no matter how far apart they are.

Scientists might be able to achieve teleportation between atoms within a few years and molecules within a decade or so, Zeilinger said.

The underlying principle is fundamentally different from the *Star Trek* process of beaming people around, but could teleportation be used on people? There's no theoretical problem with that, several experts said. But get real.

"I think it's quite clear that anything approximating teleportation of complex living beings, even bacteria, is so far away technologically that it's not really worth thinking about it," said IBM physicist Charles H. Bennett. He and other physicists proposed quantum teleportation in 1993.

There would just be too much information to assemble and transmit, he and others said.

It's not about humiliating Khrushchev. It's not about getting to the Moon and getting there first. It's not about Old Glory Up There or windup test pilots trained to treat a stroll on the Moon like a visit to the Price Club. The fantasy that drives these engineers, the future gleaming in their mind's eye, is an Aquarian-age television series.

It's a radical departure from the time-honored tradition of sci-fi culture. *Star Trek* offers a revolutionary view of technology: a mandate to press onward with research and development, walking the razor's edge until the balance of human consciousness shifts. There will be wars and disasters; there will be fallout, riots, and suffering. But the day will come when we find ourselves worthy of our tools. In the coming millennium, Roddenberry insists, technology will be our genie—and we'll have enough sense to know what to wish for.

I carry my presumptuous head of hair to the visitors' parking lot, breathing easy. America's interplanetary space program is in good hands.

AWAY MISSION I:
MAPS TO THE STARS' HOMES

London is an unlikely cybercity. Ancient streets meander haphazardly through a maze of tiny neighborhoods and districts, jamming into dead ends or curving unpredictably in the wrong direction. None of Manhattan's simple grid plan here; none of the logical, digital tap of uptown to midtown, midtown to downtown, East Side to West Side. London is analog down to its soul, from Threadneedle Street to Mile End. So daunting is the city's plan that cabdrivers, before winning their licenses, must spend two full years acquiring "the Knowledge": a Thesian command of London's proto-medieval labyrinth.

I hop off a double-decker bus at Tottenham Court Road and wander into the British Library. The first thing to catch my eye is a glass case displaying old Genoese maps: *America Unfolding*, by Vesconte di Maggiolo, and *The New World Revealed* by Battista Agnese. Drawn in the early 16th century, the maps are thrilling in their inaccuracy. North and South America reveal their eastern coastlines then fade westward, a pale wash of watercolors, into the unknown. The display stirs up deep feelings. Few documents I've laid eyes on are as seductive as these maps, their missing masses beckoning the brave and restless. It pains me to know that their boundaries have long been filled in: The rivers and lakes have been named, the deserts ensnared by flyovers and cable TV wires.

It suddenly seems natural and necessary to be faced with incomplete maps, and to go about the business of completing them. It's almost as if, by drafting such maps, we're searching for the unexplored regions of our own brains; that elusive 95 percent we supposedly never use. Much of humanity's early science, I think, arose from a hardwired drive to fill in that territory. The physical act of discovering and recording what lay upon this planet was as imperative as reckoning eclipses, bending light, and hacking away toward the atom.

Mystery despises a vacuum, but there's no vacuum worse than the absence of mystery. There will always be new maps to draw; and even as those are sketched, others will be created.

A short distance from the British Museum, the shelves at Forbidden Planet—a sci-fi, fantasy, and horror shop—are filled with such documents: atlases of distant galaxies, postcards from alien resorts, navigational star charts of the Alpha quadrant.

The specialty store opened in 1978 to serve a mushrooming market for American comics.* It rapidly expanded to include *Millennium Falcon* models, *Enterprise* schematics, light sabers, Federation passports, shuttlecraft Christmas tree ornaments, and battery-powered tricorders. It's as if the screeching halt of the manned space program caused a kind of psychological whiplash. Our bodies may have stopped, but our collective imagination sailed right through the windshield.

It's Saturday afternoon, and the Planet tumbles with a lapidary selection of stoners, slackers, and nerds. Rare groove and the high-pitched gurgle of ray guns pulse through the aisles. Brokers and bike messengers stand cheek-to-jowl, sorting through Japanese *manga* and *Batman* comics. On the main floor, shelves sag beneath a cornucopia of *Star Trek* merchandise—if I had ten pence for every image of Captain Jean-Luc Picard I could charter the Concorde home. The total effect is dazzling, maddening, and, finally, numbing. I had no idea how many Starfleet tie tacks have been produced, or how bizarre Gates McFadden looks as a ceramic coffee mug.

---

* During the 1960s and early '70s, comic books came to the United Kingdom in ships' holds, as ballast. News vendors picked up and distributed the stacks, but the selection was always a crapshoot. Forbidden Planet got a foothold by importing and distributing such pulps.

In a chaotic back office, surrounded by overflowing ashtrays and a panel of flashing "hold" lights, manager Dick Jude offers me a smoke. With his long, craggy face and thin goatee, he looks like a retired Hell's Angel. In point of fact he's a former jazz drummer, a lifelong comic book collector, and a damned sweet guy. Part of the Planet family since 1981, he watched his first *Star Trek* episode when he was fifteen—one year after the first Moon landing.

"The main reason *Trek* works so well," Jude says, "is because of its high hopes. It appeals to people like you and me, who got up at one in the morning to watch Armstrong's first step. For those of us who grew up during the space age, *Star Trek* was the only show worth watching."

"What else was on in England?"

"We had *Dr. Who* as a homegrown series which, for all its cardboard sets, still has a cult following. *The Avengers* was a different thing altogether. It was fantastic television; it was weird. *The Prisoner* came after *Star Trek*, but it was more an art project than science fiction."

It amazes me that Brits didn't chafe at *Star Trek*, with its richly American slant.

"Roddenberry was a very hip salesman." Jude grinds out his cigarette against a metallic bookmark in the shape of Pamela Anderson Lee. "He put an element of everything in there. There was Chekov, the Russian character, at a time when the cold war was still screamingly rampant. And though I imagine it was hard to get it through the networks in America at the time, he included a black woman: Uhura. There were a lot of deliberately provocative elements. The idea was to raise consciousness—but also to make it marketable around the world." He laughs sharply. "If that's not being too cynical. Anyway, they finally gave the Captain's chair to an Englishman, didn't they? And Marina

THE UNITED FEDERATION OF COMICS

In 1996, Marvel Comics and *Star Trek* celebrated their anniversaries (the thirtieth for *Trek*, the thirty-fifth for Marvel) with a joint venture featuring the ever-popular X-Men fighting beside Captain Kirk and the crew of the U.S.S. *Enterprise*. "It's a perfectly natural crossover," writer Scott Lobdell told *Entertainment Weekly*. "At heart, they're both stories about a handful of people facing the unknown. They both hit the same nerve in American consciousness."

The 64-page epic was the first ripening of a deal that Marvel and Paramount Pictures struck in January of 1995. In the story, the X-Men travel in time to the 23rd century and ally themselves with Kirk and his crew. Their common foe? An abominable hybrid of the X-Men's arch-foe "Proteus" with Gary Mitchell: Kirk's former friend, whose strange metamorphosis into a god-like being (in the original series episode "Where No Man Has Gone Before") once threatened the universe.

Sirtis is a Cockney, though they neutralized her accent. And if Klingons come from anywhere on the planet," he adds wryly, "it *must* be Scotland."

"Sure. But isn't the future of *Star Trek* still, basically, an American idea balloon?"

"Nooo . . ." Jude shakes his head slowly and gropes for another cigarette. "The world is not perceived as 'America.' It's perceived as 'the planet,' isn't it? We've all pulled together. The wars are over. We're out in space together. It's very high-end optimism. It was flawed in the original series; the planetary community was a background idea that didn't pan out through the episodes. But with *TNG* they really pursued that philosophy. They didn't have James T. Kirk, who fought or fucked everything he met; they had Jean-Luc Picard, who was very aloof and diplomatic."

The second avatar of *Star Trek*, in Jude's mind, more closely matches modern expectations of what might have been; of how the space age may have unfolded, given the direction in which humanity seems to be going. The original series was anchored in the Wild West and the cold war. But if Kirk was a hybrid of John Wayne and JFK, Picard brings Jacques Cousteau and the Dalai Lama into the mix. By the time *Next Generation* came of age, *Star Trek* was no longer about truth, justice, and the American way. It was about the global village, expanded to pan-galactic scale.

What is it about London? Rain or shine, uptown or East End, the place has a vaguely forlorn appearance. Faded trousers and Francis Bacon postures are the vogue, and you could test-drive the *Sojourner* over some of the complexions I've seen.

Despite their pallor, the locals have learned how to groove. Rumor (sorry, *rumour*) has it that every Saturday night, at a Kensington pub called Page's, London's most rabid *Trek* fans gather for a ritual viewing and Federation hoedown.

Inside Page's Bar.

Page's is unremarkable from the outside. I make my approach up Regency Street, past checkerboard housing units and sidewalks full of Bengali kids shouting at each other in Shakespearean accents. Since the bar isn't an officially licensed *Star Trek* venue, the more obvious intellectual property rip-offs—the illuminated Starfleet logos outside the doors, for example—have had to go. Inside, things are a bit looser: the blue-and-white rug is done up with a plainly Trekkish motif, and a huge model of the *Enterprise* NCC-1701-D hangs

Resistance is futile . . .

from the ceiling (it cost nearly $2,000; the bar's supporters bought it for the owner as a gift).

One entire corner of the pub is a concession stand, selling everything from Bajoran earrings to Klingon warship tech manuals. Video screens pulse with episodes from *TNG* and *Voyager*, the volume plumped to Daytona Beach disco levels. A *Star Trek* pinball machine is tucked into a nook near the "loo." There are steel chairs, chrome banisters, and a long zinc bar. But the techno-industrial decor isn't as overwhelming as one might think. There's a sense of community about the place, as if it were the only refuge for miles. It feels like I've left the streets of Kensington and beamed directly into Ten-Forward, the cocktail lounge aboard the *Enterprise* 1701-D.

About a tenth of the clients are decked out in regulation, if ill-fitting, Starfleet uniforms (the captains and commanders look half convincing if you ignore their beers, pipes, and reckless smooching). But everyone's wearing *something*, even if only a communicator badge or *Star Trek* T-shirt. The display behavior is optional, but it's more or less the point. I can't imagine anybody who isn't a fan of the show wanting to stay here more than thirty seconds.

One glaring difference between Page's and Ten-Forward is the drink list. Real Starfleet officers have to content themselves with synthahol, the cosmic equivalent of near beer. But the real booze has kept Page's from getting cozy with Paramount. The studio, hyperconscious of "family values," won't bestow its blessing on a pub.

It's odd to see guys and gals in Federation knickers puffing Camels, swilling tumblers of Klingon Bloodwine, and cheering their hearts out for one of Brannon Braga's *Voyager* episodes. But not everyone is so demonstrative. A middle-aged couple in Starfleet uniforms sits sedately

TNG Beer *Trek* Rules

http://www.planetofthegeeks.com/
trek/beertrek

Bibation occurs whenever:

The *Enterprise* is authorized to exceed warp speed limitations

The officers play poker

Data's resistance to gas/virus/bullets/etc. saves the day

Data's head is open

You see one of Data's paintings

Geordi LaForge invents something

LaForge rolls his chair from one station to another

LaForge tells the bridge, "We've got a problem . . ."

You can see LaForge's eyeballs

There's a saucer separation

Picard crosses his legs like a girl

Picard says, "I appreciate your concern . . ."

Picard says, "Make it so"

You see Picard's flute

Riker walks in like he's "Action Man"

Riker's scamming chicks

You see Riker's trombone

Troi mentions or eats chocolate

Wesley Crusher wears a sweater

Worf has a hard-on for Troi

at a table, nursing their Romulan Ales. I join them for a pint. Lorraine is a factory worker from Kent; her friend's a London software designer.

"I assemble those cardboard boxes they pack VCRs in," Lorraine stares at me through the world's thickest eyeglasses. "It's hell. This is my one treat at the end of the week. It's also my only chance to escape the kids. You better believe it means a lot to me, because it's a thirty-minute train ride just to get here."

"Why not go to a pub in Kent?"

"I'd sit alone," she shrugs.

Page's is owned and operated by Bob Benton, a tall and unpresuming barkeep who looks like a cross between Tom Hanks and *Star Trek*'s immortal "Q" (John DeLancie). He came out as a fan in 1994, when he tried to attract a Saturday-night crowd by offering an evening of vintage *Star Trek* episodes on the bar's giant video sports screen.

"I put an advert in the local paper," says Benton, "with no idea what to expect. The first night, more than two hundred people showed up."

"Don't you find it strange," I ask, "to see Brits so worked up over an American show?"

"*American?*" Benton looks stunned. "When I was working at a convention in the Albert Hall, the *Next Generation* cast said they felt the British fandom was even more ardent than the U.S. fandom."

Benton's success has spawned scores of radio and television interviews, but fame hasn't made a snob of him. During a break for announcements he barks up my visit, encouraging any and all to regale me with tales of Trek culture. I do get a few hits. A group of three people—a stout woman, a shy-looking adolescent, and a waiflike girl who introduces herself as Captain Nicole Picard—stop by to tell me about their "away teams." Members of Nicole's ship, the USS *Renault*, take monthly field trips in full-dress uniform. Last July, she informs me, they startled tube-riders at Piccadilly by chanting the *Star Trek* theme. Strange fun. When I ask why none of them are wearing uniforms this evening, Nicole lowers her eyes. "They're in the wash," she says.

Another local hero is Manny Batel, a hulking but cherubic teenager with Bengali roots. If Benton supplies Page's brainpower, Batel provides its soul. His weekly trivia quizzes and homemade *Star Trek* music videos (each one takes him at least a week to edit on a pair of VCRs in his bedroom) are a highlight of the evening. For Manny, though— and probably for a lot of these cadets— *Star Trek* is not about a longing for the stars. He shakes his head rapidly when I ask if he'd accept an assignment to Jupiter or Mars. The premise of life on

PAGE'S BAR COCKTAIL LIST
PAGE'S ROMULAN ALE **£ 2.30**
OUR OWN RECIPE · LAGER BASE **PINT OR HALF**
TRUE ROMULAN ALE **£ 5.75**
VODKA COINTREAU BLUE CURACAO LEMONADE
GALACTIC MIST **£ 4.65**
BACARDI COINTREAU GRENADINE GRAPEFRUIT
KLINGON BLOODWINE **£ 5.25**
VODKA BACARDI MALIBU GRENADINE LEMONADE

a starship moves him not at all; he's far more attracted to the idea of a future where racial boundaries have evaporated, and people of all colors (and belt sizes) live together peaceably.

Along with Manny's videos and the high-tech decor, Page's big draw is that Benton previews episodes of *Voyager* and *Deep Space Nine* well before they appear on British television. (CIC, the U.K. production company used by Paramount, provides him with promotional tapes of upcoming shows.) There's also the fact that legendary *Trek* stars (including George "Sulu" Takei, James "Scotty" Doohan, and Majel Barrett Roddenberry) have been known to drop by the pub and raise a pint of Romulan Ale with their fans.

The chief reason for Page's popularity, though, is the obvious one. If you're one of Britain's million-plus Trekkers, it's a great place to meet fellow fans—and not all of them are dressed like 24th-century space cadets.

Sally Oberstein-Smith is a riveting blonde in a black bustier; she also happens to be captain of the starship *Juno*. With three hundred members, her "ship" is the second largest of Britain's one hundred-plus fan clubs. Her mate, Chris Boyd, has a shaved head with multiple piercings; he's worked as a model-maker for ILM (Industrial Light & Magic) and has left his mark on several *Star Trek* films.

The Captain of the starship Juno.

"If you're a stranger, and you go into any other bar, here or in the U.S.," Boyd shouts, "the music stops. You get looked at, *severely*. If you walk in this place, and you like *Star Trek*, it doesn't matter who you are. Everybody is a big family. That doesn't work out just for the U.K.; it works out worldwide. We believe it's going to carry on forever." He's talking to me, but other carryings-on have caught his eye. There's some heavy petting, I notice, in progress behind the view screen.

"*Star Trek* represents a vision of a society without boundaries; whether racial, sexual, what have you." Sally agrees. "It doesn't matter about the color of your skin, what you do for a living, or where you come from. *Star Trek* may have started in the U.S., but it's become a universal phenomenon. You might walk in here a stranger, but you'll leave with a dozen new friends."

Moments later, in a kind of spontaneous baptism, she spills her Chablis onto my lap. She spends the next five minutes mopping my pants with a hankie, her designer cleavage pressed against my face.

"Your crew must be very happy," I murmur, coming up for air.

"They certainly are." She smiles, giving her chest a little hike. "Worth every pence."

And it's not just her. In the far corners of the pub, intoxicated fans play out their own holodeck fantasies. There's rave-caliber smooching, and a tangled threesome cavorting on the carpet. The myth has exploded into real time. No network, no studio, no sponsors; just a room full of tanked-up Starfleet officers a long, long way from home. Not exactly Paramount's idea of family viewing, it's an equally plausible interpretation of life aboard a 24th-century starship.

Cheers, Gene; this may be as close to your *real* vision as I'm ever going to come.

THE SOUL OF A NEW MACHINE

I suspect (although I have no way to prove it) that, aside from *Titanic*, the starship *Enterprise* is the most famous vehicle ever created. I've been making a list of heroic vehicles. Not in order of importance, or even by category, but just as they enter my mind.

It's tougher than I'd expected. My first thought, oddly, is the Batmobile. Man, what a car! I owned the vintage Corgi miniature, from the campy television show of the '60s, when I was a kid. It would be worth a fortune now if my parents hadn't put it in a sack with all my rare comic books and baseball cards and hurled the whole lot into the fourth dimension. The new Batmobile's pretty good, too, though it does look disturbingly like Alien's dildo.

What else? *The Spirit of St. Louis*, *Freedom 7* and *Friendship 7*, *Apollo 11*'s *Eagle*, Darwin's *Beagle*, and the rugged lunar module that rescued *Apollo 13*'s crew. The *Mayflower*. Amundsen's sled. The *Niña*, *Pinta*, and *Santa Maria*. *Chitty-Chitty Bang-Bang*. The *Millennium Falcon*. The Black Stallion, Secretariat, and Trigger. And yes—oh, mama—the fabulous, option-packed Aston-Martin wrecked by 007 in *Goldfinger*.

It's amazing to realize that, during the past four decades, the ship has survived six captains and six reincarnations. She's been around almost as long as rock 'n' roll. Her transporter, early-warning, and propulsion lingo are probably more familiar to most Americans than the Bill of Rights, and her mission—*To boldly go where no one has gone before*—better known than the recipe for Play-Doh.

According to the *Star Trek Encyclopedia*, the very first *Enterprise*—NCC-1701, flown by Captain Kirk in the original series—will be commissioned in the year 2245, at Starfleet's San Francisco Yards. Those future engineers will be assembling an antique; the ship was actually designed in 1964, by *Star Trek* art director Matt Jefferies (the narrow "Jefferies Tubes" that serve as the starship's conduits are named in his honor). His concept for the spacecraft was an ingenious one, marrying the classic saucer motif with wingtip "warp nacelles." (Jefferies' original sketch put the saucer on top, with the nacelles underneath, like skis, but Roddenberry liked it better upside down.)

Despite its pedigree, the *Enterprise* was the first science fiction rocket ship that didn't look like a flying saucer or mutated cigar. It has no retrorockets or landing pads. The reason is obvious: a true starship will be assembled in orbit. It need never touch the ground, or enter a planet's atmosphere. It is hard to imagine what the stuffy execs at NBC made of this design back in 1964, but, like so many other things about the original series—from Spock's ears to the black female lieutenant on the bridge—they probably thought it wouldn't fly.

Over the years innumerable improvements have been lavished on the Federation's flagship. The *Enterprise* NCC-1701-D, of *Star Trek: The Next Generation* fame, was designed by Andrew Probert in 1986 (unlike its predecessors, 1701-D will be commissioned in 2363 at the Utopia Planitia Fleet Yards orbiting Mars). Volumes have been written about the starship's architecture and systems. Even those with absolutely no interest in science fiction will admit that the fifth *Enterprise* drips with elegance: a quality defined by biologist Edward O. Wilson as, "the right mix of simplicity and latent power."

If a single factor makes *Star Trek* believable, it's the confidence with which all this 24th-century technology is portrayed. From the jargon rattled off in engineering to the animated displays flashing on *Voyager*'s main bridge, the show has a *look,* an atmosphere within which the most far-fetched scientific miracles seem plausible.

Two men, primarily, are responsible for this. Rick Sternbach and Michael Okuda, the show's longtime illustrators and technical advisors, are the wizards behind *Star Trek*'s curtain. Together, they've created a nearly seamless illusion of life aboard a stadium-sized starship.

Entering *Star Trek*'s art department at Paramount Pictures, I find the two techs on their feet, watching television. The program, of course, is *Star Trek*—and their rapt expressions indicate that they're utterly entranced by their own illusions.

Sternbach and Okuda are both in their forties. Physically, they're polar opposites. Sternbach is stocky and Germanic, with a rusty blond mustache and slight double chin. He looks like he could be a fireman, or part of a barbershop quartet. Okuda is Japanese, about a foot shorter than Sternbach, with a round, unlined face and the vaguely myopic gaze of a man who spends too much time in front of CRTs.

Still, they have remarkably similar backgrounds. Both identify themselves as children of the post-Sputnik generation: an era when, as Okuda puts it, "the nation still realized that science, education and technology were priorities." Both grew up devouring sci-fi, building Estes rockets, and chanting the satirical ballads of songwriter/mathematician Tom Lehrer.

Careerwise, they took different tacks. While Sternbach moved into magazine and book illustration, Okuda focused on commercial graphics and community theater—learning skills that would serve him well in the world of television production. "You've got to come up with creative solutions," he explains, "and there's no money."

Sternbach was drafted onto the *Star Trek* team in 1977, designing spaceships and props for the first feature film. He left Paramount, but was called back in 1987 for *The Next Generation*. Okuda—who'd contributed to *Star Trek IV: The Voyage Home*—returned to invent *TNG*'s graphics. "The similarities between us were very scary," Sternbach recalls. "We've been fortunate to converge on this show and achieve a high-tech critical mass."

"Fortunate" doesn't come close to describing the union. Playing with the props and models on Okuda's shelves and leafing through Sternbach's sketches of the latest Romulan weapons, I'm floored by the sheer *fun* these guys are having. They're the luckiest nerds in the world.

An enormous poster of the *Enterprise* NCC-1701-D, cut away to show the decks, hangs on the office wall. Over the past ten years Sternbach has made numerous modifications to Probert's design. He's also sketched out dozens of smaller Starfleet vehicles, and concocted an armada of alien battleships, shuttlecraft, and cruisers. As challenging as it is, he admits, it's nowhere near as tough as the real thing.

"Designing real spaceships is for people with real mathematical and engineering backgrounds," says Sternbach.

"We're safe because there are no peer reviews," Okuda jokes. "There are no wind tunnels. You can't test the *Enterprise* to destruction."

Ratings, however, do act as a kind of peer review. If the starship didn't hold together visually and conceptually, it would've been blown off the air years ago. In some ways, the original *Enterprise* had it easy; it flew in the 1960s, before the era of personal computers. In the world of Pentium processors and Iomega Zip drives, technical credibility is a must.

> "When you're that far out [with imaginary physics], you can make your own rules, and that's okay. It's just fun. And if some kid now, in public school, can be inspired by that challenge, great! It'll keep 'm out of law school!"
> —Dr. Leon Lederman
> 1988 Nobel Prize
> winner in Physics

"We could, of course, come up with things the audience couldn't really identify with," Sternbach observes. "Driving the ship by brain waves, for example. But we don't. Instead we jump way ahead—then step back a few paces."

Since most of the action aboard the ship takes place on the main bridge, one key to the *Enterprise*'s success lies in its visual displays: the consoles and blinking screens that summarize information about the ship's tactical, scientific, and environmental status. All of these, along with the video clips appearing on the ship's monitors, are Okuda's brainchildren. His style is so distinct, in fact, that the graphics are called "Okudagrams."

"One can easily imagine control panels a hundred times more complicated," he says, unrolling a large transparency that, backlit on the bridge, will serve as one of the *Enterprise*'s computer consoles. "What I'm trying to imply here, by these sweeping curves and clear lines of organization, is that Starfleet has put an enormous amount of thought into figuring things out. Each task has been broken down into highly simplified steps. The software reconfigures itself to relate to what you're dealing with *now*. The computer knows what you want to do before you know you want to do it."

Any way you look at it, running a starship will require vast amounts of RAM—and the computers on board the *Enterprise* make today's most advanced mainframes look like pocket calculators.

"We have mass storage on both sides of the bridge," Sternbach says. "Lots of parallel processors, plus connections we haven't even thought of today. There are massive amounts of computing power distributed throughout the ship and concentrated in three central cores. Each core," he notes casually, "is about the size of the Capitol Records building."

"Every once in a while," Okuda elaborates, "we have to describe the processing capacity of the shipboard computer. The first few times we did so in terms of bits and bytes: *quadrillions* of them. It was like trying to describe the speed of the Concorde in inches per fortnight. So, we came up with

Rick Sternbach and Michael Okuda.

units called *kiloquads*. What's a kiloquad? What does it translate to in bytes? I don't know. I don't *want* to know. If I say it's equal to four hundred gigabytes, six months from now Motorola will introduce a four hundred gigabyte chip—and we'll be obsolete."

The tendency of life to imitate art is one of the most uncanny aspects of the *Star Trek* universe. The holodeck, a virtual reality playground that crew members use for everything from martial arts training to erotic distraction, may still be a century away, but some of the original series' gizmos—like transdermal hyposprays and folding cellular "communicators"—are already in common use. A Canadian firm has developed the first working tricorder, and Apple Computers —directly inspired by *Star Trek*—has come up with a version of the PADD (Personal Access Display Device): a palmtop computer used by Starfleet personnel.

"When Rick first designed the PADD, my reaction was, 'Shouldn't this have more buttons?'" Okuda laughs. "Then we saw the prototype *Newton*, and I said, 'Oh . . . *no* buttons!'"

Such situations also beg the question of obsolescence: a big sand trap when you're designing a starship that won't be launched for another four centuries.

"We try to stay reasonably well informed of things that are likely to happen in the next five, ten, or twenty years," Okuda says. "But at the same time, a lot of the [*Enterprise's*] computer systems are archaic, even now."

The key to staying on top of things, Okuda and Sternbach have realized, is anchoring the foundations of the 24th century in cutting edge theory. Although the show is filled with wild terms—wormholes, antimatter streams, and dilithium crystals (see the *Star Trek: The Next*

Generation Technical Manual for details)—the physics behind them is impressively robust. Technical consultants have included Dr. Robert Forward, widely known for his "hard" science fiction; Dr. Robert Bussard, who came up with the concept of harvesting interstellar gases as starship fuel; and Dr. Gregory Benford, a scientist and sci-fi writer at the University of California at Irvine. British astrophysicist Stephen Hawking not only contributed the foreword to Lawrence Krauss's *The Physics of Star Trek*, he starred as a poker-playing hologram in a *TNG* episode called "Descent."

"A lot of the engineering inspirations come from G. Harry Stine, a former White Sands missile engineer," adds Sternbach. "He's got a very practical view of large aerospace projects. It's a very long design process. In some cases, you have to order materials five *years* before you start cutting parts. That's why, as per the *Manual*, constructing a Sovereign-class starship—like the *Enterprise* 1701-E appearing in *First Contact*—is a twenty-year effort. Even with fabulous, computer-assisted systems, it would take longer than one would believe."

One of the most impressive things about Sternbach and Okuda is their command of fictional physics. They can lecture for hours about warp drive, list the sixteen power settings of Type II and Type III phasers, and explain how Romulans drive their ships with quantum singularities. It sounds very convincing. In fact, it sounds *inevitable*. But are there some technical aspects of the show that, given the laws of physics, will *never* be possible?

"Never—as Arthur C. Clarke would say—is a term you want to stay away from." Okuda grins. "But there are things like the transporter, which is essentially a molecular fax machine."

"Superluminal [faster-than-light] travel may never come to pass," Sternbach concedes. "And the replicator is another magic box. But I think that seeing these things, week after week, is a tribute to the potential ingenuity of future generations. And if we don't do exactly those things—well, we may do other things that are just as magical."

"Don't you sometimes feel convinced," I say, "that after so many years designing the *Enterprise* you could put together a real starship?"

The two men look at each other, shaking their heads in a silent "No way."

"You try to make the design look credible," declaims Sternbach. "But we're not kidding ourselves. We haven't filled in the details."

"The most powerful device in television, and in all of drama, is the viewer's mind. We can suggest and imply that a tremendous amount of work has gone into all this . . ." Okuda gestures at the blueprint with a sweeping hand that embraces all forty-two decks of the *Enterprise*. "But if Rick or I actually knew how to make warp drive work, we'd be polishing our Nobel acceptance speeches."

———————

Sound Stage 29 is a whale-gray building big as a city block, with giant Helvetica-style numbers tattooed on its side. A short flight of steps leads to an industrial-strength door, and into the vast hangar where the *Enterprise* 1701-E is under construction.

A Galaxy-class starship may require two decades to build, but this one's got to be finished in a week. Power drills and buzz saws shriek through the haze; a worker in overalls carries a stack of phaser rifles toward the prop room.

Braga and Moore lead me through an opening in a high plywood wall, and we emerge onto the main bridge. The place is a mess. Plastic sheets cover the consoles and noodles of snipped electrical insulation litter the floor. Despite its rough edges, the set radiates a mythical panache.

"Here's the observation lounge," indicates Moore, pointing to an adjoining room containing a long, glossy table. He nods back to the rectangular hole we climbed in through. "That'll be the main viewer . . ."

There's a creaking sound, and the floor rumbles alarmingly. I'm ready to bolt—but it ain't no earthquake. Herman Zimmerman, *First Contact*'s solidly built production designer, eases up through a trapdoor and wipes his hands on his overalls.

"You see us in a bit of a disarray here." He grimaces. "We had all the chairs in place, and the consoles in place, but now we're diggin' holes in the floor to put all the electric to 'em. So it's kinda messy."

Braga tilts his head. "I think the crushed Pepsi can over there in the replicator is a nice touch."

Zimmerman laughs. "We always try to keep the product placement in."

We follow him off the bridge and into the captain's "ready room," where a haunted Picard will receive orders from Starfleet during the film's opening scene. "We'll have his bed over here," Zimmerman says, gesturing with flattened palms, "and two chairs over there. There'll be an aquarium in this corner, and a model of the *Enterprise* over there . . ."

Braga ducks through an adjacent door, and gestures me in. "Here's

TOP 10 SIGNS YOU'VE WATCHED TOO MUCH *STAR TREK*

http://www.halcyon.com/zylstra/
comedy/star/too-much-trek.txt

10. You send weekly love letters to the actress who played the green-skinned Orion slave girl in TOS episode #7.

9. You pull the legs off your hamster so you'll have a Tribble.

8. You tried to join the Navy just so you could serve aboard the USS *Enterprise.*

7. Your wife left you because you wanted her to dress like a Klingon and torture you for information.

6. You went to San Francisco to see if you might bump into Kirk and crew while they were in the twentieth-century looking for a whale.

5. Your masters thesis was, "A Comparison of the Illustrious Careers of T. J. Hooker and Captain Kirk."

4. You fly into a homicidal rage any time people say "*Star Trek*? Isn't that the one with Luke Skywalker?"

3. You have no life.

2. You recognize more than four references on this list.

1. You join NASA, hijack a shuttle, and head for the coordinates you have calculated for the planet Vulcan.

the bathroom. Hey, there's a mirror in here! It feels *real*!" He spies the toilet, and calls to Zimmerman with mock exasperation. "Herman . . . people don't poop in the 24th century. This is not consistent with Gene's Vis——"

"Yeah, well, it's just a little touch of realism for Patrick."

The PD's beeper chirps, and he hurries away. Ron, Brannon, and I wander into the maze of *Enterprise* corridors and pause at the entrance to the transporter room. It's impossible to resist; I fiddle with the controls and hop onto the biofilter footpads, trying to fax myself into Uma Thurman's shower. As I wait, futilely, to dematerialize, Braga points out an interesting fact: The "phase transition coils"—i.e., the opaque glass circles above my head—were the actual transporter footpads used on the very first *Enterprise.*

We continue our stroll in silence. The carpet is plush and the sets look terrific; it would be a pleasure to spend a tour of duty on this vessel. The feeling is so compelling that I experience a dizzy moment of temporal disorientation. I get an unsettling feeling that Zimmerman, Okuda, and Sternbach are actually *creating the future*; that if there ever is a real-life *Enterprise*, it's going to look exactly like this.

Braga stops short, and stares down the long, curving corridor. "Look how great that is. Just that *sweep*." He's whispering. "Every direction you look, you're on a starship. You are *actually on a starship*."

Ahead lies engineering, its illuminated "warp core" activated and pulsing. Blue deuterium flows from above, red antimatter seethes from below, and the two meet in an opaque central chamber that sloshes and churns like a vintage Maytag. These sets are finished; with their seamless control panels, communicator panels, and glowing schematics, they look absolutely real.

The poignancy of the illusion isn't lost on me. "It almost makes you feel," I muse, "like we've still got a real space program."

Moore nods ruefully. "Both the space program and *Star Trek* were ending just as I was becoming aware of life. Technically speaking, I was born in the last year of the baby boom: 1964. So I've got all these memories of the '60s, but I wasn't really *there* for any of it. Yet I became fascinated by the music, the Kennedys, by all that stuff. I still am."

"I find it *shocking* that the space program has dissipated," Braga erupts. "A lot of people don't realize that everything from Velcro to computers—from the most inane technologies to the most important—came out of it. Things developed for the astronauts found their way into the mainstream, opening new technologies and industries . . ." He fumes, picking at a Starfleet sticker on the wall.

Now Moore gets into it. He tells me about his childhood fascination with the Moon shots—he was five when the *Eagle* landed—and his memories of the motorized rover. He would have been an astronaut himself, but his eyesight wasn't good enough. Instead, he read about rockets, built plastic models of the lunar lander, and collected those books you paste picture-stamps into. Moore's not an emotional guy, but *Apollo 13* moved him deeply. During the movie's *Saturn V* launch sequence, he found himself in tears.

"There was a sense of, 'God, the space program used to be so *great!*' It was just this amazing adventure." Moore sighs, and shrugs with ennui. "But it got boring, somehow. The missions got less sexy. There's not the sense that we're pushing the frontier back like we were."

"Unfortunately," says Braga, "the problems here on Earth are so horrible and complex that people have turned their eyes away from the stars. They're looking down, instead of up. Meanwhile, *Star Trek* represents that adventure—and we all need adventure in our lives."

AWAY MISSION II:
ROCKET MAN

Riding the rails north from London, after departing King's Cross on the dot of seven. The thrill of quick, efficient mass transit is something most Americans, for all our space-age pretensions, can only dream of. Then again, if Los Angeles had built a good light-rail system, Roddenberry might never have dreamed up the transporter.

Fifteen minutes north of the city, there's already a hint of manure in the air. And always that pall of dampness, as British as Earl Grey tea. Small round clouds paddle across the sky, a parody of British landscape painting. A bright yellow backhoe sits isolated on a hilltop amid big green fields: plenty of spots for flying saucers to land. We pass through a small town without stopping. I spot a red MG parked outside the Macclesfield Borough Council; a narrow, empty street; a van emblazoned with a postal horn. *There's something familiar about this setting* . . . then it comes to me. This is *Avengers* country.

But John Steed and Emma Peel are ancient history now, the chaste collaboration of their 1960s television series eclipsed by darker avatars like *The X-Files*. Across the decades, twixt Nixon and Netscape, as Vietnam puckered into a pink scar and idealism drove off in a Land Cruiser, a few remnants of 1960s culture survive. You never know what's going to make it. *Star Trek's* creator was a motorcycle cop, but his sketches of the future outlasted Communism, free love, and Nehru jackets....

The train rolls past farms radiant in the late afternoon sunshine, past stone estates lost in copses of trees. Cattle graze in the fields. I wonder about their fate. Technically they should be bound for slaughter, their possible contamination with BSE (bovine spongiform encephalitis) making them unfit for consumption. The karmic tragedy seems yet another step toward the inevitable realization of *Star Trek*'s meatless future; a time when Yorkshire steer ranchers, willingly or not, will learn to settle for computer-replicated gluten in place of blood-rare beef. I think to myself: *When hell freezes over.*

But *Star Trek*'s charming vanity lies, perhaps, in its refusal to explain the economic transition that will supposedly occur between our present century—with its corporate body tattoo—and the liberated 24th, when money is obsolete and Burger Kings are overgrown with foliage. "This may be difficult for you to understand," Captain Picard tells techno-scrounger Lily in *First Contact*, "but we don't use money in the 24th century."

Where to, then, these cattle ranchers and leather tanners? Where to, the tobacco growers? What fate awaits the people who now sweep bank lobbies and repair ATMs? All of them erased, downsized by the anonymous cataclysm that, according to *First Contact*, will drive humanity into the woods by 2061. But none of this really matters, of course. Like Edward Bellamy's 1888 classic, *Looking Backward*—the memoirs of a utopian century, with a preface written on "December 26, 2000"—*Trek*'s mission is to posit the world as it *could* be, and let the generations between sort out the details.

The Manchester Museum of Science and Industry has a vast annex devoted to legendary aircraft and spacecraft. Bombers and biplanes rest on a broad cement deck, their wingtips nearly touching. Suspended from the I beam struts, running lights aglow, hangs a scale model of the starship *Enterprise*.

Between the two generations of vehicles, pointing toward the skylights, sits a two-story rocket called *Starchaser II*. Its wasp-waisted fuselage rises above four delicate fins. Along its length are small British flags, and the stenciled logo of Tate+Lyle: the rocket's local sponsor.

On a chilly February morning in 1996, *Starchaser II* rose from

Steve Bennett, Britain's foremost rocketeer.

a Northumberland launchpad and soared nearly 2,000 feet before parachuting back to Earth. The moment made history. *Starchaser* was the largest private rocket ever to be successfully launched in Europe, and it carried its designer—thirty-two-year-old Steve Bennett—one small step closer to attaining his lifelong goal: do-it-yourself spaceflight.

Bennett is stocky, of medium height, with swept-back silvery hair. His mustache is still red, though, and his face radiates a babylike calm. "How does it feel," I ask him, "to be sharing museum floor space with the world's most famous starship?"

He rests a hand on *Starchaser's* glossy white fuselage and beams. "This rocket here," Bennett says, "shows where I'm coming from. And that one there—" he points upward, to the *Enterprise*—"shows where I'm going."

The concept of a backyard rocket able to lift its builders into space is nothing new; it's been around since Jules Verne wrote *From the Earth to the Moon*. For a while, though, it seemed like Heathkit spaceships might not be necessary. The near-future visions presented by popular culture were so vivid and compelling that orbital sightseeing seemed imminent. Pan Am, playing off the popularity of their Space Clipper in *2001: A Space Odyssey*, even started a "First Moon Flights Club" in the late 1960s, issuing membership cards and creating a waiting list for their imminent lunar routes (I joined in 1969—and my number is 11,311).

"When I was growing up," says Bennett, "everything seemed possible. Men were landing on the Moon, and each mission was more spectacular than the last. I really thought we were going places. I thought, *I could grow up and train to be an astronaut—but I'll be* too late *to go to Mars.* Had the space program kept going, people would have been walking on the Martian surface by 1981.

"Later on, I realized that they'd pulled a plug on the Apollo program. I thought, 'God, there's nothing left. It's all gone.' That's about when we started to get *Star Trek*. And I thought, 'Wow, this is great!' *This* is where we should be: setting off in spaceships, and landing on strange new worlds.' A bit like Captain Cook, a couple of centuries ago."

For Bennett, though, the passive posture of couch potato is not enough. His desire to experience actual spaceflight remains an overwhelming passion. To this end, the rocketeer —a quality-control engineer who samples and lab-tests huge vats of Colgate-Palmolive toothpaste by day—has devoted every spare moment of the past seventeen years to fulfilling his lifelong dream of placing himself in Earth orbit.

Starchaser's success vindicated not only its builder, but scores of other like-minded designers as well. For Bennett is not alone: a new international space race is in full swing, with Do-It-Yourself rocketeers in Britain, Australia, and the United States locked in fierce competition.

Steve Bennett with *Starchaser II.*

An awesome payoff awaits the victor. In 1996, a consortium of astronauts and business moguls—inspired by Dr. Peter H. Diamandis—banded together to create the *X Prize*: a $10 million bounty for "the first private spaceship capable of lifting three humans to a sub-orbital altitude of 100 kilometers, on two consecutive flights within two weeks." The vehicle, needless to say, must also be able to return its passengers safely to Earth. As of 1998, Steve Bennett was one of fourteen entrants in the competition.*

As we quit the museum and hop into Bennett's Rover, I ponder the contest. The requirements seem far too severe. It wasn't even until Project Apollo that the United States shot three-person crews into space. Personally, I'd be floored to see a private company replicate even Alan Shepherd's 1961 Mercury flight: one astronaut, up and down in a phone-booth-sized capsule.

Bennett enters a parking lot, and leads me into a popular fish-and-chips joint. The menu enumerates the simple culinary pleasures of Britain: breaded cod, warm stout, and "mushy peas."

The liftoff of the rocket destined to snag the X Prize may be years away, but competition in the United States and Europe is already well established. "There's also a group in Australia working on pretty sophisticated rockets," Bennett says. "But they've had a lot of bad luck, because they tend go up a few hundred feet and explode. I've perfected the art of recovering my rockets safely. *Starchaser II* cost £13,000 to build—but if I want to fly it again, I could do so for a few thousand pounds."

---

*The X Prize Foundation Inc. is a non-profit educational foundation; readers are invited to visit their Web site at www.xprize.org

To Bennett, the incentive represented by the X Prize makes perfect economic sense. "As an individual I can design my project from the ground up. I don't have to cut dead wood away. As a result," he claims, "we'd be able to launch payloads for a fraction of what NASA charges. And there's obviously a market for space tourism: charging people for going up on suborbital flights. There's millions of pounds to be made, but no one's willing to take that risk yet."

And when they are? In the beginning, of course, the only thing truly astronomical will be the liability insurance. But however dragged-out, perilous, and litigious the process may be, the privatization of space travel is inevitable. There will come a day when the Moon has its own zip code, and teenage warp rats are naming their backyard starships after the *Enterprise*, *Nostromo*, and USS *Minnow*.

For now, though, the effort required to create a backyard Cape Canaveral is commensurate with the prize. Designers must perfect not only the launch vehicle, but its computer programs, recovery systems, and propellant as well.

Standing twenty-one feet tall, *Starchaser II* took fifteen months to build. It breaks up into portable modules, the longest piece just four feet long. "That facilitates easy transportation," notes Bennett. "It also means I can work on the various bits just about anywhere I want to."

The rocket is made of fiberglass and phenolic tubing, a lightweight material manufactured exclusively for use in amateur rocketry. Its total cost, about $21,000, was borne by Tate+Lyle—a British sugar company enticed into sponsorship by the fact that many of Bennett's original rockets were powered by his secret formula: a cunning blend of sugar and other chemicals.

Bennett's medium-term goal, and a crucial step toward that X Prize, will be building a rocket that actually penetrates "space": an ambiguous domain that, as defined by European scientists, begins 100 kilometers (62 miles) above the Earth's surface. American astronomers place the threshhold at 50 miles, or 300,000 feet.

"But it's difficult," Bennett says, "to make the leap from *Starchaser II* —which is in effect a giant model rocket—to an actual space-faring vehicle." To bridge the gap, he's designed an interim rocket called "*LEXX*": a three-stage vehicle designed to reach an altitude of 25 miles and recover by parachute. "I've got a team of fifteen people working on it," he states. "We're at the top of the tree in the field of amateur rocketry."

The waitress arrives, bearing a steaming bowl of mushy peas. There's no art to the dish; it is simply a bowl of boiled green peas, mashed to a peristaltic pulp. I stare at the gruel; a thin film congeals on the surface. Bennett attacks his portion with gusto.

"Try some?"

I do. It tastes very much like it looks. I make a silent vow never to grow old in England.

"The thing I've got to prove," Bennett continues, "is that we can *do* it. Nobody's going to give me a wad of money and say, 'Hey, Steve, here's a satellite. It's worth two million dollars. You launch it for me.' They won't do that unless I've got a track record. That's what amateur rocketry is all about: building a track record. So that if an opportunity comes along I'll be able to say, 'We've got the infrastructure in place. We can launch your satellite—and for a fraction of the price the European Space Agency would charge."

"But what about the rockets themselves? Where do you get the parts?"

"Everything is available right off the shelf," Bennett declares. "If I need a sophisticated piece of electronic or computer equipment, I simply buy it on the open market. Same with propellant. Why waste my effort and resources trying to perfect a solid propellant, when I can go to the people that supply NASA and get the same fuel used in the space shuttle boosters?"

So where does the ingenuity come in? It seems what Bennett's saying is that anyone with a wad of cash could assemble a spaceship and walk off with the X Prize.

"That's *exactly* what I'm saying. The biggest obstacle is finance. Full stop. I've been working on amateur rockets for twenty years, and I'm telling you: it's raising the cash that's the problem." He orders another pint.

Bennett's success owes as much to fund-raising skills as to rocket science. He persuaded Tate+Lyle to sponsor *Starchaser II* and persuaded his employer, Colgate-Palmolive, to grant him the six month's paid leave he'll need to put *LEXX* together. He's cultivating a relationship with one of Britain's leading publishers and is wooing any number of other corporations (including the *Star Trek* franchise itself). All this despite a maddening Catch-22: companies not involved in aerospace are completely ignorant of the possibilities of such a venture, while aerospace firms themselves are far too aware of the dangers involved.

A fine example of such a hazard—and Bennett's worst humiliation as a rocket scientist—occurred in November 1995, during the inaugural flight of *Starchaser II*. "I don't know if you're aware," Bennett begins, "but on November 5 we celebrate Guy Fawkes Night in Britain. Fawkes was the guy who tried to blow up the Houses of Parliament. Every year, up and down the country, thousands of bonfires are lit, effigies of Guy Fawkes are burned, and we have fireworks and traditional foods—like mushy peas."

"What a treat."

"Yes. Anyway, my sponsors thought it would be a good idea to tie in the launch of *Starchaser II* with Guy Fawkes Night because that's the time when we traditionally launch rockets."

Since *Starchaser* was financed by Tate+Lyle, Bennett wanted to power the rocket using sugar-based propellant. A couple of weeks before the launch, though, he received a grim piece of news: The authorities in charge of the site wouldn't provide insurance if he used his homemade fuel. So Bennett scrambled for a new propulsion unit. "I got in touch with a fireworks manufacturer, and paid them £1,000 to build the rocket motor for the test," he recalls. "It looked the business; it was a big metal thing."

Finally the big day arrived. "There must have been a hundred news media people there: journalists, TV, radio, everything. There were also about two thousand members of the public. We give the countdown, I press the button, and the motor just fizzles. No power. The rocket stays where it is. So everybody has to go home, and there's me with egg on my chin. I could've *killed* the guy sold me the motor . . ."

When his rage subsided, Bennett examined his failure. "I learned never to have all my eggs in one basket," he reflects, "and never to entrust the success of an entire mission to one individual."

He ordered a new batch of propellant from the United States and reserved a military testing site where he could use any kind of fuel he liked. A second launch date was scheduled for February 1996. This time there was less media, and no public—but liftoff was flawless. *Starchaser II* made the front page of nearly every British newspaper, and secured Bennett's reputation as the dean of Do-It-Yourself rocketeers.

Bennett's home is located in Dukinfield, an enclave of looping streets and brick homes built on the site of a former farm. He lives with his wife, Adrianne, and their six-year-old son. Their two-story house is small but homey, crowded with space age and fantasy imagery. Above the couch and easy chairs hang framed photos of the American space shuttle and the Mir space station. The dining room wall is papered with a blowup mural of earthrise, seen from the Moon. Downstairs, every spare surface is crowded with Adrianne's "Myth and Magic" collection: a menagerie of pewter wizards and miniature dragons.

Bennett throws his jacket over a chair. "I like working around the house," he says. "Otherwise I'd probably never see my wife and child. I do the clean stuff in the living room, the nastier stuff in my shop, and the *really* nasty, smelly stuff in the back garden."

His "shop," I discover, is nothing more than a corner of the garage. Sections of rocket fuselage share space with motorcycles, welding gear, and rakes. In the center of the room sits a small steel safe. Bennett cranks it open, extracting with both hands an American-made, military-grade rocket engine. The squat fuel cylinder looks innocuous enough—a thick cardboard tube stamped *M-1939* and packed with a chalky white compound—but it's all Bennett needs to power a rocket the size of *Starchaser* beyond the stratosphere.

"It cost me £25,000," he says, moving out of the garage onto the outdoor patio. "But my original fuel was more powerful. I'll burn some of it for you. . . . Would you like to see that?" I nod eagerly.

Bennett hurries off and returns a minute later wearing a white lab coat and safety goggles. He squeezes a stripe of homemade propellant (it looks like very abrasive toothpaste) onto a squarish pylon of cement, leans over and lights the end. It burns slowly and blindingly bright, an arc of ambitious combustion amid the soccer balls and trikes littering the yard.

Bennett peers at me devilishly. "Even Klingons would be proud to use the sugar propellant I invented," he chortles.

His office, on the upper floor of the house itself, is a cramped room papered with pencil drawings, mathematical equations, and thick tomes with titles like *Rocket Propulsion Elements*. "The rocket scientists' Bible," Bennett assures me. I survey the clutter, wondering if this is truly how it starts. Will Steve Bennett be the one who breathes life into our television fantasies? Will he be our Zefram Cochrane? Will this unpresuming toothpaste-tester, with his modest cottage and plastic spaceship models, be immortalized as the godfather of civilian space travel?

Before leaving the office I scan Bennett's desk. Amid the pencils and paper clips sits a red lapel pin in the shape of the *Star Trek: The Next*

Generation emblem, bearing the simple imperative immortalized by Captain Jean-Luc Picard: *Make it so.* I say the words out loud. Bennett nods, suddenly wistful.

"I don't normally tell people about the interest I have in *Star Trek*," he says, "but it's fundamental to what I do. I find it inspirational."

"How so?"

"I've always felt that our future lies in our ability to exploit the resources of space. We either expand into space, or we'll die." He shrugs his shoulders. "That's it. There's no middle ground."

He pauses, seeking a foothold. "Look. I don't put on a Starfleet uniform and go to Star Trek pubs and stuff like that. It's a bit of fun, but some people take it too seriously. In my view, *Star Trek* is a projection of where we want to go. I'd like to make that vision a reality. I'm only thirty-two; I can make a significant contribution over my lifetime. Just as Gene Roddenberry did, but in a different way."

"Do you have a long-range plan?"

"Absolutely." The hesitation leaves Bennett's voice. "I want to start a company that facilitates the launch of small payloads into orbit. I want to make a lot of money doing that. Then I want to rally people together: people who share the *Star Trek* dream, who feel that we've got some sort of future in space. If we could get £10 off each person, we could raise enough money to build an interplanetary spacecraft..."

He senses a limit, the membrane between obsession and lunacy, and stops. I fish into my pocket, and hand him a ten-pound note.

AMONG THE GREAT APES

Brannon Braga owns a Spanish-style home in Hancock Park, an exclusive neighborhood not far from Paramount. His party is starting to hop when I arrive. In the living room, a bowl of M&Ms sits beside a platter heaped with party favors: Nitro Nub Cock Rings, Amazing Elephant Clit Critters ("for untamed clitoral stimulation"), and a tangle of Groucho Marx disguises. Ethan Hawke and Sarah Jessica Parker fork cold cuts on the back patio. Warm water spills from sculpted jets into a swimming pool lined with Spanish tiles, and a disembodied mannequin's head glares vampishly amid flaming tiki torches. Ron Moore reclines on a lounge chair. Savoring a cigar, he looks more like a junior senator than a space brat.

Braga takes my bags and carries them up to the guest room. He's got the charm of Sir Galahad—and the mind of Rasputin. A few days ago we'd dined out together at a swank hotel in West Hollywood. Two gorgeous women were sitting at the next table; the eye contact was intense. After dessert, we stopped by to chat them up. It was starting to look a lot like Christmas—until Braga leaned over their table.

"Hey, we're making a porn film up in Room 227. Care to come up and join us?"

They fled so fast their plates were spinning.

There's no trace of the rude boy as Braga greets his guests. He's supersolicitous, hanging up jackets and pouring eighteen-year-old scotch. One minute he's leaning in a corner, listening intently to Moore's wife, Ruby; the next he's working the room with an ice bucket. He strolls past the pool, kicking at a huge inflatable *Enterprise*, and finds me bent over his telescope, focusing on Jupiter and its moons.

"Nice place," I say. "Can I ask a rude question?"

"Please do." His voice is vaguely conspiratorial; he always seems ready to confess some heinous crime.

"How does it feel, being this loaded at thirty?"

Braga lights a Marlboro. "Ten years ago, I was sorting mail at a publishing house. I was happy. I never really fantasized about having money. When I started working at Paramount and found out how much they were going to pay me, I was *stunned*." He glances around with a hint of restlessness. "I still feel kind of weird, having all this *stuff*. Sometimes I feel like it's not really *me* who owns it. I have much more nomadic tendencies."

"This is a pretty deluxe yurt." I don't bother mentioning his pack animal: the fully loaded BMW 840ci in the driveway.

A pod of starlets arrive; all their clothes put together couldn't keep a pygmy warm. "The way I see it," Braga says, "I'm paid in Hollywood lira. You might pay two dollars for a cup of coffee in Oakland; I pay a thousand Hollywood lira. My mother's house in Ohio cost forty thousand dollars. Mine cost a million—but that's in Hollywood lira."

———

Braga grew up with his mother, Scherry, on the edges of L.A.'s Venice canals: a south-coast version of Haight-Ashbury. A single mom, she raised Brannon and his younger sister with money she earned as a portrait artist. Brannon found his own focus early on. At six, he borrowed an Underwood from one of the neighbors and taught himself to type. The plays he churned out—calling for buckets of stage blood—were performed by the neighborhood kids.

"Brannon was always obsessed with the macabre," Scherry told me during a phone conversation. "He loved *The Twilight Zone* and worshiped Alfred Hitchcock. And he knew that Hitchcock, before making a movie, drew by hand every single scene that was to be filmed. So Brannon took up drawing."

"What did he draw?"

"Typical kid things. People with their heads cut off. A lot of bloody, gory stuff. He once did a brilliant cartoon comic book about going into a Denny's and being accosted by a born-again Christian. He ends up chopping the guy into pieces." She laughed. "When he was little, I wondered if he was going to grow up to become a mass murderer."

She needn't have worried; Braga can't stand the sight of blood. Though he'd spend hours mixing up gory concoctions in the kitchen, the genuine article made him queasy.

He saw a lot of body parts, though. "Things were pretty crazy," admits a family friend from the canals. "Sex was totally out in the open. I remember that my dad used to pull out his dick and chase us around the house with it. It must have had an effect on Brannon," she remarks offhandedly. "It certainly had an effect on me."

"I was exposed to everything," Braga confirms. "Maybe that's why I gravitate now towards something a little off the beaten path."

Rumors about Braga's private life pulse around him like a plasma storm. They buzz through the *Star Trek* fanzines and rattle the Web; they pursue him through the corridors of the Hart Building. When I first met Braga, in 1995, I heard about his famous orgies: between seasons he'd fly half a dozen of his sweethearts to an island retreat and frolic with them in inventive configurations until their juices ran dry. Even his boss seemed in awe.

"With the microphone off," Rick Berman confided, "I could tell you Brannon Braga stories until the morning. And the ones that would come at 5 A.M. would still have you awake. Brannon and his ladies . . ." He whistled through his teeth. "It would be like listening to the O.J. tapes."

This evening won't do much to quell the rumors. The place is dripping with evidence of Braga's obsessions. Polaroids of once and future lovers adorn his refrigerator door, and X-rated magazines slide from a table onto the living room floor. Gorgeous women pass through the kitchen in a steady stream, each one pausing long enough to embrace their host in a lascivious body lock. His latest girlfriend—an exotic dancer with Bambi eyes—seems miffed, but Braga defends his appetites.

"Look," he says. "I'm just an adventurous, experimental person who's striving to live out whatever fantasies I might have. I'm not into bondage and S&M. I'm not into voyeurism—in the traditional sense of the word." He lowers his voice. "I *am* something of an amateur gynecologist. I have been known to utilize a speculum now and again. The female body, as a

HOLODECK

SCOTT ADAMS

from *The Dilbert Future* published by
HarperBusiness © United Media, 1997

For those of you who only watch the "old" *Star Trek*, the holodeck can create simulated worlds that look and feel just like the real thing. The characters on *Star Trek* use the holodeck for recreation during breaks from work. This is somewhat unrealistic. If I had a holodeck, I'd close the door and never come out until I died of exhaustion. It would be hard to convince me I should be anywhere but the holodeck, getting my oil massage from Cindy Crawford and her simulated twin sister.

Holodecks would be very addicting. If there weren't enough holodecks to go around, I'd get the names of all the people who had reservations ahead of me and beam them into concrete walls. I'd feel tense about it, but that's exactly why I'd need a massage.

I'm afraid the holodeck would be society's last invention.

functional instrument, obsesses me. If I were on the *Enterprise*'s holodeck . . ." He grins, eyes glazing. "My greatest fantasy is to be with that fifty-foot woman from those schmaltzy 1950s sci-fi films. That would be the ultimate: to actually *crawl up into a vagina.*"

Braga knew he'd end up in Hollywood, but his tour aboard the *Enterprise* was unplanned. He graduated from the film program at the University of California at Santa Cruz in 1989, and was placed on *Star Trek*'s doorstep as an intern with the Academy of Television Arts and Sciences.

"I met him his first day," Ron Moore recalls. "Most of us were writers, and we thought, *Wow! A* film school *graduate!* He seemed very intelligent, though."

For Brannon's first assignment, TNG producer Michael Piller asked him to collaborate with Ron on a script for an episode called "Reunion." Their chemistry was terrific, and, in the seasons that followed, Braga continued to shine. Rick Berman took notice, ultimately embracing Braga as his protégé. *Star Trek: Voyager* is now essentially in Braga's hands. When Jeri Taylor retires, at the end of the fourth season, he will become the show's executive producer.

Jupiter sets, and the spa fills with a ratatouille of naked humans and spilled beer. Across the yard, a woman gives her boyfriend head against the ivy-covered wall of the garage. The Clit Critters have vanished, and the doors to the guest bedrooms are locked. I enjoy a sizzling flirtation with an up-and-coming actress, but she runs off in tears when a co-worker unmasks her as one of the caterers.

The party is over by three, but Braga's still wired. He digs through his videotape collection and shows me *System Error*, a short film he made at Santa Cruz. It features a stodgy executive (played by Braga himself) who goes inexplicably mad and literally devours himself in a gruesome, blood-soaked orgy—leaving only a glistening eyeball for the office cleanup crew.

I'm ready to spew, but Braga interprets my silence as awe. "I wanted to make a film with pure, visceral dream logic," he explains modestly. "I'm very attracted to surreal imagery."

Braga's screenplays for *Star Trek* strike similar chords. In a TNG episode called "Phantasms," Data—the ship's mild-mannered android —starts having terrifying nightmares and embarks on a murder spree. "Projections," from *Voyager*'s second season, finds the ship's virtual doctor trapped within a malfunctioning holonovel, unable to distinguish between truth and illusion. In "Non Sequitur," another *Voyager* episode, Ensign Harry Kim is jarred through a spacetime glitch and awakens in 24th-century San Francisco. "Deadlock" forces Captain Janeway's crew into a plasma cloud, where they confront a duplicate *Voyager* with an identical crew.

"Many of my shows involve characters struggling to maintain their sanity as reality crumbles around them," says Braga. "I think that's a very effective departure for *Star Trek*, because the show is so controlled. The environment is so perfect. Everything is so *right*." His girlfriend slinks into the living room in her nightgown and drops irritably into a chair. Braga gives her a look, and I know our chat is just about over.

"I'm amazed you've survived there as long as you have."

"When I first landed at *Star Trek* as an intern," he nods, "I felt like I was this weird kid being adopted by a straight-laced family. This franchise has such a strong spirit to it—a moral code, the Starfleet way, its thirty-year history—and a lot of it was created and cultivated by Gene Roddenberry. I thought, *How am I ever going to write for this show? It's so . . .* square.

"But *Star Trek*, I've discovered, allows me to do anything. I can get as wild and weird as I want to be. There are really no constraints. There's a simple premise, and the characters have to act a certain way. But they can find a new phenomenon every week. So I manage to wedge my own twisted vision in there," he says. "And shake up this square family from time to time."

———

The next day—or maybe the day after that—Braga and Berman climb into the backseat of the studio's Ford Crown Victoria and depart for the Angeles National Forest. Charlton Flat, a picnic area at 5,300 feet, has been dressed up as the location for *First Contact*'s Montana scenes.

The rugged, pine-covered hills, an hour northeast of West Hollywood, lie at the limit of the "drive-to" zone. For out-of-town location shoots, Berman explains, the guilds require extra travel pay. Today's destination in Angeles Forest is as far as Paramount can go without incurring such costs.

On first impression, Rick Berman seems like a big teddy bear. He's boyish and fleshy, with baggy trousers and a sensitive, ironic smile. *Another transplanted New York Jew*, I think to myself. *We'll get along fine.*

It's a long drive, and there's traffic. I'm in the front passenger seat, minding my own business and reading sections from the *First Contact* script. We're out of the ratlands and well up the mountain when Berman, who's virtually ignored me until this moment, leans over my shoulder.

"What is that?," he asks quietly.

I lift up the script innocently, my index finger holding my place.

"Where did you get that?"

It's a tone of voice I haven't heard for at least three decades; not since Uncle Saul found me hiding in a closet with his stack of *Screw* magazines.

Where did you get that? My impulse is automatic: I'll never tell. It occurs to me to ask him who the hell he thinks he's talking to, but I chomp on my tongue; it's a long walk to the nearest 7-Eleven.

"Give it to me." Berman snatches the script out of my hand. At first I'm too shocked to react. I'd gotten the pages, of course, from Braga; nothing about the transaction was the least bit underhanded. On the contrary, it seemed the most natural thing in the world for me to read the scenes I was about to see filmed.

I seethe, half ready to jump out of the car, hitchhike back down, and blow the whole thing off. But thirty seconds later Berman is smiling again, joking with Braga as if nothing had happened. I suddenly understand: The episode was not about the script at all. Nor did it have much to do with me. It was a display of primate posturing, directed at Braga. Big ape shows little ape who gets to pee where. Spooky—but very, very Hollywood. *Fuck the Borg*, I'm thinking, *these guys are the real aliens.*

Our hierarchy established, the ride proceeds smoothly. Berman and Braga run a steady stream of dialogue, flipping between shoptalk and inane banter. Their heads lean together. Sometimes they whisper. One minute they're hotly debating the Vulcan hand greeting (thumb in or out?), the next they're churning out Tom Swifties:

" 'I don't like the angle of that shot,' Rick stated obliquely."

" 'I'm allergic to shellfish,' Brannon said clammily."

" 'I can't believe my condom broke,' Rick ejaculated."

" 'I'm a heterosexual necrophiliac Hemingway,' Brannon remarked earnestly."

As the miles dwindle they obsess on the minutiae of the film. At the eleventh hour of production, the beauty is in the details. What does a 21st century jukebox look like? Will the visiting Vulcans raise their eyebrows? When does Jerry Goldsmith's theme music start in? I listen to them volley back and forth. Brannon's got a great sense of story, but especially of the story-within-the-story, the disparate elements that bring a scene to life. Berman's approach is more holistic. He circles the armature slowly, adding here and trimming there, like a sculptor modeling clay.

In an industry full of Alpha males, their relationship is remarkable. It's more than friendship; they're alter egos who have miraculously found each other. Berman is the family man, twenty years Braga's senior, with a wife and kids in tow. Brannon, meanwhile, is the antic fledgling: flitting through the L.A. underbelly of starlets and strip clubs, then flying home to nest beneath the eagle's wing.

A mile above the Los Angeles Basin, the air is as hot and dry as a Finnish sauna. Alternating breezes carry the odors of pine, fuel, and Port-a-Potties. Director Jonathan Frakes has set up on a flat spot. A narrow creek runs below a dry, tick-infested slope, trickling over stones and disappearing into the trees. A million dollars' worth of film equipment is clustered near the bank, shaded by a gossamer tarp. The electrical cables, silver reflecting scrims, and Panavision cameras look as out of place in this wild country as the junk we left on the Moon.

I got through enough the script to know what's up. The *Enterprise* has traveled back in time to 2063 and is orbiting Earth. An away team has beamed down to Zefram Cochrane's Montana refuge. The fate of the world depends on this drunken scientist; for "first contact" to occur, he must launch the *Phoenix*—his experimental warp-drive rocket—the next day. But Cochrane (James Cromwell, in a very silly hat) doesn't want to be a hero. He runs away, hip flask in hand.

"What people will learn from *First Contact*," Brannon tells me, "is how the *Star Trek* world came to be. One of the ironies, of course, is that the people who give birth to that world were suspicious, unhappy, and greedy; everything that Star Trek *doesn't* represent."

Frakes's character, Commander Will Riker, actually appears in several of today's scenes. He and Chief Engineer Geordi LaForge (LeVar Burton) chase Cochrane to the creek. They try to reason with him, but he breaks away. Riker, exasperated, sets his phaser to stun and brings the scientist down. Cromwell himself doesn't take the fall; when the scene cuts, after the phaser blast, a stuntman replaces him. The surrogate collapses onto the embankment, rolls through the brush and flops into the water.

There are long shots of Cochrane on the run, medium shots of Riker firing his phaser, and close-ups of LaForge's bionic eyeballs. Since all three actors have lines—and each character is on-screen when he speaks—the scene must be filmed from every imaginable point of view.

Edited together, the showdown at Charlton Flat creek will occupy forty-four seconds of the finished movie. It takes five hours to film.

There's no pretty way to say it: I'm bored stiff. There's a certain point that arrives in almost any peak experience—from a gourmet dinner to a parachute jump—where your brain simply stops being thrilled. With luck, you stay interested; dessert's on the way, or you're drifting toward high-tension lines. On a typical outdoor movie set, the glamour lasts about an hour. Then you're collecting pinecones, or carving your initials into a tree.

That's my first confession. Here's another: *The scene that follows did not actually occur.* The conversation took place, all right, but in a very dull office. But hey! This is Hollywood. If Frakes can convince audiences everywhere that Cochrane rolled into that creek, I can demand a little suspension of disbelief as well.

And so, grabbing a cranberry Calistoga and poppy seed bagel from the catering table, I wander away. A hundred yards from the site, at the crest of a bare hill, I find Berman. He's sitting on a rock, squinting toward the pasty sprawls of Alhambra and Whittier. He seems to be talking to himself, until it dawns on me: The unobstructed ridge is the best place around to use a cell phone.

I approach him slowly, showing my teeth and making appropriately nonthreatening noises.

Twenty-five years after *Star Trek's* birth, Rick Berman received the mantle from the so-called "Great Bird of the Galaxy"—a moment he remembers well. "It was a Thursday morning," he deadpans, "and Gene knocked on my door carrying this huge mantle. I had no idea what he was doing; he just passed it to me and left."

The facts of the matter are only slightly less bizarre. Berman had formerly been an independent producer in New York, specializing in educational programs (including the Emmy-winning children's series *The Big Blue Marble*). He arrived at Paramount in 1984 and rose rapidly through the ranks.

By 1986, Berman was vice president of special projects. That's when Roddenberry announced, to the world in general and Paramount in particular, that he wanted to give *Star Trek* another shot, this time as a syndicated television series. (Paramount did not yet have its own network; Roddenberry hoped they would produce the show, which could then be peddled to networks and other stations.) The studio was well aware that *Star Trek* had become a hot property. They were also aware that Roddenberry could be a real prick—so they handed him over to their greenest VP.

"I went," Berman recalls, "with an unnamed executive who was above me, to the first meeting. Roddenberry was very ornery, and this executive decided to get his dander up. He started challenging Roddenberry a little bit, which Roddenberry was not about to have. I just sat there benignly and smiled at Gene at the right time, with a look that said, '*Can you believe that asshole?*' "

Sometimes a look is all it takes. Roddenberry bonded with Berman, and asked him to lunch the next day. During that second encounter, Berman told Roddenberry about his personal history. "I was honest and told him I knew nothing about *Star Trek*," says Berman. "I'd maybe seen one or two episodes when I was a kid, but it was not something I was familiar with." Berman did, however, claim a familiarity with the world-at-large. He'd done a lot of location work and considered himself well-traveled. Roddenberry, himself a seasoned traveler, smirked.

"Oh, yeah? So what's the capital of Upper Volta?"

Berman smirked back. "Ouagadougou," he replied.

That was it. Twenty-four hours later, Roddenberry invited Berman to leave his post at Paramount and help produce the new incarnation of *Star Trek*.

It was a high-risk proposition. At that point, a syndicated television show had never been successful in the one-hour format. *The Next Generation* also would be a sequel, which had never been successful in *any* format. Finally it would be science fiction, which had not been a successful television genre for many years. "I would be leaving a vice presidency at a major motion picture studio for a job that could've lasted four months." Berman laughs. "But I took it."

During *TNG*'s development, Roddenberry surrounded himself with veterans of the original series. Berman was an outsider. But he was new blood, and that's what Roddenberry wanted. Berman worked on casting and advised Roddenberry on scripts. He and Gene spent a full day going through hundreds of audio samples, searching for fresh bleeps and chirps for the new *Enterprise*, its transporter, and its high-tech toys.

Berman became Roddenberry's right-hand man. He was among the few people who could challenge the Great Bird outright. "Which I did," he admits, "out of benign ignorance." One such showdown came shortly after producer Bob Justman had rushed into Roddenberry's office, convinced he'd found the *Enterprise* a new captain: a Shakespearean actor he'd seen lecturing at UCLA. Roddenberry mocked Justman, refusing to even consider casting "a bald British guy" in the role.

Justman backed out of Roddenberry's office, resigned to failure. He warned Berman not to go in: "Gene never changes his mind." But Berman gave it a shot—and the rest is history.

From 1988 onward, Roddenberry's health declined. He suffered a minor stroke, diabetes, and a host of other ailments. During TNG's second season, confident that Berman had a firm grip on the business, Roddenberry surrendered the helm.

On October 26, 1991, Gene Roddenberry died, and Rick Berman stepped in as *Star Trek*'s executive producer. During the next seven years, he would oversee the production of three series and three feature films—more than three hundred hours of *Star Trek*—outdoing even the Great Bird himself.

We leave the ridge and drop back down the hillside toward the shoot. In the distance, by the creek, Frakes and Braga are laughing like hyenas. Berman squints in their direction and waxes philosophical.

"I remember talking to Jason Alexander," he remarks. "The guy from *Seinfeld*. He's a big *Star Trek* fan. I said, 'You may have three times the fans we have, but ours are more loyal, and take it far more seriously.'

"Because we not only get to entertain, but to influence people as well. People don't look to *Seinfeld* for answers. They do, for whatever reason, look to *Star Trek*. Not for answers, but for direction. For course corrections. For things that will cause them to think abstractly, or metaphorically, or in a lateral sense."

"What about you? Has producing the show changed your outlook at all?"

"It has." He skips down a short slope, raising clouds of ocher dust. "I'm dealing with something that means a tremendous amount to millions of people. There are people around this planet who are moved, and whose lives are to some degree steered, by what *Star Trek* gives them. They write to me by the hundreds—and it definitely gives me a sense of responsibility. I'd be a fool not to take that responsibility seriously."

Berman stops to shake a pebble out of his shoe. "And it *has* changed my life. It's like being an author, or a musician, who knows that there's an audience out there—an audience that's looking to them for enlightenment, or some kind of clarification."

As he's yanking his shoe back on, Berman loses his balance. He stumbles sideways, hopping toward a scraggly bush. Just as he's about to plunge into the shrub, a terrifying sound—the chattering of demonic dentures—pierces the air. It's a rattlesnake, coiled to strike! Thinking only of *Star Trek*, I launch myself toward Berman like a short-range missile. The force of the collision sends us flying out of range, where we land in a heap. We watch in silence as the serpent retreats, then dust ourselves off and continue down the hill with our eyes wide open.

A few miles south, across a wide val-

DONDE MUY POCOS LATINOS HAN IDO (WHERE FEW LATINOS HAVE GONE BEFORE)

FRANK DEL OLMO
Los Angeles Times, March 19, 1995

Word is getting out among Latinos who are also fans of *Star Trek*—like me—that we're finally a big part of the science-fiction universe envisioned by the late Gene Roddenberry.

I have been a loyal Trekker ever since the very first *Star Trek* TV series in the late 1960s, but I confess that it was sometimes a bit painful to note how the racially mixed crew on the original starship *Enterprise* hardly ever included Latinos.

Jesus Salvador Treviño, a veteran screenwriter and director, wrote in the *Times'* Calendar section some years ago that he was still waiting for the *Star Trek* episode that would explain how all the Latinos in the universe had been "wiped out by some horrible intergalactic disease."

[Treviño was overstating things, but] Latinos had no continuing role until the premier of *Voyager*. Robert Beltran plays the starship's first officer and the chief engineer is named Torres. So finally Latinos are on a par—if not exactly of the same rank—with Capt. James T. Kirk, the macho American who commanded the original Starship *Enterprise*, and Capt. Jean-Luc Picard, the erudite Frenchman who took over the bridge on *The Next Generation*.

These things do add up in their small way. No less than the Rev. Martin Luther King, Jr. once told actress Nichelle Nichols that her continuing role as Uhura was an important milestone for African Americans. . . . If an actor named Beltran and a character named Torres give some Latino kids the idea of having a career in space science—or even science-fiction—they will represent a breakthrough that Gene Roddenberry, who once worked as a Los Angeles cop and knew this city's tough barrios, would surely have appreciated.

ley, the white domes of the Mount Wilson Observatory hang above the tree line like lost volley balls. "It must strike you as strange, and a little bit humbling," I say, "to know that two generations of astronomers have grown up on *Star Trek*. Dark matter and superstring theories come and go, but the *Star Trek* cosmology is remarkably stable."

Berman nods, a bit distractedly. He hasn't uttered a word about the snake. "One of the things that makes the show successful is its consistency, and its sense of history," he says. "There's hardly a person in this country who doesn't know what 'Beam me up, Scotty' means. There's hardly a person who doesn't know what a phaser is, what warp speed is, or who Spock is. These terms are embedded in the American mythology." He waves his hand, dispersing the constellation of gnats above our heads. "All of that is because *Star Trek* has been around for thirty years—and has remained true to what Gene created."

That said, he's ready with the down side. Everything people admire about Roddenberry's credo, he reminds me—from the Prime Directive of non-interference to the goody-two-shoes conduct between Starfleet officers—limits the arena for conflict. Working for the show is like driving a Maserati through a school zone—and Berman's the town sheriff.

"Gene's ghost is my greatest inspiration, and my greatest limitation," he admits. "He had incredibly harsh rules. Gene believed, when he created *The Next Generation* (though he didn't feel this way with the original series) that Starfleet officers didn't squabble. They were above all that shit. That sounds great, but it's terrible for writing drama."

After years of squeezing the franchise into Roddenberry's conceptual corset, something had to give. *Deep Space Nine*, created by Berman and Michael Piller in 1991, was the answer. The darker, grittier series, set on a remote space station staffed by wily and rebellious aliens, allows a few lucky writers and producers to let their hair down. But even DS9, Berman insists, merely *bends* Gene's rules. And that's as far as it's going to go, at least on his watch.

"Because *Star Trek* is a formula," he declares. "It's not my idea, it's not your idea, it's not Paramount's idea. It's Gene Roddenberry's idea of the 24th century. And it's very important for me to remember that. Not because I'm 'faithful to Gene's legacy,' as people love to write in magazines. It's because that's what *Star Trek* is. To change that is to not be doing *Star Trek* anymore."

As we approach base camp, Berman stops me. "You saved my life back there," he says at last. "How can I possibly repay you?"

That's easy. For years I've had a mad crush on the actress who plays Jadzia Dax, the beautiful Trill lieutenant on *Deep Space Nine.* "All I ask," I reply, "is a week in Tahiti with Terry Farrell."

Berman, a shrewd negotiator, looks at me with narrowed eyes. "Dream on," he says. "How about lunch with Quark?"

AWAY MISSION III:

KLINGONISCH

Morning fog—*nebel*—evaporates from the banks of the autobahn. Painted smokestacks pierce the mist, vertical billboards silhouetted against the sky. The highway itself is arterially smooth, as if it had been laid down overnight. Bright corpuscles—BMWs mostly—fly past our Volkswagen, bearing their chubby nuclei to shifts at Bayer, Mercedes, Siemens.

Despite the eternal industrial landscape, this is a far cry from the Germany I toured in 1971—the summer after my high school graduation. Even through the window of a moving vehicle, I get it: the nation is retooled and revitalized, a model of safety-goggle efficiency, dressed up and eager to please.

I flew into Düsseldorf and was met at the airport by Torsten Frantz, a tanky, twenty-six-year-old computer scientist from nearby Dortmund. Frantz organizes the town's monthly *Star Trek* dinners. Described by Frantz as a "non-organized culture," the dinners are endemic in Germany. More than a hundred of them happen each month, in cities and villages across Germany.

My original plan had been to join Frantz and about sixty of his buddies for their Friday night gathering. Since then, I'd been invited to attend a big Klingon feast—a weekend-long *Qet'lop*—in the forests near Trier. My visit to Dortmund, I confess to my host, will be a short one.

With sun-starved skin, floppy blond hair and wire-rimmed glasses as wide as television screens, Frantz is a certified member of Neogeeks Anonymous. Smart and serious, he bends over backward to make my stopover productive. Our program begins with a lunch visit to Gaststaette Wuestefeld, the restaurant where the Dortmund dinners are held. Frantz proudly shows me the custom menus printed for the monthly events. A disclaimer appears on the bottom of the last page:

> Dishes are served in the Klingon manner if the waiter is asked to do so—but you'll have to look for a location far away from the other guests.

Among the incomprehensible menu selections, Frantz recommends the Uhura-schnitzel. It tastes a bit like chicken.

———

Star Trek was postwar Germany's first real introduction to sci-fi. Frantz doesn't count *Shuttle Orion*, a homegrown program from the early 1960s: "It had such a small budget that electric razors, radio microphones and irons were used as props."

Before the mid-eighties, he explains, science fiction was considered entertainment for children. "*Star Trek* first appeared here in 1974, but you would not have recognized it. The censors of the German Public Network cut out the violence and changed the dialogue, smoothing whole episodes to make them suitable for kids."

German morality, along with humiliating memories of the Holocaust, gave the censors plenty to do. They nipped away at the racy American import, shortening some episodes by as much as ten minutes. They wrote fresh, wholesome dialogue and dubbed it in wherever sexual innuendo might intrude. There is a famous episode called "Amok Time," Torsten reminds me, in which Spock goes into "heat" and must fight Captain Kirk to the death. The dialogue was rewritten to make it sound as if the Vulcan merely falls ill and has a series of amusing dreams. Another episode—"Patterns of Force," in which Spock and Kirk visit a planet knuckled under a Nazi-like dictatorship—was banned for many years, and aired for the first time in 1996.

To further illustrate this butchery, Frantz hands me a typewritten translation of the *Star Trek* teaser, as recited on German television:

Space. An infinite area.
We write the year 2200.
These are the adventures of the spaceship Enterprise,
which, with its four-hundred-man crew
is five years long underway, in order to explore new worlds,
new life, and new civilizations.
Many light-years distant from the Earth,
the Enterprise forges ahead into galaxies which no man has seen
before.

"Pure nonsense," Frantz grunts. "Four hundred *men*? And it takes the *Enterprise* years just to cross *this* galaxy!"

In 1985 the first *Star Trek* movies—and unexpurgated videotapes of the original television shows—made it across the Rhine. Episodes of *The Next Generation* began airing on private channels in 1989, though hardcore fans were already trading bootleg videos from the United States and England. The fan club dinners started in southern Germany in 1981, many years before Frantz got involved. "So there were already lots of fans in Germany," he said, "even before TNG."

That evening we visit Frantz's friend Andreas, a gangly, gregarious Trekker with a huge beer cooler bolted into a corner of his living room. He shows me his bedroom. The walls are papered with photographs of Rosalind Chao—the obscure actress who plays Keiko O'Brien, wife of the chief engineer, on *Deep Space Nine*. A satisfied feeling envelops me as I behold this shrine: I am in the presence of true obsession.

Surrounded by a dozen bags of potato chips and enough beer to fill Picard's aquarium, I flop onto an overstuffed couch to watch the Friday night, prime-time broadcast of *Voyager*.

"I don't know if I have the courage to show you the German treatment of *Voyager*." Andreas hesitates apologetically, fiddling with the remote. "The voices have nothing in common with the American version . . ."

We watch it anyway, as well as a taped episode of *Raumschiff Enterprise*

STAR TREK PEWTER LIDDED STEINS
from http://www.cui.com/startrek.html

"Even in the bucolic future of *Star Trek*, manly men (and other rough and tumble entities) have been known to down massive quantities of beverages. Now, just to make certain that you can follow their example in true *Trek* style, Metallic Impressions offers these cool pewter steins. Each stein features a full-color, wraparound image from classic *Star Trek*, as well as a lid upon which perches a famous *Star Trek* spaceship! Kick back, relax, and beam a beverage down! Limited to 1,996 of each stein."

(i.e., *The Next Generation*) and the censored version of "Amok Time." It's the first time I've seen *Star Trek* in a foreign language. German works; the orders barked by Picard on the bridge—especially during a Red Alert—seem far snappier in *deutsch* than in English, and the banter between Spock and McCoy has a sharper, more diabolical edge. *Voyager* is especially weird. Kate Mulgrew's reedy elocution, problematic as it may be, is infinitely preferable to the voice of her dubbed replacement, who sounds like Olga of the SS.

My hosts bristle when I call the series an icon of American pop *kultur*. *Star Trek* is the cutting edge of a universal vision, Torsten explains; a mythos that owes no allegiance to borders or politics. It's a template, a role model for an enlightened contemporary lifestyle.

"It's more than a hobby for me," Andreas says. "It's not exactly a religion either, but something in between. It shows me how to understand other cultures; how to solve my own problems in a way of peace and not always with aggressive methods."

My hosts agree that *Star Trek* has been an inspiration for Germany's postrecovery generation. But they don't see it as a blueprint for the human future in space. A myth spawned by the Apollo era—which ended when Torsten was an infant—need not compel its viewers toward cosmic journeys, any more than reading the *Odyssey* makes us want to cross the Aegean Sea on a raft. To Americans, *Star Trek* reflects a manifest destiny, a new space age to be finessed with American technology and know-how. For my German hosts, the focus is different: it's the recipe for courage and resourcefulness quilted into each episode.

Late that night, while Torsten snores, I contemplate how Starfleet, with its Prime Directive and multiracial crews, is the polar opposite of the Third Reich. *Star Trek's* huge popularity in Germany reflects a generation's complete rejection of the Aryan *übermensch* philosophy that led to World War II. It is the irony of ironies that the first real flowering of rocket science occurred during the same insane epoch—with the deadly technology of von Braun's V2 rockets.

The *Josef Haydn* rolls south from Cologne, hangs a right at Koblenz and swoops down the Moselle valley, clinging to the river. The hillsides lie emerald green, candy-striped with grapevines. This is true rustic Germany: steeples everywhere, the houses as severe as Mennonite barns.

A turn and a tunnel carry the train away from the Moselle, and we race among fields. Horses graze between white fences. The sun, intense but uncertain, shimmers behind a cirrostratus veil. Every kilometer brings us nearer to the Luxembourg border, another of Europe's odd corners. Once a Roman stronghold, Trier marked the last of the empire's conquests on the Continent.

The perfect location, I reflect, pulling my bags off the train, for a Klingon Qet'lop . . .

My instructions, delivered via E-mail from a Munich Internet jockey named Ralf Gebhart, are simple: Take a local bus to the edge of town, and walk toward the forest. Follow the signs to the Qet'lop.

The bus ride continues for nearly an hour, much of it spent grinding up streets so twisted and narrow there are mirrors on the corners. Past the homes and streets and hidden drives, the land bursts open into wet rolling countryside, fragrant with pine. A feral cat streaks across the road. There are no other passengers on the bus.

The driver pulls over. There is a hydraulic hiss, and he thrusts his thumb toward the open door. He speaks no English; I, no German. I step off, hauling my bags, and he drives away. There isn't a car in sight. A sign along the road says *Auf wiedersehen*, though I've had no sense of being anywhere for a good half hour.

I start walking.

Rain falls. I get wet. Voices filter down from the hills, but I see no humans. There are signs I can't read. The road changes to gravel, then dirt; the wheels of my flight bag are sucked into the muck. Weak with irony, I recall Gene Roddenberry's initial *Star Trek* sales pitch: a "*Wagon Train* to the stars." It is difficult to convey how stupid I feel at this moment, wet hair hanging limply across my face, pants soaked, dragging forty kilos of carry-on down a bad road toward a dubious encounter with a bunch of Worf wanna-bes . . .

I'm not an obsessive enough fan to know how many times the term *Qet'lop* has been mentioned on *Star Trek*. Part lodge meeting, part bacchanal, a Qet'lop is a sporadic festival at which the might of the Klingon fleet is celebrated. The European events are held twice yearly, in spring and fall, when cold weather makes the heavy Klingon costumes sensible. I first heard about this Qet'lop via the Internet, and spent many anxious e-sessions lobbying for permission to attend (hard-core Klingons are reluctant to allow journalists into their private functions). Last-minute clearance had arrived while I was in London, approved by one Admiral Qor-Zantai Haqtaj (don't ask me how to pronounce it) and delivered by Ralf Gebhart.

An hour later, and still no sign of the event. I've given up hope of ever finding the party when I hear an extended crunching sound, and an American-made Jeep pulls up beside me. A freckled, earthy-looking blonde sits behind the wheel; there are saddles in the back. Christine—she introduces herself—understands English, and I convey my dilemma. She listens to my half-crazed

You know you've arrived when . . .

description of an alien warrior picnic and seems to wrestle with her better judgment before motioning me in.

We follow the road another few miles. It turns toward a canyon, meets the anchorage of a collapsed bridge, and disintegrates into the tangled concrete of a construction site. I shudder, imagining my fate if I'd reached this place alone. But Christine shoots off along a spur, directly into the woods, and we spend the next ten minutes bouncing over rocks and logs.

We emerge, miraculously, at the entrance to what is apparently a regional park. A hand-lettered sign, drawn on a paper plate, points us toward the Qet'lop.

"Yes," Christine observes, perplexed, "but how do we know when we . . ." Then she slows the jeep to a crawl, her jaw slack, as we approach an open area filled with tents. Banners with sinister lettering flap in the wind; the low sun glints off *bat'telh* swords.

Here, within a circle of trees, among picnic tables and barbecue pits, are the Klingons.

"Jag mobogh puuuu' . . . ! Jag mobogh puuuu' . . . !"

The strangely familiar musical refrain pounds throughout the grove, blasting from an industrial-sized boom box suspended between two trees. In a campsite at the foot of Germany's Moselle valley, eighty snarling warriors raise goblets of crimson "bloodwine"—shots of colored vodka, each containing a writhing worm—and toast the glorious Klingon Empire. For the moment, all is laughter and fun; later they

will engage in contests of brute strength and eat broiled Wiener schnitzel with their bare hands.

This is the third Qet'lop held in Germany thus far, drawing warriors from as far as Switzerland and Scotland. It's a highly deconstructionist event: Walking up the crude wooden steps leading to the picnic area, I pass a table loaded with makeup, glue, and sewing kits. A young man sits on a bench, stitching a wig onto the latex headpiece that will transform him from an anonymous Austrian accountant into a warlord from Qo'noS—the Klingon home world.

He is the rule rather than the exception. Out of costume, few of the men or women attending this celebration would merit a second glance at an outdoor café. It's amazing how the ridged brows and black lipstick, the spiked boots and fangs, lend these bankers, students, and computer nerds a savage panache. Ralf Gebhart himself, a grunge beanpole in street clothes, spends nearly an hour squirming into a costume of leather and latex that transforms him completely. What was geeky becomes diabolical; his whole personality rises to the role. Ralf is dead and buried, and I find myself facing Q'Eltor, a Klingon lieutenant capable of eating live spiders.

The change is even more amazing in Astrid, Ralf's American-born lover. Astrid is the first to admit her own plain appearance, and it's tough to argue with her. But in full Klingon gear, with her small breasts pushed up in a tight leather teddy and her gnomic head expanded by a black wig and cartilaginous brow, she is a consort worthy of a warrior.

"What do I call you now?" I ask.

"I'm taj'IH."

"Can you spell that for me?"

She takes my notepad, supports it on my back and scrawls the odd hybrid of capped and lowercase letters. "In the Klingon language it means 'beautiful knife.'"

I scan her hips for weapons. "Are knives a big part of this event?"

"No." taj'IH shakes her head emphatically. "One of our strictest rules is, 'no live steel.'"

"What's 'live' mean?"

"Sharp enough to cut your throat."

Astrid is an M.D., currently working as the director of an on-line medical service. Her family moved to Europe from New Jersey twenty-two years ago, when she was twelve. As taj'IH, she is captain of a Munich-based "Bird of Prey" named *quv'a'* (literally, "Honor"). The ship is part of the Khemorex Klinzhai: the European "Dark Vengeance Fleet" to which all these warriors belong. Its four hundred-plus members hail from England, Germany, Austria, Switzerland, and Scotland. Taj'IH herself joined in 1994.

Taj'IH (left) and Q'Eltor.

Taj'IH first met Q'Eltor in March 1996. Ralf—a longtime fan just coming out as a Klingon—had been surfing the Web in search of kindred spirits and found the Khemorex Klinzhai's home page. A picture of Astrid, resplendent as the warrior Taj'IH, pulsed on the screen. Ralf spent the next two weeks tracking her down. The first few times they went out, both wore full Klingon costume. Astrid barely recognized Ralf when she finally saw him as "his real self."

She leans toward me, lowering her voice. "Wanna hear a Klingon joke?"

"Sure."

"Okay. Why are Klingons born with ridged foreheads?"

I shake my head.

"Because Klingon pussies are so tight!"

We yuk it up. I inquire—with the barest hint of lechery—how her relationship with Q'Eltor gets on.

"In a normal way," she replies testily. "We know who we are. Listen, I keep a healthy gulf between my civilian life and my Klingon existence. Though a great deal of my time *is* devoted to my ship . . ."

I ask taj'IH if she can shed some light on why the Klingon mystique is so appealing here in Germany.

"Absolutely," she laughs. "Germans have a very anal, regimented existence. They're stiff, they're quiet, and they drink hard. This is a chance to break away. To enjoy a little anarchy. To . . ." A command, barked in fluent Klingon from the picnic table, draws her attention. She responds in kind, and turns back to me. "Gotta go," she announces. "It's time to stuff the Romulan."

The dummy, an effigy of an alien race despised by all Klingons, figures prominently in the afternoon's decathlon. Befanged contestants chafe and stomp, waiting for the privilege of hurling the mannequin to the ends of the earth—a feat performed to the accompaniment of bloodcurdling battle cries. That competition is followed by an "obs-Tribble" course, in which merciless warriors walk a crooked line while balancing furry Tribbles on spoons. Next comes balloon slashing, accomplished with crescent-shaped bat'telh swords.

It's a lot to absorb. I approach the bartender—by now a fond acquaintance—and order another bloodwine, straight up. Nem'Roc grins, reaching for the tweezers, but I grab his wrist: "Hold the worm."

Just then the music starts again: "*Jag mobogh puuuu'* . . . *!*" at volume ten. It's so familiar, and yet . . . "What *is* that song?" I demand.

"You don't know?" Nem'Roc throws back his head and laughs. "It's 'Born to Be Wild,' translated into Klingon!"

Pork steaks broil above a barbecue pit; prune juice flows like wine. Along a groaning board loaded with Klingon and Terran delicacies, fourscore warriors heap their plates with stuffed *to'baj* legs, *gagh*, and mixed bean salad.

RaH'el Qvl'n cha', the Klingon Defense Force weapons officer, stands beside me in line. She's lithe, dark, and savagely beautiful. Her jet-black hair ripples like Nefertiti's. The look fits; by day she's an Egyptologist, employed by the University of Bonn.

"Your nameplate isn't bilingual, only Klingon."

She shrugs. "I forget the German names anyway."

"Are you fluent in Klingon?"

"I love the language. There are so many similarities between Klingon and Egyptian. For example . . ." She spoons what looks like fresh placenta onto her plate. "This—'rokeg blood pie'—is a famous Klingon dish. In Egyptian, *rokeg* is also a kind of pie, made with meat and vegetables."

"Sounds like you're leading two parallel lives."

"I try to." She smiles, her teeth a gleaming ripsaw blade. "The name RaH'el, for example, means 'to be violent'—and I am." She grabs my arm and yanks me a few steps away from the feeding masses. "I'm addicted to weapons." She lifts her leather tunic, displaying the Klingon *d'k tahg* against her skin. The ritual dagger is a beautiful piece of work:

well balanced, razor sharp, and unquestionably lethal. So much for 'no live steel. . . .'

There's an awards ceremony at twilight. The top Klingon officers, dressed in thick regalia, assemble on a crude cement stage beneath a canopy of trees. The formalities are conducted under the glowering eye (and crustacean brow) of Toqduj Zantai JonwI: the fearsome fleet admiral of the entire Khemorex Klinzhai. Bats swoop around his ears, feasting on invisible gnats.

Ten warriors are called up in turn and honored for outstanding service to the fleet. Finally, Q'Eltor himself is summoned. Along with a promotion to Lieutenant Commander, Ralf receives the Qet'lop's coveted *SuvwI'a'* Award. "The literal translation," taj'IH explains proudly, is, '*That's* a warrior!' "

There is more drinking, more singing, and drinking again. When darkness falls, the warriors reconvene for a Klingon wedding. Qor-Zantai Haqtaj, commanding officer of the Dark Vengeance Fleet, will wed the half-Klingon, half-human B'Elanna Torres. The bride and groom look marvelous. Haqtaj struts among the picnic tables in his armadillo-like jacket, bedecked with medals and pins; B'Elanna, (named for the half-Klingon engineer on *Voyager*) adjusts her head-piece, and applies dark makeup to her nose.

Though the ceremony won't have the blessing of the holy church, it's carried out in reverent Klingon style. Haqtaj literally battles his way to the altar. He's a big man and brooks no nonsense. Thick-suited warriors tumble over park benches (and each other) with loud shouts, their swords clanking into the dust. When the couple is finally united, taj'IH—master of ceremonies for the evening's events—presents them with small tokens: an amulet for her, a nose ring for him. They exchange vows and drink together from a silver chalice. Finally the bride and groom snarl at each other and share a savage kiss. Blood (or something close) flows down their chins. They exit the stage amid roars of congratulations.

To love, honor, and obey—or else.

By the time the ceremony ends, it's

bitterly cold outside. I join a pack of Klingons standing around the pit fire, singing battle songs and roasting marshmallows. RaH'el appears beside me, palming her dagger.

"The wedding was great." I sigh.

"Yes." She leers, fangs glinting in the firelight. "But the divorce will be better."

An hour or so later, I find Supreme Admiral Toqduj Zantai JonwI—a.k.a. Andy Wilson—sitting alone on a picnic bench. I take a seat beside him. In his other life, Wilson is a rough-looking Scot, born in Paisley. A former cop, now a mechanic, he shows up at the Qet'lops "whenever I can afford it."

Wilson first saw Klingons on TOS in 1966, when he was fifteen. "I've never been a Federation fan," he sneers. "It's like cowboys and Indians. I've always sided with the Indians—and Klingons are definitely the Indians."

Wilson and his buddy, Robert Kirkwood, started the Khemorex Klinzhai (literally, the "Klingon spirit that grows") in 1993. It was an act of treason: a mutiny from the U.S.-based Klingon Assault Group (KAG). Klingons in the U.K. and Europe cheered the move, shifting their allegiance to the local leaders. From its seed group of "ten Scottish guys," the KK membership spread like wildfire. There are now more than four hundred members throughout Europe.

"America-based fan clubs tend not to be a great idea for the U.K., or Europe in general," Wilson tells me over a Styrofoam cup of wild prune juice, "because communications are difficult. Also, American Klingon groups tend to have a very short life span. They last a year, eighteen months at most, and then they fold. Compared to that, the Khemorex Klinzhai's been going a very long time."

The author enjoys a morning shave.

There was probably another motive for the split as well. Personalities attracted to the Klingon mystique, obviously, prefer being in charge. It's hard to blame them, especially the Scots, whose great heroes have been in small, marauding bands rather than united armies.

"Scots are born warriors," Wilson confirms, puffed up in his flamboyant uniform. "We've *always* been warriors. It's in the bloodline. And if y'hear two

Scots arguin'—why, it even sounds like Klingon!"

"Do you feel," I ask, "like a fleet admiral?"

Wilson laughs, rolling a smoke. "When there are other Klingons about, yes."

"Otherwise?"

"Otherwise I'm just Andy Wilson, mechanic."

A pod of warriors walk by, saluting smartly. Wilson nods in response and strikes a match with his thumbnail.

At 2 A.M., music is still blasting through the trees. The late-night anthem is *Tek for Trek*, a heavy metal CD produced by a band of musicians from Berlin. Everyone present knows the songs by heart, and their *Klingonisch* howls could rouse a rotted skunk.

I slink off into the medical tent and collapse onto one of the army surplus cots, shivering under a borrowed sleeping bag. The music pounds on through the night. When I wake at dawn, breath steaming, I see a Klingon asleep in the cot next to mine. His black leather tunic, metal sash, and molded brow piece are covered with frost.

That's a warrior.

HEART OF A WARRIOR

"If Klingons come from anywhere on the planet," Dick Jude had told me in London, "it *must* be Scotland."

He was referring, or course, to the Scottish reputation for hard-edged, high-grade toughness. Maybe so; but there's nothing brutish about the way Scottish loyalty to the Klingon clan is celebrated. Their ships meet monthly in Glasgow, where a primary activity of the fans is to raise money for charity.

Charity! Not exactly a tradition on Qo'noS (the Klingon home world), but it works for the Kingdom of Haggis. Both the Khemorex Klinzhai and Klingons Unite! (a breakaway Scottish fan club) have done successful promotions for a variety of human and animal causes—including the SPCA and the Brittle Bone Society.

Worf, Son of Morg, might curl his lip at such shenanigans (true Klingons are a pitilessly Darwinian lot) but he'd be outnumbered. There are now at least threescore Klingons in Scotland, from Paisley to Glasgow.

It's an impressive invasion—even the Romans never made it north of Hadrian's Wall. Guess they just weren't tough enough.

WORF FACTORS

Springtime in Los Angeles can be beautiful. Pacific breezes cool the air, and the broad canyon boulevards stretch luxuriously beneath canopies of purple jacaranda leaves. For brief, terrifying moments, it's possible to imagine living here.

I rent a Romulan-green Grand Am and drive twenty minutes (without traffic, everything in Los Angeles is twenty minutes away) to the Pasadena Convention Center, where the fourth annual "Grand Slam" convention is underway. The three-day event will feature dozens of stars and staff from *Star Trek*'s multiple incarnations. Everyone from René Auberjonois (the shape-shifting Odo in *Deep Space Nine*) to *Voyager*'s Garrett Wang will mount the stage, making grateful speeches and fielding questions from caffeinated, corn-dogged fans.

Ever since I got lost in the Roosevelt Field Mall as a child, crowds of garishly dressed people have terrified me. Maybe that's why, contrary to all expectations, *Star Trek* conventions are not my thing. They're a giddy distillation of Witches' Sabbath and Cub Scout jamboree, staged in hyperfunctional civic centers with peach fuzz carpeting. Small toys covered with beady-eyed LEDs chirp and rattle at me from every direction, recalling the terrors of the primeval forest. The fluorescent lighting makes me dizzy, and I keep bumping into obese Klingons and spilling their nachos.

So what am I doing here? Let's just say it's an anthropological expedition—and a chance to catch up on some shopping.

After carousing amongst the vendors (you can never have too many United Federation of Planets shot glasses), I make my way into the auditorium. There's a place open in the fifth row, beside a tall, curly-haired woman wearing a powder blue Starfleet uniform. She sewed it herself, she declares proudly, with a pattern she ordered from *Communicator*, the official *Star Trek* fanzine.

We're waiting for Michael Dorn to appear. The Texas-born (but Pasadena-raised) actor, who flies military jets in his spare time, is the first big name of the day. A seven-season veteran of TNG (and now a regular on *Deep Space Nine*), Dorn plays the immensely popular Worf: a full-blooded Klingon who, orphaned as a child, was raised by Russian parents on Earth. Tenuously balanced between his warrior heritage and Federation loyalties, Worf may be the most complex and sympathetic character in the history of *Star Trek*.

> **TOP TEN THINGS OVERHEARD AT THE THIRTIETH-ANNIVERSARY STAR TREK CONVENTION**
>
> http://simtel.coast.net/~amanda/humor/trek.html
>
> 10. "I just got Shatner to autograph my tush!"
>
> 9. "I think you're right, the hot chicks hang out at the *X-Files* convention."
>
> 8. "OK, a Vulcan, a Betazoid, and a Klingon walk into a bar . . ."
>
> 7. "But Ma—you said I could have my own phaser when I turned forty!"
>
> 6. "Oh darn, James Doohan is stuck in the door again."
>
> 5. "OK, men, set your phasers on zit removal, and let's go get us some chicks."
>
> 4. "Not to boast, but I played the unnamed, red-shirted security guy in the landing party killed in episodes 4, 7, 15, and 29."
>
> 3. "No, really, Fibercon IS better than Metamucil."
>
> 2. "Wow! Two girls! That's twice as many as we had at the Twentieth-Anniversary Convention!"
>
> 1. "Live long and purchase."

Before his appearance, though, we are awarded a "special treat": a visual homage to the character and his role.

The theater darkens, and the video begins. It is a montage, a cloying compilation of the warmest, most poignant moments from Lieutenant Commander Worf's space-faring career. To ice the cake, the whole thing is set to "Why Should I Cry for You," by Sting.

"Now and forever . . . I will always be with you . . ."

My embarrassment is extreme. I grit my teeth, and lean toward the Starfleet cadet beside me. "Can you believe how *schlocky* this is?"

But she turns to me incredulously, her face streaked with tears.

Cut to: the Paramount lot, four weeks later.

With *Deep Space Nine* in hiatus, Ron Moore has a small day. He agrees to introduce me to Dorn, who's filming a scene with Patrick Stewart. We leave the Hart Building and walk up Avenue C toward Stage 29, dodging studio go-carts filled with tourists.

Moore is considered, by staff and fans alike, to be *Star Trek*'s resident Klingon cultural expert. Introduced during the original series as straight-up villains, the Klingons have evolved—largely in Moore's hands—into a race of fierce, honor-driven aliens who live for battle.

"Exactly how much of what we see of the Klingon race is your creation?"

"Quite a bit," Moore says. "To be brutally honest and immodest, quite a bit. I wrote an episode called 'Sins of the Father,' in TNG's third season. It was the first time we went to Qo'noS, the Klingon home world. So I made some decisions early on that became how we defined the Klingons."

"I don't remember much about them from the early days," I say.

He shrugs. "In the first series, they were just villains. They were cool villains; they had a great name; their ship was great. That's all there was, really. When we were doing 'Sins'—which was about Worf going back home because his dead father had been accused of treason—I decided to make them a cross between the samurai and the Vikings. A warrior's honor was their guiding principle. But I also wanted them to be 'eat, drink, and be merry' guys, so that we could do scenes where, after a battle, they come back and party like Hell's Angels.

"That was how it started," Moore concludes. "After that episode, it was natural that I do the follow-up to it, and the follow-up to that—and before you know it, I was the Margaaret Mead of the Klingon empire."

I glance at Moore sidewise. "Do you think of Worf as your alter ego, the way Gene Roddenberry thought of Spock?"

"To a certain extent, sure. I'm fascinated with the military, and history. More specifically, I've always been interested in morality plays, where a sense of duty conflicts with personal desire. That's always at play with the Klingons—especially with Worf. It's always his family, and his honor as a Klingon, versus what the Federation says is right.

"It's an interesting synthesis," he continues, stepping over a loop of cables. "One difference between Spock and Worf is that Spock was pretty much the only Vulcan we saw. He was the funnel for that entire race, whereas we spend a lot of time with Klingons who are different than Worf. And Worf stands out because he's not like them. He's the guy who grew up in the Federation. He's always holding back, and repressing his inner turmoil."

We pass the studio powerhouse and turn left on 12th Street. Behind us lies the "N.Y. District," a near-perfect duplication of streets in SoHo, Brooklyn, and the Upper East Side. They're eerily empty, as if an air raid were in progress. "How do you feel about Dorn himself?" I ask. "Is there much synergy between your process as a writer and his portrayal of Worf?"

Dorn has shared ideas, admits Moore, of how he's wanted to play things. During the making of TNG, for example, he expressed a wish to fight differently. In the early episodes, Worf's fighting was an out-of-control, berserk kind of thing. Dorn felt that the Klingon should be like a martial artist: very precise.

"That registered with me, because I was also starting to think in those directions. So I started writing that Worf was a guy who would do T'ai Chi-like exercises by himself. That was a good note from the actor; it helped us both."

The rapport between Dorn and Moore is unusual. As a rule, *Star Trek's* writers are faceless and anonymous—even to the actors. At the *Deep Space Nine* cast party last Christmas, Ron proved the point. He and the other writer/producers got up onstage, each wearing a number. They challenged the assembled actors—who'd been playing these writers' scripts for three years—to identify even a single writer by name. Not one of them could.

"We're just a bunch of guys with short hair and glasses," Moore says, pulling out his *First Contact* security card.

The red light above the soundstage door is off; shooting has not yet begun. Moore banters with the guard, and we enter the cavernous room. The makeup mirror lights glow softly; extras in Starfleet uniforms slouch in folding chairs, crossword puzzles spread on their laps. Just ahead of us, within reinforced plywood walls, lies the set that unit publicist Alex Worman so accurately calls the "oval office of science fiction."

As many times as I've visited this stage, it never fails to hike my pulse. Here is ground zero of a cultural ritual that defined my childhood as much as Little League, Hebrew school, or orthodontia. Every Thursday night my father, brother, and I would open a box of Mister

Salty pretzel stix, pile onto the couch, and flick the dial on our black-and-white Zenith to NBC. We watched every episode of the original *Star Trek*, every single week, for three years. Then we watched the reruns. We saw every show a dozen times, until my brother could identify each one from the first ten seconds of teaser:

> "Captain's log, Stardate 4523.3. Deep Space Station K7 has issued a priority one call. More than an emergency, it signals near or total disaster..."

Thirty years later, the icons of that universe remain tattooed on my psyche. Never mind that the ceiling is a web of wiring, klieg lights, and cranes. Forget that the stars shimmering outside the view screen are bits of silver mylar, glued to a rotating black scrim. And ignore the fact that Patrick Stewart, whom viewers in more than one hundred countries revere as Captain Jean-Luc Picard, is wearing his Starfleet uniform over a Beavis and Butt-head T-shirt. Walking toward the bridge of the *Enterprise*, I feel like I'm stepping directly into the Great American Myth.

First Contact, Scene 233, is in rehearsal. It's a highly charged moment. The Borg have taken over the *Enterprise*. Worf and the crew want to blow up the ship—marooning themselves on Earth, but destroying the Borg in the process. Picard, in an Ahab-like fever, insists on facing his adversaries in single combat. He and Worf square off on the bridge, locked in a potentially lethal confrontation.

"You're a coward," Picard mocks, serving his Klingon security officer an intolerable insult.

"Jean-Luc . . ." Beverly Crusher, the ship's doctor, starts forward in alarm.

Worf glares back at the captian, death in his eye. "If you were any other man," he whispers, "I would kill you where you stand."

Picard sneers at his security officer, unwavering. "Get off my bridge."

"Perfect!" Jonathan Frakes yells to the actors from his seat beside the view screen. He's wearing a blue short-sleeved shirt and khakis; a wooden shiatsu massager hangs over the back of his chair. The *First Contact* script has his character—Commander Will Riker—on Earth, dealing with Zefram Cochrane, through most of the story. This gives Frakes total mobility while directing the scenes onboard the *Enterprise* itself.

His approval cues the production team to prepare for actual filming. An effects man starts pumping smoke onto the set. "Non-carcinogenic," Herman Zimmerman assures me. Electric is up; the Red Alert spotlights flash rhythmically, backlighting the Plexiglas wall panels. Two gaffers stand on ladders, tacking big sheets of white cardboard to the ceiling of the bridge. A primitive tactic, but it bounces more light onto the actors.

Frakes darts around the set with manic energy, ribbing the cast and crew. He's been directing for six weeks now, fifteen hours a day, but his humor seems unflappable. I catch up with him near the replicator, which is stuffed with cans of solvent and spray cleaner. "How do you do it, Jonathan? What's your secret?"

He grins diabolically. "Yohimbine."

I laugh out loud. The nutrient is an African bark extract, used by porn actors to sustain their erections during long workdays.

Back at the command cluster of chairs and monitors, a pod of production assistants pores gleefully through a box of photographs. The pictures are rejected portfolio stills, submitted by actors and actresses hopeful for parts in the film. As the PAs poke fun at the portraits—the cruelest sport I've seen this side of Thailand—the two principles wander by. When they see what's up, they grimace with revulsion. "It touches a deep fear," Stewart remarks. Dorn nods. "That's what they once did with ours."

They move hastily away, taking cover in the doorway leading from the starship corridor onto the bridge. Dorn has been aspirating too much; in an earlier part of the scene he had some trouble with a line about phaser rifles. He uses the lull to improve his diction, with Stewart as doting schoolmaster.

"Whhheapons," Dorn hoots. "Whhea-pons. Wea. Pons. Weapons?"

"Yes!" Stewart croons, much like Anne Sullivan in *The Miracle Worker.*

Matt Leonetti, the no-nonsense director of photography, interrupts the lesson. "Picture's up!"

The set—a zoo ten seconds ago—is now dead silent. Stewart and Dorn position their toes by the masking tape on the floor and run through the scene several times, nose to nose under the hot white lights. Frakes calls for action and the cameras roll.

Wardrobe girls wielding lint rollers run onto the set between takes, attacking the actors like cleaner shrimp on steroids. Stewart tips his pate toward a makeup girl, a steed nodding absently for the brush. "We need a director!" Frakes cries suddenly. He launches himself off his

Is *Star Trek* in Need of Affirmative Action?

Leah Garchik
San Francisco Chronicle

Donald Frew, scholar of religions and member of the Bay Area Interfaith Council, has come to the conclusion that *Star Trek* has a Jewish problem.

A recent story in the *Jewish Bulletin* notes that in four prime-time series and seven movies, *Star Trek* has had not one Jewish character. McCoy had a Southern accent, Scotty played the bagpipes, Uhura spoke Swahili, Sulu spoke Japanese, and Chekov spoke Russian, says the *Bulletin*, "but no one has even mentioned a bar mitzvah."

After studying all 250 characters in the series, Frew concluded that not a single one is Jewish. To make matters worse, a "villainous group of aliens," the Ferengis, are described in terms reminiscent of historical bigotry.

Ferengi are "short, swarthy, and shifty-eyed," notes Frew, "have big ears, wear a distinctive piece of headgear" and "are wanderers without a home." They are depicted as greedy merchants and "social pariahs. . . . It could just as easily be a description of the Jewish people from a Nazi propaganda tract," he told the *Bulletin*.

chair and disappears through a backdoor; Jerry Fleck steps in. A minute or two later Frakes returns, hiking his fly with a contented mien. "Now I can do a few more takes."

It's a meaty scene, and the boys are into it. Frakes is soon satisfied, calling for one last effort before the break. The cameras move into position, and the officers face each other like rutting elk.

"You're a coward," Picard hisses.

Worf bares his teeth. "If you were any other man—" his arms snake out, embracing Stewart—"I would *kiss* you where you stand."

The crew cracks up, and Frakes takes the hint. They break for lunch. Patrick Stewart makes a beeline for the catering table; Dorn pulls off his Klingon beard and steps down to where Ron and I are waiting.

Who do we talk about when we talk about aliens? Ourselves, of course. Our concepts of extraterrestrials are total projections, as subjective (and probably as ridiculous) as our notions about God. The cold, hard fact is that we have not one shred of evidence that life of any kind exists anywhere outside our own miraculous biosphere. For all our fantasies of what such creatures might look like—from dirigible-sized gasbags to saucer-eyed ETs—we know no more about the possibility of their existence than we do about life after death, or what dogs think about when they dream.

Despite their popularity, Klingons may be the most hackneyed extraterrestrials ever created. I don't know any more about "real" aliens than Carl Sagan did, but I'll bet you dinner at the Space Needle that, when we encounter them, they will look, act, and think absolutely nothing like Worf. The Klingon race was inspired by cold war paranoia; they were everything we needed the Soviets to be. When Ron Moore fleshed them out nearly fifteen years later, he used more timely (but equally earthbound) models. Appearancewise, they're ridiculous—a cross between "gangsta" rappers and elephant seals. They are such a cliché, such a bit of Hollywood vanity, that the only appropriate response is to laugh in their faces.

Which makes it difficult to expain why, shrinking beneath Worf's dark gaze, I'm ready to shit my pants . . .

On stage at the Pasadena Civic Center, Michael Dorn had looked like a well-dressed investment broker. But in full makeup, Dorn *is* Worf. He's 100 percent Klingon, and it's impossible to accept that's he's simply a human being with a pound and a half of latex on his face. My journalistic objectivity has evaporated; I'm alone with an alien warrior whose exploits I've followed for a decade. The spell is broken, thankfully, when a production assistant walks up and hands the Klingon a cupful of carrot sticks.

I bring up the conversation I had with Moore on our way to Stage 29. Aside from the martial arts suggestion, how has Dorn brought more subtlety or development to the role?

"I'm basically a cowboy," he answers. "A wrangler. I keep Worf within certain boundaries. Sometimes the writers will write things like, 'Worf smiles broadly, and does this or that.' And I say, 'No, Worf *doesn't* do that. He doesn't act that way.' I have a very clear picture of who Worf is. If you take him out of those boundaries, what happens is, he becomes un-Worf. People won't gravitate toward him as much as they do."

"They'll stop believing in him?"

"It's not a matter of belief, as much as it is that there's no *edge* anymore. There's no reason to go, 'Oh my God! Here comes Worf! What's he going to do?' If he's just one of the guys, you take the teeth out of the character."

Dorn was born in 1952 in Luling, Texas, a small town not far from San Antonio. Though he watched *Star Trek* as a kid, he really got into the show during college. His initial training was not in acting but in music. He played piano and bass and sang in rock bands well into the first season of TNG. Dorn didn't begin full-time acting until the mid-seventies, when he landed steady roles on *The Mary Tyler Moore Show* and, a few years later, *CHiPs.*

"Worf is *big,*" the six-foot-three Dorn observes, "and he's totally alien. I think he's probably the most alien of all of our aliens, because we always tend to have our aliens be humanlike in a lot of ways." He grins, but can't help looking sinister. "I think that's always been his charm."

"One thing about Worf," I say, "and I wonder if you feel it as well, is the mythical quality about his character. He seems to resonate on a very deep level with a lot of viewers."

Dorn nods thoughtfully. I resist the urge to poke my finger into his ridged brow, which appears to be made out of Play-Doh. "He's like all the great epics, in one character," he says. "He's Shakespearean in a lot of his language; he's samurai in his loyalty and nobility. And he's Greco-Roman in his basic sentiments of 'What is man? What is life's essence?' and that type of thing."

Gene Roddenberry was initially against the idea of a Klingon officer on the *Enterprise*. As a result, Worf's character took shape slowly. Dorn originally played the role as a brutish and aloof barbarian—not very difficult after sitting in Michael Westmore's makeup chair from 5:30 to 8:00 A.M. every morning, and spending each day with his face shellacked in irritating glue.*

Producer Robert Justman's original concept for Worf was a sort of "Klingon marine." Worf is still the most militant of *Star Trek's* players, the one who would just as soon negotiate with an armed phaser or sharpened bat'telh. In later episodes of TNG, though, and especially in *Deep Space Nine*, it's possible to see him demonstrate introspection—and take a longer view of his warrior's destiny.

"Do you know," I ask, "where you're taking this character?"

"The thing I created for Worf is, I made him a guy who's trying to be the best soldier he can. Deep down inside, he wants to be remembered as the greatest soldier *ever*. Even bigger than Kahless [the mythic warrior-hero of the Klingon race], even bigger than Picard." Dorn's eyes flash, and I pull back. It's amazing how, in Klingon makeup, even natural gestures seem threatening. "It's a lofty goal," Dorn laughs, "and who knows if he's going to achieve it? But I think Worf really wants to be remembered as somebody you can look up to and go, '*That's* the guy I want to pattern myself after.'"

"Do any aspects of Worf's character infiltrate your personal life?"

---

* Artist Michael Westmore has been designing *Star Trek's* special makeup effects since 1987. Although the concept of a ridged Klingon brow predated him, the look was perfected by Westmore—who drew his inspiration from cross-sections of dinosaur vertebrae.

"No. Because me, Michael Dorn, it doesn't matter if I'm remembered." He leans forward, elbows on his knees, right fist in left hand. "I'd love people to say, 'He was a good actor. He did some nice work.' But I don't have any lofty aspirations. I'm not like that. I'd like to be remembered as a guy who retired early and spent the rest of his life raising his family on a tropical island and flying jets around. Enjoying life to the fullest."

The conversation turns toward my travels and my perception of *Star Trek* as a real time international myth. When I ask Dorn about the gap the show might be filling in the collective psyche, though, he snorts in dismissal. "*Baywatch* is filling a bigger space than . . ."

"Yeah," I counter, "but *Baywatch* hasn't lasted for thirty years."

"But in terms of it being global, *Baywatch* is a bigger show. Look." Dorn turns up his hands. "I think that people who are obsessed with *Star Trek* would like to attach some importance to it—more than what it is. But I think Gene [Roddenberry] would be the first person to tell you, it's a *people* show. He was just doing great television."

"Well, it certainly transcends the medium for a lot of the people I've spoken with."

But Dorn's not having any. "I've heard," he says, "that people think [*Star Trek*] really shows the future that we hope for. God, I hope not! I hope our future's a lot better than this one!" He tilts his head toward the darkened set. "They also say, 'Oh, the stories are moralistic, they're all morality plays!'

"But me?" He shrugs. "I think that if somebody cures cancer by watching this show, if they're inspired to go beyond their physical limitations or abilities, that's great. But if you're asking honestly, I think it's great television—and that's just about it. It's something everybody can relate to. You can sit down and escape, after eight hours of fighting all day."

"Still," I insist, "the show is one of the only programs with a consistently positive ethical premise. Meanwhile, the rest of television is dumbing off into vaudeville-type comedy, hospital dramas, cop shows . . ."

Dorn stares at me; his eyes are unblinking and intense. "This is a bone of contention for me. Television is entertainment. It's great if it educates; I'm all for that. But I don't think you can educate through sitcoms, or even through dramatic shows, because they're written for a particular reason. It's *entertainment*. Same with this movie. If you want an education, you should go to PBS, or a library, and read about real heroes. Otherwise, I think entertainers should entertain—and TV should be television."

Worf smiles broadly, and finishes the last of his carrots. "Now I'm going to climb down off my soapbox," he says. "But that's the way I feel. A lot of people come up to me and say, 'Oh, Michael, [*Star Trek*] really has opened up this . . . it really showed me that . . .' I want to say, 'Really? Well, have you ever read this book? Or do you know about that guy who gave his life to help out indigenous people in South America?' *Those* are heroes," Dorn states with conviction. "*That's* awe-inspiring stuff."

Dorn wishes me well, and departs to forage at the catering table. On his way back toward the main bridge, he spies Moore. Dorn spends the next ten minutes towering over the writer, pitching arcs for Worf's character development on the upcoming seasons of *Deep Space Nine*. Dorn envisions a trajectory of tense and dynamic conflict, with Worf and Commander Benjamin Sisko (Avery Brooks)—the space station's leonine overseer—locked in a battle for Alpha male dominance. Dorn gestures with his hands, voice booming, eyes flaming with enthusiasm beneath the massive Klingon brow.

Moore listens silently, nodding. I happen to know that he has nothing of the sort in mind. In the upcoming years, Sisko will embrace his role as the prophet and visionary of the Bajoran religion; Worf will marry Dax, reunite with his son Alexander, and reconcile his Klingon heritage. Still, Moore doesn't burst Dorn's bubble—but he doesn't encourage the actor, either.

"It sounds," I comment as we exit the soundstage, "like Worf wants to be co-captain of *Deep Space Nine*."

"Everyone wants to be captain," Moore confirms dryly. "Not enough Indians, and too many chiefs."

AWAY MISSION IV: HUNGARIAN GOULASH

I cross into Hungary, leaving Germany behind. The Brothers Grimm scenery degenerates into a series of gray, grafitti-covered tunnels reminiscent of Spanish Harlem. Riding the rails into Budapest is like slouching toward Manhattan on Metro-North: you get that sense of inexorable decrepitude that you pray will shift once you arrive in the city's center. And so it does. Budapest's Eastern Railway Station, despite rows of withered hanging plants, is an Art Deco masterpiece: a tribute to the quasi-romantic Hapsburg era, before Hungary's spirit was pounded down by Stalinist repression, Soviet tanks, and debilitating corruption.

But that seems ancient history. Budapest is once again a charming city. I'm sitting on a webbed metal chair in a cobblestone square lined with stalls selling doilies, Soviet leader nesting dolls and other ill-conceived tourist goods. Stone lions dribble geriatrically into a modest fountain a few yards from my table. Couples neck at outdoor cafés, pausing in their mutual adorations to answer chirping cell phones. Sunlight leans in between the high blockish buildings, amber and angular, as if Mondrian had loaded his palette with honey. If I squint down an adjoining street I can just see the trees that block the Danube—here called the Duna—from my view.

The setting is a perfect fit. Strauss's "Blue Danube Waltz," evoking the aardvark-nosed Pan Am Space Clipper, will always be the anthem of my personal longing to orbit Earth. Seeing *2001: A Space Odyssey* at age fourteen was a pivotal event in my life, the seed that would eventually bloom into my obsession with space travel.

I stroll along the Pest bank of the Duna to the old Chain Bridge, crossing the river on foot, gazing at Buda Castle as the two "speechless" guardian lions (the artist forgot to sculpt their tongues) glower over my shoulders toward the Gothic spires of Parliament.

A funicular railway carries me up a steep grade to the palace itself, now a museum full of Hungarian art. I study the dark, heroic paintings: agoraphobic landscapes in which doomed Magyar soldiers, about to be slaughtered by Turks, put their lovers to the sword.

This is clearly a nation with some issues to work out.

Hopping off a tram outside the entrance of Kentucky Fried Chicken, I marvel at the honor system on Budapest's mass transportation system. No one punches tickets aboard the city's streetcars or subways; the drivers in particular couldn't care less. Some of the stops have vending machines that sell the required chits, but there are no guards, gates, or turnstiles to enforce the law. People simply pay for what they use, supporting a system that benefits all. Socialism, I reflect with admiration, had some lasting benefits.

There must be a dozen KFC franchises in Budapest alone. The branch along Teréz *korut* is perhaps the largest, occupying an entire corner of busy midtown Pest. The Colonel's stenciled face—the high-contrast 1990s version—grins hospitably from the window, inviting one and all to experience Hungary's grotesque travesty of his original recipe.

Eighteen members of the local fan club await me in a far quadrant of the eatery, surrounded by mirrored wall tiles and diet Sprites. They range in age from seventeen to about thirty. Only two are in Starfleet uniform, but everyone wears some sign of otherworldly affiliation. One man displays a Lego model of the *Enterprise*; a woman carries a *Star Trek* role-playing game that club members play on rainy days.

My point man for Hungary was Péter Porkoláb. He's the youngest of the bunch, but very tall—about 6'4"—and unusually self-possessed. His e-mail had reflected a James Dean–like cool, an unrattled response to my zealous glad-handing. Face to face I find him quite likable, with a keen sense of irony and bone-dry wit.

He introduces me to Emese Felvegi, captain of the U.S.S *Àrpàd* (the fan club's "ship" is named for the conquering chieftan who unified Hungary in the ninth century). She is heavyset, almost butch, with limpid, intelligent eyes and the hangdog expression of a career Eeyore.

"Hungary is a peripheral country," she admits, "with a lot to learn. We have to adapt to the other countries in order to fit in, to become as mainstream as Germany or Austria. There is a parallel, I think, between the *Star Trek* characters and the Hungarians in many ways. The theme of our last convention, in fact, was, 'The Outsiders.' "

"Outsiders?" If it's a *Star Trek* term, I'm not familiar with it.

"They are the characters who see humans in a different way. The ones who can give an objective opinion about us, and see flaws that we ourselves might not see. They want to be like humans, but something stands in their way."

The characters Emese (pronouced *em-mesh*') most closely identifies with are indeed outsiders. There's Odo, the protean, shape-shifting constable on *Deep Space Nine*, forced to live among "solids"; Data, the clever android who longs for human sensibilities; and the holographic doctor on *Voyager*, forever aware of the illusory matrix that sustains him.

But all of these characters, I point out, have powers and abilities that humans lack—attributes that place them in a class by themselves.

"I think that the Hungarian culture is also extraordinary in every respect," Emese agrees, making the connection. "Our novels are some of the best in Europe. Hungarian literature is outstanding—but most people don't know it, because there are few translators who can put the words as they are in Hungarian. And our music, or course, is world famous."

In fact, there is music everywhere. This morning, at every stop on my rushed bus tour of Budapest highlights, violins serenaded me with a canned repertoire of regional music: a little Liszt, a bit of Bartók, and a smattering of Strauss (Austrian though he was). Equally ubiquitous was Alan Sherman's infamous "Hungarian Goulash" theme, immortalized on *My Son, the Nut*.

The Hungarian Star Trek Fan Club boasts about one hundred members, including a handful of Germans and Romanians. Their last convention attracted hundreds of people, many of whom came to meet

Diane Carey's *Ghost Ship,*
translated into Hungarian.

special guest Gyula Szersen—the Hungarian actor who dubs the voices of both William Shatner and Charles Bronson.

The funny thing about all this is that neither the original *Star Trek* nor *The Next Generation* have appeared on Hungarian television. Three of the films—the first (*Star Trek: The Motion Picture*), the second (*The Wrath of Khan*) and the fourth (*The Voyage Home*)—have been shown on television, and *Generations* strutted and fretted in Budapest theaters for two weeks. The USS *Árpád*, I learn, is powered via the Internet—and by videotapes and fanzines sent by friends in the U.S. and England. For most Hungarians, though, science fiction is limited to the *Star Wars* saga and a homegrown, *Nova*-like series that Emese refers to with contempt.

"If you translate it," says Emese, "it sounds like *Space Gammas*. It wants to teach little children chemistry and math and literature, but it fails to teach anything, because it's so dull."

My hosts are eager as pups for the inside scoop on *Voyager,* and for any behind-the-scenes gossip I can provide about *First Contact.* I regale them with minor anecdotes, painfully aware that I'm not the Paramount insider they imagine me to be. A comeuppance of sorts arrives when I promise that the movie has a surprise ending which I cannot, under any circumstance, reveal.

"We already know the ending," Péter Porkoláb states wearily.

"That's not possible." I remember Rick Berman's wrath when he saw me leafing through Braga's script. "The security around that script is watertight. No one outside of Paramount . . ."

"The whole screenplay is on the Internet." Péter yawns. "It has been for months." To prove his point he recites the film's climatic scene from memory. I snort in amazement, and fall back in my chair.

Emese introduces me to Tamás Szoboti, an earnest young man who sits down before me, wipes off the table with a fistful of napkins, and presents me with a portfolio of pristine schematics.

The drawings portray the pride of the Hungarian Star Trek Fan Club: the USS *Árpád* itself, NCC-75011. Tamás has married *Voyager's*

STAR TREK

THE
HUNGARIAN
DIVISION

The logo of the USS
Árpád.

oblong saucer to an innovation of his own: triple-warp nacelles (those long, hotdoglike protuberances that channel warp power). It's an ingenious design, clean and sleek.

Along with the ship's elevation and floor plans, the portfolio includes drawings of the *Àrpàd's* crew quarters, shuttlecraft, main bridge, sick bay, and corridors, as well as designs for hand phasers. They're expertly rendered, as credible as anything I've seen on Rick Sterbach's desk.

"They took me twelve months." Tamás admits.

"Good God. What inspired you to spend a year of your life designing this ship?"

"The *Enterprise*," he says. "I love the design. I love the ship. It's large and it's small. If you look at the space around it, it appears small, but when it moves around a planet, it's wonderful. It's like nothing you have ever seen before." He leafs slowly through his drawings, enraptured by his personal Pygmalion. His eyes glaze over. I know where he is, and it ain't KFC.

"I don't know," he says, returning to Earth. "All I can say is that Picard is like a father to me, and Riker like a brother. Watching *Star Trek* is like going home."

Next up is Kata Kovacs, a mousy woman wearing Vulcan ears. She takes Tamás's place and leans toward me with her hands clasped against her breastbone, speaking in an imperative whisper.

"I don't know why, but nearly every person in this group is trying to *do* something. Trying to draw, to be creative. I've been a Trekker for a year only, but this club has inspired me as well. Before I came here I didn't draw. I didn't write. But I saw what the others made. I saw their drawings, I saw their models, I saw their articles and games. And I said to myself, Why not? Now, even I draw. I made a portrait last fall, for example. Not with a pencil, but with a match."

"I see." Nodding at this woman and her rubber ears, I feel like a fin-de-siècle psychoanalyst, confronting a fresh twist on the Wolfman syndrome.

A gangly teenager with an oval head, prominent nose, and tightly mown hair takes the seat beside her. He nods

Hungarian Trekkers display their otherworldly Lego creations.

grimly to Kata, and hands me a card. It identifies him by his Hungarian name, Zsolt Sárközy, as well as by his Federation alias: Lieutenant Commander Q. "Q" is an archetypal prankster, introduced in *The Next Generation*, who delights in annoying the crews of both the *Enterprise* and *Voyager*. By way of greeting, Q hands me a cassette of Klingon language lessons, narrated in Hungarian. "You can learn both languages at once," he jokes.

Kata puts her hand on Zsolt's arm, a gesture of friendship rather than intimacy. "A lot of people in this group were lonely souls before they came to the club," Kata says. "He, too, was such a lonely soul. But we are together and we are happy now. We can sow friendship, real friendship. We were looking for it, and we found it here."

Zsolt admits this is so. He had never really been a social person, he says; people intimidated him. But *Star Trek* gave him the ability to view his own personality in a different light. "I see characters on the show that are very familiar," he says in a low, nasal voice. "I can see myself in them."

"Anyone in particular?"

"The junior Starfleet officers. They're young, a bit scared, yet ambitious. It's a big future."

"What part of the future appeals to you the most?"

"Interstellar peace," he replies.

"That," I observe, "entails interstellar travel."

"Yes! That part is very important to me: the first contact missions, the explorations, the dramatic dialogues—those things. I like the stars and I watch the sky. It's beautiful. I want to go out there. I want to get to Mars or the Moon."

"Do you think that's possible?"

"One chance in a hundred." He smirks with resignation. "I do not live in America. I don't have the possibility of joining NASA and training to be a crew member. To be a passenger someday is my only hope. I will have to earn a lot of money to achieve that . . ."

"Zsolt," I ask, "do you think that *Star Trek* has a special message, a special meaning, for Hungary?"

"Yes." His eyes blaze with conviction. "Hungarians are very pessimistic. If *Star Trek* ran on Hungarian TV, there would be a possibility, a chance, for optimism. Not for money, not for work, but for the good things in life. The Hungarian people might see their future as a bit happier."

"What," I ask, "is happiness?"

He laughs. "Well, at the age of seventeen, happiness is having a girl-friend. At the moment, I am searching for one. But in the future, I want to have enough money to achieve something, and relax. Not by sitting on a beach, but by giving people something I have made. Perhaps a series like *Star Trek*. That would give me a sense that I have lived; a sense of *why* I have lived."

"If you had never seen *Star Trek*, would you be a different person?"

Zsolt ponders this, folding his empty french fry bag into triangles. "I think something would fail, would miss, in my life. I would be empty. I would go out with friends to a pub, and drink, and think nothing. I would live for music, or be a student—always studying. But that's a parallel universe," he says, brightening. "You ask, 'what is happiness?' I'm happy that I'm a Trekker. It gives meaning to my life."

———

After a face-off with an inedible order of mashed potatoes (think wall-paper paste), I coax the club out onto the sidewalk and take a few snapshots with Colonel Sanders in the background.

"I still can't understand," I say to Emese, "why you meet at this place. Is it because you think the food tastes like the crap that comes out of a starship replicator system?"

"It's because they don't throw us out. And the food is cheap. It's lousy," she concedes, "but it's cheap."

The photo-op seems clever at first—eastern European Trekkers posed beside another American icon—but I'm soon bored by it. I want something fresh, a more typically Hungarian background.

"How about Burger King?" Q suggests.

With Emese's help, I convince the club to take a short field trip. We move en masse to the streetcar stop, and board the first tram toward the river. I jostle aboard with the other members, and wind up in the center of the car.

"Let me off," I whisper to Emese. "I forgot to buy a ticket."

"Are you crazy?" She looks at me with bewilderment. "Nobody buys a ticket."

"But . . ."

"Don't worry about it!" A middle-aged man nudges me and winks. "No one ever checks."

Arriving downtown we stroll south along the Danube. Emese leads the group toward the Chain Bridge, where their Starfleet uniforms elicit amused glances from passers-by. We mount the stairs and flow

GEE, WOULDN'T THAT MAKE A GOOD BOOK??

Reuters, 8/4/98

HOLLYWOOD—Looking to keep its most lucrative franchise in the family, Paramount Pictures has paid $1.25 million for "Trekkies," a documentary about diehard fans of the *Star Trek* television series and films.

The film, which was directed and edited by Roger Nygard in 1996–97, incorporates interviews with stars of the *Star Trek* movies and series, including Leonard Nimoy, Brent Spiner, and Kate Mulgrew.

But the most arresting footage comes from the devotees who follow the voyages of the Starship *Enterprise*, including:

- A man who changed his name to James T. Kirk in 1974.
- The founder of the Interstellar Language School in Red Lake Falls, MN, who teaches people how to speak Klingon.
- A dental-care facility in Orlando, Fla., where all the staffers wear *Star Trek* uniforms.

Paramount Picture Group Vice Chairman Robert Friedman said he was not concerned that the film would offend Trekkies, the core fan base of the studio's biggest cash cow.

"We've done a lot of homework on that front," he said. "*Star Trek* fans love it. It's not condescending, it's a celebration."

out onto the pedestrian walkway. It's a great place for a group portrait, with Buda Castle illuminated on the eastern hills and Strauss's river waltzing below. But this spot above the Danube, I learn, has a symbolic meaning for the Trekkers as well. The Chain Bridge, Emese reminds me, is Budapest's "main bridge."

The sun falls behind the Parliament, and Buda Castle descends into shadow. The sky is lit with thin clouds, twisting red streamers that fade toward violet as we march back toward the tram.

Outside the Atrium Hyatt, between two riverside cafés, a stationary mime stands frozen on a low platform. No one seems to know what to make of him. Péter breaks away and circles the performer. He doesn't need a tricorder to make his diagnosis.

"Transporter accident," he declares.

On Sunday afternoon, Emese, Péter, and his new girlfriend, Dorina—a quiet, perceptive woman with straw blonde hair and the eyes of a Madonna—meet me in front of the Pizza Hut on Thököly út. We board a local bus and then another, bound for the outskirts of Budapest.

As we pass over the Danube and out of town, my chaperones summarize a century of Hungarian history for me. It is a tragic saga, filled with invasions, violent oppressions, and names I cannot pronounce. The common themes seem to be despondency and defeat, punctuated by the rise of well-meaning Communist leaders—often trained as writers, lawyers, and artists—whose ideological wind vanes collapsed amid the gales of rhetoric that whistle continually over eastern Europe.

"You'll meet them all," Péter assures me. "In the flesh. Or rather, bronzed."

Indeed; for our destination is Statue Park, a landscaped "Lenin Garden" where scores of Socialist era statues have been gathered together and put out to pasture.

The bus deposits us by the roadside. We cross the street toward a high brick wall of recent pedigree. Above the wall rise the black metallic heads and raised fists of Communism's deposed heroes. Entering the grounds, we follow a broad dirt path. The grass is dry and withered, and the weathered statues posture upon the parched earth like huge, discarded hood ornaments.

The space itself, conceived by literary historian László Szörényi and designed by Hungarian architect Àkos Eleöd, is an open-air theater of meaningful conceits. From the *Szobopark* guidebook:

> This crude, monumental brick wall has all the characteristic elements of socialist realism (pillars, arches, wall spaces). It wishes to create the illusion that it is a natural successor to classical architecture, but in its own legitimate terms.
>
> The imposing facade has only one "small fault"—the building behind it is missing.

Péter and Dorina are in a world of their own—exchanging glances, touching fingers, exhaling pheromones into the dry, conductive air. It was Emese who introduced them, just a month or two ago. She's predictably uncomfortable; the success of her matchmaking has left her in the cold.

We stop at each statue, reading the description in the English-language guidebook. There are monuments to martyrs, militias, even conceptual movements. Here is Georgi Dimitrov, a trade-union organizer turned revolutionary; Béla Kun, a journalist-turned-propagandist who was liquidated by his Stalinist comrades; Ferenc Münnich, a former armed forces minister whose statue was painted red, sawed off at the feet and toppled in 1990 by a methodical mob. Most of these former heroes appear poker-faced, with glassy, smoothed-over features.

"Shape-shifters," Péter comments, referring to an ancient and powerful race featured on *Deep Space Nine*. Composed of protean soup, Shape-shifters can assume any form they wish. They can be animal, vegetable, or mineral, changing their appearance as circumstances dictate. In human form, their features are as minimal as the bronze faces surrounding us. Péter has lit upon a shrewd metaphor; we nod in admiration.

It is surreal to wander among these unflinching ruins. I find it strange that they've been allowed to remain standing at all. *Those who remember the past*, the poet Gary Hall once remarked, *are condemned to remember it*. Not only that; it may be careless to leave the images of these once magnetic leaders in plain sight. History shifts, and another anti-Capitalist backlash could see the images trotted back into the squares and placed along the avenues again. *When smashing monuments*, Polish science fiction writer Stanislaw Lem has quipped, *save the pedestals. They always come in handy.*

The sun is in our faces. I turn to Dorina, who has allowed Péter to take her hand.

"Is there such a thing," I ask her, "as Hungarian popular culture?"

"I don't think so," she laughs.

"No rock 'n' roll bands? No Budapest lifestyle? No special style of dressing?"

"I have no idea. Sorry . . ."

"I suppose there's not, then. You would probably know if there was."

"I'm not sure I would."

"Jeff is correct," Péter interjects. "We don't have any Hungarian pop culture ideas."

"Does it feel at all awkward, then, to embrace American popular culture as your own?"

"I like American popular culture," Dorina says. "I mean, I love McDonald's and that sort of stuff. So for me, it's really easy."

"So you think *Star Trek* is kind of like McDonald's? Fast brain food?"

"No, no; I just meant that McDonald's is American as well. It's part of the American culture."

"I don't see *Star Trek* as American," Emese retorts. "It's built on Shakespeare. It's built on Greek mythology. It's built on details collected from around the world. And the characters are not all Americans. They are from France, from Britain, from Japan, or Africa. They are from outer space; from Vulcan, from Qo'noS, from Bajor. These characters are not saying how to fit into American society, but how to fit into *any* society. That's why we like it."

"And what will it take to make Hungary fit in?"

Emese shrugs wearily. "A new government, maybe. The cultural base is here, but the government is not as good as it was a couple of years before. We have some resources. We have some metals. But mostly we have agriculture: corn, wheat, and animals. A lot of animals. Lots of spiders." She shudders. "But trade is a very big problem. The government wants it, of course, but they already have big debts they can't pay back. They need new loans to support the changes they want to make—but that only brings more debt."

Star Trek's appeal, as Dorina sees it, is based on what I've seen in Germany and England: Gene Roddenberry's vision of an idealistic future, a human community where kindness, tolerance, and patience have superceded brutality and greed. Emese and Péter agree.

"Is it important," I ask, "that the show takes place on a starship? What if the show was set in, say, a bar in Boston?"

"Like *Cheers*?" Péter peers at me slyly. "No, that wouldn't matter."

"Not very much," Dorina agrees, stopping in the shade of the enormous Republic of Councils Monument. Thirty feet tall, it portrays a screaming bronze colossus with a banner clenched in its fist. "I really think the concept of visiting outer space and meeting new species is meant to show us how tolerant humanity can become. How understanding, and how . . . *human*. So in that sense, yes, the people in the *Enterprise* are important; they are people who are *doing* something. In a bar they are just . . . *simple* people."

"Do you ever think about going to the Moon, or to Mars? Does it interest you at all?"

Emese is suddenly animated. "I've always wanted to go to outer space," she declares. "I want to see what's out there. It is stupid to think that we are the only intelligent life forms, even in this humanoid form, in the universe."

I turn to Péter. "Would you go up if you could?"

He regards me quizzically. "To do what?"

I grapple with this. "On a 'five year mission?' "

"No! Never!"

Dorina shakes her head. "No way."

"Not alone," Péter adds.

"But you would be with a whole ship of people!"

Peter hesitates. "Well, maybe if Dorina was going . . ." They exchange loving looks; Emese rolls her eyes.

We have reached the limit of the park. The path leading from the entrance ends at a brick wall, crowned by gleaming curls of razor wire.

To our left is a fourteen-foot-high statue of Osztapenkó, a Red Army captain who was killed while negotiating for Budapest's surrender to Soviet forces in 1944. To our right stands Captain Sandor Mikus Steinmetz, Osztapenkó's colleague, killed by a mine in the same conflict.

We stare at the statues. Like the captains of the *Enterprise*, *Voyager*, and *Deep Space Nine*, these were reasonable men, men with enough courage to walk into a line of gun sites with white flags and letters of negotiation clutched in their hands.

> The path, which has guided the visitor so far, goes past the two statues of the negotiators, which have become a symbol for "farewell," and then a few metres farther, travels smack into the end wall.
> You can progress no further. You have to turn back.
> It is a dead end.

I reflect for a moment on the militaristic nature of *Star Trek*: the uniforms, the command structure, the hard knocks of Starfleet Academy. It occurs to me that none of that stuff is especially useful, and that Roddenberry, for all his imagination, failed us on this point. Or perhaps *failed* is too strong a word. Roddenberry, was, after all, a consummate television hack. The Great Bird of the Galaxy could sell the networks a future without war—but not without war's trimmings.

"Why on earth do you put on the Starfleet uniform," I ask Péter, "if you don't even want to go out into outer space?"

"We are showing that we are part of this whole idea of *Star Trek*," he replies simply.

"And what does that mean?"

"You want me to summarize? In one sentence?" He squints at the ground. "I think that, for me, the most important line in any *Star Trek* movie—one that describes the whole vision—is in *Star Trek II*. There is a scene at the end, where Spock sacrifices his life to save his shipmates. 'The need of the many,' he explains, 'outweighs the need of the one.'"

"Isn't that also the motto of Communism?"

Péter kicks at the ground. "Yes."

"But even in democracy," Dorina says, "the masses decide . . ."

"A Federation starship," I remind her, "is not a democracy."

"No," she admits. "It's not."

Péter laughs, picks up a stone, and throws it with all his might over the razor wire and the high brick wall. "It's not a democracy," he repeats. "But it's a very good tyranny. A good, working tyranny."

We return to Budapest and say our farewells. Emese places a few copies of *Trekker*, the "Magyar Star Trek Fanzin," into my hands. Péter presents me with the paperback edition of Diane Carey's *Ghost Ship*, an original *Star Trek* novel translated into Hungarian. It's signed by the entire Hungarian fan club. Péter flips to the back of the book. I'm amazed to see that he has authored the epilogue, a commemorative essay called "Thirty Years of *Star Trek*."

I thank him sincerely. We clasp hands, and I kiss Emese and Dorina, Russian style, on their cheeks. As they go, I raise my hand in the traditional Vulcan farewell, forming a ∨ with my fingers. "Live long, and prosper."

Péter grins at me wryly. "I would return your salute," he says. "But we have no word for 'prosper' in Hungarian."

I depart from the Eastern Railway Station at 0620 the next morning, passing through a landscape at first industrial but soon almost mystical. The morning mists rise above Lake Balaton, above gilt fields of ripening corn, above the onion-domed steeples in the distance. Rocking and rolling, we approach a border post. A mountain of turnips rises in the station's lot. Workers tramp toward a lumber mill; a boy rides a bicycle in the opposite direction. We enter Slovenia, another of those vast European unknowns that have failed to raise a float in the great parade of Western civilization.

The longer I stayed in Hungary, and the more I spoke with young Trekkers, the better I understood how odd it must be to grow up in an "outsider" country. Hungary's every attempt to rise into the mainstream has been trampled down—by the Turks, the Hapsburgs, the Soviets, and finally by the Realpolitik of global economics.

To the Budapest Trekkers, *Star Trek* is not about easy travel to other planets. It's about acceptance, emergence, and hope. On the rare occasions that *Star Trek* appears on Hungarian television, it is a glimpse through spacetime; a porthole onto an epoch where even Hungarians are consummate insiders.

HE IS NOT SPOCK

Standing on the threshold of Leonard Nimoy's Beverly Hills office, I make an effort to dismiss my preconceptions. It's a tough thing to do. Though we've never met, the man awaiting my visit has been a part of my life for more than thirty years.

Earthlings are fickle. We adopt our heroes briefly, trading up for fresh ones as we move from childhood to adolescence, from college into professional life. How many of our role models survive the long hot drive from our preteens to postpuberty? How many continue to be interesting, or even diverting, into adulthood? Among musicians, I can think of a few: Mick Jagger, Leonard Cohen, Aretha Franklin, John Lennon. In sports, three: Willie Mays, Muhammad Ali, and Jacques Cousteau. But who from the land of television?

I enter, knocking lightly on the open glass door. The fellow standing beside the broad curved desk is not alien to me at all. Pensive and intense, his eyes slightly magnified behind octagonal lenses, Leonard Nimoy at sixty-six looks like someone you might bump into at a Vulcan bar mitzvah: Mr. Spock's uncle.

My encounter with Nimoy grew out of a serendipitous exchange. I'd held no real hope of interviewing him. Shatner turned me down flat, and I suspected that his co-star would be equally disinterested. What happened, however, was this: For several months, I'd been engaged in a snappy and seductive e-mail dance with a woman who'd enjoyed my second book (a travelogue called *Shopping for Buddhas*). After much soul-searching, we decided to meet face-to-face.

The encounter didn't live up to our cyberchemistry, but we had a nice dinner anyhow. Over coffee, our conversation turned toward my book-in-progress. I told her about my interviews, and also about my frustrations—including the fact that I'd been unable to speak with anyone from the original *Star Trek* cast.

"Like who?" she asked innocently.

"The ultimate," I laughed, "would be to interview Leonard Nimoy."

"He's an old friend of mine," she declared. "I'll call him tomorrow." And so she did.

Nimoy is casually attired in a Monterey Bay Aquarium sweatshirt and blue running shorts. His long rabbinical face has wizened with age, and a salt-and-pepper stubble scratches the folds of his neck. The actor is indeed Jewish, a fact of some significance. Early in my *Star Trek*–watching career, I recognized that the traditional Vulcan salute was a gesture borrowed from Judaism. Nimoy himself first suggested this touch, in an original series episode called "Amok Time."*

"During the High Holiday services," he explains in his book *I Am Spock*, "the *Kohanim* bless those in attendance. As they do, they extend the palms of both hands over the congregation, with thumbs outstretched and the middle and ring fingers parted so that each hand forms two vees. This gesture symbolizes the Hebrew letter *shin*, the first letter in the world *Shaddai* (Lord). In the Jewish *Qabala, shin* also represents the eternal Spirit."

Over the years, numerous actors and actresses have been defeated by the difficult hand position. Celia Lovsky, who played the Vulcan matriarch on "Amok Time," was barely able to manage it. William Shatner could not. When he was required to give the greeting in *Star Trek III: The Search for Spock*, his fingers were lashed together with fishing line.

I, however, mastered it—and find myself hoping for a chance to

* The first-season episode, written by science fiction great Theodore Sturgeon, also introduced Mr. Spock's most enduring line: "Live long and prosper."

DOES THE REPLICATOR KNOW FROM MATZOH BALL SOUP?

These are discussion subjects taken from *Trek-cochavim*, an unmoderated Internet chat room for those who wish to discuss *Star Trek* from a Jewish or Israeli perspective. As of mid-1997, the Trek-cochavim Web site had more than 150 subscribers.

1. Are Worf's religious practices based on Jewish mystical traditions? What would a Jewish Klingon be like?

2. Is the portrayal of Ferengi monetary practices based on anti-Semitic stereotypes? If the Ferengi used the Jewish tradition as a basis for their Rules of Acquisition, what would the rules be?

3. The Maquis's circumstances are often seen as a thinly veiled representation of the current situation on the West Bank. Do you think this is true? If so, how should the situation be solved?

4. If there were a Jewish element in the training at Starfleet Academy, what would it be? What aspects of the training given to the Israel Defense Forces would be used?

5. In which segments of Starfleet would Jews want to participate? Would they want to be doctors, therapists, computer experts, and lawyers, as a lot of Jews are today?

impress this fact upon Nimoy. But he offers only a handshake, and installs himself behind his desk.

Immediately, an air of formality is established. I have been granted an audience. Not for the first time on this project, I feel I'm visiting another country; a kingdom where the customs are far different from my own. This will be a no-nonsense interview: no doughnuts, no coffee. We'll have an hour together, and then our allotted time will end.

"So," Nimoy asks, "how can I help you out?"

For a moment I'm speechless. His voice, so resonant and familiar, awakens a keen nostalgia. I want to fly out of my chair, and grab him by the arm. *Spock! Is it really you?*

I squash this impulse and tell him instead about my visit to JPL and the esteem in which the NASA engineers hold Spock's memory. Nimoy nods attentively. Back in 1967, I recall, he wrote an incredulous letter to Gene Roddenberry, recounting the royal reception he had received at NASA's Goddard Space Flight Center:

> I do not overstate the fact when I tell you that [NASA's] interest in [Star Trek] is so intense that it would almost seem they feel we are a dramatization of the future of their space program, and they have completely taken us to heart. . . . They are, in fact, proud of the show as if it in some way represents them.

"I've always felt there was a specific and easily identifiable symbiosis between NASA and *Star Trek*," Nimoy agrees. "Certainly, we've been welcome at NASA because of that. And, certainly, NASA was useful and helpful to the *Star Trek* process."

"In what respect?"

"*Star Trek* went off the air in 1968," recalls Nimoy, "after three years of piddling along at the bottom of the ratings list. In 1969, we landed men on the Moon. I've often speculated on how much effect that had on the future success of *Star Trek*. Because shortly after that, *Star Trek* started to take off in syndication. It's quite possible that the Moon landing cast space travel in a whole new light. Suddenly, the starship *Enterprise* became a more viable entertainment idea."

A bit different, admittedly, from my own theory—that *Star Trek* actually became a surrogate space program—but interesting. *I shall consider it.*

Nimoy's career has been highly eclectic. When TOS died, he starred for several seasons in *Mission: Impossible* and appeared with Ingrid Bergman in the made-for-TV movie *A Woman Called Golda*. He directed a successful comedy—*Three Men and a Baby*—and a rather disturbing drama, *The Good Mother*. He also acted in a number of theater projects, including *Fiddler on the Roof, Equus*, and *Vincent*, a one-man show drawn around the relationship between Vincent van Gogh and his brother, Theo.

I'm aware that Nimoy has traveled widely, and ask about the response that people have had to Spock—and to *Star Trek*—in the far regions of the world.

His immediate response, strangely, is to talk about the *lack* of attention he has drawn while traveling on business and pleasure. During three separate trips to Israel, he was approached only by a handful of American tourists. In Italy and France, virtually no one accosted him. Nor was he recognized in China, or in the former Soviet Union.

"That's surprising," I say, "because I know that the original series is shown in England, Europe, even parts of Asia . . ." The more I look at him, though, the more I'm forced to admit: the actor is thirty years and a few hundred haircuts removed from the fresh-faced Vulcan science officer.

Still, I press him. He must have seen *something* to indicate why, after so many years, the show has attained global popularity. Nimoy squints, palms pressed together beneath his chin. It is a function, he states, of critical mass. *Star Trek* is popular because, like Shakespeare, it is ubiquitous. There's just no avoiding it.

BRITISH CUSTOMS OFFICIALS CONSIDER MR. SPOCK DOLLS TO BE ILLEGAL ALIENS

DANA MILBANK
The Wall Street Journal, August 2, 1994

EU officials in Brussels, on their continuing mission to boldly go where no government has gone before, have applied the Vulcan death grip to *Star Trek* hero Spock. Likenesses of the pointy-eared Spock and of other "nonhuman creatures" have fallen victim to an EU quota on dolls made in China.

As part of an effort to establish Pan-European quotas on various products, the EU Council of Ministers in February slapped a quota equivalent to $81.7 million on nonhuman dolls from China. But it left human dolls alone.

This has put British customs officials in the unusual position of debating each doll's humanity. So far, they have blacklisted popular nonhuman dolls Noddy and Big Ears; they've cleared Batman and Robin. Although they've turned away Spock because of his Vulcan origins, they will admit *Star Trek*'s Captain Kirk. Teddy bears have also fallen to the quotas.

Star Trek fans say the governments should not be meddling with the final frontier. Dan Madsen, president of *Star Trek: The Official Fan Club* in Colorado, said the customs officials "ought to cut Spock some slack" because his mother, Amanda, was human. But Britain's customs office is standing firm on Spock. "We see no reason to change our interpretation," says spokesman Dez Barrett-Denyer. "You don't find a human with ears that size."

"There must be more to it than that," I say. "I've been in contact with people all over the world who have expressed a profound emotional connection to the show."

"Are you talking about the original series?"

"I'm talking about the whole, thirty-two-year-old franchise. Somehow, something has clicked on an international level."

"Well, then, I must plead ignorance." Nimoy shakes his head, befuddled. "There may be something in *The Next Generation, Deep Space Nine,* or *Voyager* that has triggered this. I'm not in touch with that." There's something ponderous, almost gruff about him. Mr. Spock may be less emotional, but he's somehow more *animated.* "My foreign experiences with *Star Trek* have been very sketchy, and I often wonder whether we're being successfully translated. You know, *Star Trek* is a language show. At least *our* episodes were very much a language show."

"What do you mean—the banter? All that heel biting between Kirk, Spock and McCoy?"

He nods. "Also, a lot of ideas on *Star Trek* were expressed verbally. It has been said—and I think it's true—that if you didn't *listen* to *Star Trek*, you couldn't follow the stories very well. It's not a cinematic show. At least, not the episodes that we did."

Nimoy recalls two specific incidents where translation had a direct impact upon the popularity or perception of *Star Trek*. The first occurred in France, years after TOS aired in America. Nimoy tried to find out, at Paramount's request, why the original series had done so poorly there. He learned that, early on, Paramount had cut corners by importing the Canadian, Quebeçois-dubbed version of *Star Trek* to France. One can imagine how the French reacted; the show went over like yak-wool panties.

The second incident occurred in Japan, during a promotional tour for *Star Trek III: The Search for Spock*, in 1984. On his way to a book signing, Nimoy met the translator of the *Star Trek* novels in Japan.

"We had an interesting conversation, to say the least." Nimoy laughs, a gesture that transforms his entire appearance. "He was *extremely* chauvinistic. He said—" Nimoy frowns and furrows his brow like a Hokusai samurai— " 'I must make changes in the *Star Trek* novels, for Japanese audience!' I said, 'What kind of changes?' And he said, 'Aaahh! Too much, ah, *familiarity* with crew and captain! Japanese culture does not accept this kind of easy familiarity: Dr. McCoy and Mr. Spock with Captain Kirk! Authority figures demand more respect. Not appropriate conversation in *Star Trek*!'

"I told him that one of the things *Star Trek* was *about* was the camaraderie between these people. 'Not acceptable for Japanese audience!' said he.

"I came back and told this to Gene Roddenberry. I was shocked by it. I thought, *This is an amazing misuse of power by this man—to decide how* Star Trek *should be interpreted for Japan!*"

As Nimoy speaks, I find myself stealing glances at his ears. They are large, beautifully shaped, and, for the moment, perfectly human. They may be, I realize, the most notorious ears in history. Nearly every book about the making of *Star Trek* describes in exquisite detail the agonies these poor ears have suffered: the endless plaster castings, the rubber molds, the fittings with foam rubber and glue; month after month of trial and error, culminating at last in the otherworldly appendages familiar to everyone from Dennis Rodman to the Dalai Lama. Seeing those famous ears this way—in their natural, unguarded state—is vaguely shocking, like seeing God without his beard.

"You know," I say, "what you've done may be unique in the history of entertainment. You've created a mythological character as compelling as any in world literature. But have you given any thought as to *why* Spock strikes such a universal chord? What is it about Spock himself that resonates so deeply with people?"

"I think it operates on a lot of levels," he reflects. "Early on, when the show first went on the air, I was receiving mounds and mounds of fan mail from little kids. They couldn't have had any concept of what

Spock was about, except that he was a strange and interesting-looking man, one who didn't *frighten* them."

The children sent him thousands of drawings, all of Spock. Something about the Vulcan's image—the ears, the eyebrows, the bowl-cut hair—was tremendously compelling to them.

"Which was very interesting, because NBC was very trepidant about the ears and the eyebrows." Nimoy leans back, his arm draped casually behind his head. "They especially thought Spock might be problematic in the Bible Belt, where people would see him as a devilish character." He smiles faintly. "It was quite the contrary, of course."

Nimoy swivels slowly in his chair. I peer around the office, noticing a 1951 pulp poster from *Kid Monk Baroni*. This was Nimoy's first starring role; he was twenty. Like Spock, this character had an odd appearance. The "Monk" was a slightly disfigured Italian boxer, a forceps baby from New York's Lower East Side.

"And then there's the aspect of Spock's distance, Spock's *coolness,*" Nimoy continues. "Which played well in the sixties, when 'cool' was important. I've also read pieces by women, that describe Spock as someone whom women wanted to nurture, as he seemed to need the warmth that a woman can offer. There was also the challenge of, 'Could I be the one to "awaken" Spock? Could I be the one who can help him get in touch with his sexuality, and with intimacy?'"

I was hooked on Spock at twelve—but it obviously wasn't about sex, or nurturing. And although I never trotted out my Vulcan Green Crayola, he definitely got under my skin. He's there still—and I admit as much to Nimoy. He nods sympathetically.

"That's because there is also a sensitive side to Spock, to which a lot of people, male *and* female, responded. Also very important—at least *I* thought it was, because it was what I was constantly playing—is the yin/yang balance between our right and left brains. How do you get through life as a feeling person, without letting emotions rule you? How do you balance the intellectual and emotional sides of your being? I think people identified with that and understood that, in that sense, Spock is a very *human* character. He chooses to downplay, ignore, deny, his emotions—but he *has* them."

Nimoy scratches his chin, and I notice his arm. He's wearing, of all things, a Micky Mouse wristwatch. The juxtaposition of these two characters, these two familiar icons from the American mythos, is transcendentally weird. I try to imagine the reverse: Steamboat Willie, whistling off to work with a *Star Trek* lunch box.

"I think Spock was a proud alien," Nimoy concludes. "Proudly alien-ated. And kids still identify with that. I see kids today with strange hair, strange piercings, tattoos; this is all about alienation, and establishing a separate identity. 'I am *not* one of the crowd. I am different. I am spe-cial.' And Spock always *was* different and special. Jokingly, to Dr. McCoy [DeForest Kelley], he would say, 'This is the way I am, and I don't have a problem with it. If you do, it's *your* problem.' I think that resonates for young people. Teenagers, adolescents, who are trying to play out their own identity in the world, without getting sucked into the mass culture."

But it is mass culture, of course, that has given them Spock in the first place. Beaming from television sets and theater screens from Darwin to Dubuque, Nimoy's alter ego was the harbinger of a future in which logic would reign over emotion and rational thought triumph over blind faith. He was a digital being in an analog world, the Pied Piper for the wired generation.

Anyone who watched the original series with any regularity knows how magnetic Spock's charisma was. For many of us, he was nothing less than a role model. If there were two characters I wanted to be dur-ing the sixties, they were Mr. Spock—and James Bond. The relation-ship is quite logical. Both displayed total self-confidence and amazing problem-solving skills. Both traveled to exotic locales, surviving any number of deadly perils. Both were irresistible to women. And both shared a quality that my generation lacked completely: *composure.*

Bond, of course, had his weaknesses; his tackle rattled like a crib toy at the sight of a well-filled bikini. But Mr. Spock was virtually unassail-able. The most startling marvels in the cosmos were "fascinating." Disasters were "unfortunate," perhaps even "tragic." The raised eye-brow, the vaguely sarcastic mien—these were coins of the realm to my circle of adolescent friends. How did we weather the terrors of grade school? We became Spock. How did we survive the irrational outbursts of our parents? By invoking Spock. Who served as our logical, enlight-ened counterpoint to the madness of the late 1960s? Who else, I say, but Spock?

If Spock had this effect on his viewers, imagine the impact on the man who wore the ears. For Nimoy, the relationship was often hellish. Even out of costume, there was no time off. People on the street addressed him as Spock; he found his responses to friends and family mirroring the Vulcan sensibility. For ten years—from the end of TOS to *Star Trek: The Motion Picture* in 1979—Nimoy struggled to shake off his alias. It was more than a matter of altering the public's perception; he needed to exorcise the emotionally distant Vulcan from his core. This is when he wrote *I Am Not Spock*, a rejection so bilious that Paramount had grave doubts they'd ever reprise the role again. He also bared his soul in reams of verse, published in a volume entitled *Warmed by Love*. That did the trick. Nothing in the galaxy would send a Vulcan to flight faster than these saccharine love poems, profusely illustrated with birds, butterflies, and flowers.*

But time blunts all edges, and a true bonhomie now prevails between the Boston native and his Vulcan twin. So completely has Nimoy made peace with his doppelgänger that he published, in 1995, a second autobiography, *I Am Spock*. Punctuated with dialogues between Nimoy and his alien avatar, the book acknowledges the debt the two owe each other. It is the inevitable reconciliation between a mortal actor and his immortal role.

I ask Nimoy if his dialogue with Spock continues. His reply—a curt "yes"—makes me wonder if I've overstepped my bounds.

"Would you say, then, that there's something Spock has ultimately bequeathed you?"

Nimoy grunts at the question, as if answering will cost him physical effort. Is he annoyed? I'm finding it difficult to gauge his mood.

"I'm sure," he replies at last. "I didn't used to think about these issues quite so consciously." A pause. "I *have* been changed by him. No question about it. I guess that's the reason I finally wrote *I Am Spock*; I discovered that I had come full circle, and come to terms in a kind of convergence with the character." He revolves to face me and leans forward over the desk. "There was a moment, making *Star Trek VI: The Undiscovered Country*, where I had a scene with Bill Shatner. Spock, somewhat disillusioned by what's happened in the plot, says to Kirk, 'Is it possible that we two, you and I, have grown so old and inflexible, that we have outlived our usefulness?' I was talking, obviously, as Spock to Kirk; but as I said it, I realized that I could also be Leonard Nimoy, talking to Bill Shatner."

The Undiscovered Country, released in 1991, was the last *Star Trek*

---

* I might also mention that, during the 1970s, both Nimoy and William Shatner released pop albums. *The Two Sides of Leonard Nimoy*, which includes the inexplicable "Ballad of Bilbo Baggins," is not to be missed. Shatner's effort, *The Transformed Man*, is a minor classic as well. El Capitan's ranting cover of "Lucy in the Sky with Diamonds" may be described, without a shred of exaggeration, as the low watermark in a decade defined by bad taste.

movie Nimoy worked on. His final portrayal of Spock came later that same year, when he guest-starred in a TNG cliff-hanger called "Unification." Previous to that he'd appeared in all the Trek films, and directed two of them: *Star Trek III: The Search for Spock* and the immensely popular *Star Trek IV: The Voyage Home*, which he co-wrote as well. I'm fascinated to learn that the idea behind *Star Trek IV*— the recovery of two humpback whales from 20th-century Earth—owed a debt to biologist Edward O. Wilson. "It was his book *Biophilia* that inspired me to deal with the subject of endangered species," Nimoy confirms. "Specifically with the *loss* of species and its potential impact on humanity."

In early 1994, Nimoy was offered the opportunity to direct and appear in *Star Trek: Generations*, the first film to include the *Next Generation* cast. The screenplay, by Braga and Moore, was a done deal. Nimoy read it and turned the project down. Spock's role was no more than a cameo, he said, and there were other problems with the script as well. (His final decision, though artistically sound, opened a serious rift with Rick Berman; particularly when DeForest Kelley, a loyal friend of Nimoy's, shunned the production as well.)

When all is said and done, though, no one—with the exception of Gene Roddenberry himself—has had a longer, more vital, or more *intelligent* relationship with the show. Acknowledging this, I ask Nimoy for his sense of what *Star Trek* is—and what it could be.

"For me, it always goes back to the basic ideas we were dealing with when I was very active with the show. The *Enterprise* crew was a professional team of people solving problems. Those problems had relevance in this culture, even though they were placed in the 23rd century. And it was always a very *humanistic* show; one that celebrated the potential strengths of mankind, of our civilization, with great respect for all kinds of life, and a great hope that there be communication between civilizations and cultures.

"Stories that grow out of that kind of an ethos are what *Star Trek* should always be about," he concludes. "And I think that resonates throughout the world."

"Are those your own sentiments as well?"

"They're very important to me." He raises his eyebrows—both of them at once. "That's why I felt so much at home doing the show. Maybe once in a while we'd go astray, in various ways, and sometimes it was very successful. 'The Trouble with Tribbles,' for example, had nothing to do with anything I'm talking about. But it's fine. You lighten up once in a while, have a romp, and then go back to the other kind of stuff."

———————

At this writing, Nimoy's current project is a recording venture called "Alien Voices." Working with actors drawn from the *Star Trek* stable— John deLancie, Roxann Dawson, and Armin Shimerman, to name a few—he is producing two-hour-long dramatizations, on compact disc and cassette, of such science fiction classics as H. G. Wells's *The Time Machine,* Jules Verne's *Journey to the Center of the Earth* and *The Lost World.*

"From the Arthur Conan Doyle novel," Nimoy clarifies quickly.

"Not the *Jurassic . . .*"

"No." He closes his eyes and shakes his head. "Wow. Wow. Wow. Oh, oh, oh. Deadly. Terrible."

The Voices project has been a lot of fun, he says. No money, yet, but lots of fun. To me, the concept seems bizarrely retro. Will people shell out hard cash for passive, audio-only media in this brave new age of Tamagotchi cyberpets and action-packed CD-ROM games?

The truth is, it matters not. Three decades of *Star Trek* residuals have given Nimoy the freedom to experiment. Alien Voices, he feels, is a project with integrity and sizzle. It is, essentially, a labor of love.

The glorious illogic of it!

Nimoy glances at his Mickey Mouse watch. Our hour is up. "Okay!" he announces. I tuck away my microphone and compile the souvenirs he's given me: two Alien Voices CDs and an autographed copy of *Warmed by Love.* His assistant snaps a picture of us in a corner of the office, and I bid the actor farewell.

When I recall our parting later, I experience a moment of regret. It was an opportunity, I realize, for perfect literary closure: I could have offered *him* my long-practiced hand salute. At the time, of course, it never occurred to me . . . And maybe I'm glad that it didn't. Leonard Nimoy, after all, is not a Vulcan; and I'm certainly not a rabbi.

BAD NEWS FROM IVOR PRIME

Jonathan Frakes has been in the director's chair for nearly eight hours by the time I arrive on Stage 29. I walk quickly past the catering table and makeup stations to the radiant corner where filming is underway. The main bridge is dormant, lit only by auxiliary lights. Peering over the soundman's shoulder, I read the daily call sheet. They're shooting Scene 17, the last work of the day.

The action takes place in Jean-Luc Picard's ready room, stage right of the bridge. Patrick Stewart is inside, separated from the film crew by a cutaway wall. The space is jammed; he's barely visible through the clutter of lights, cameras, and cables. I sneak up behind Frakes and watch the action on the director's twin Sony monitors.

Stewart currently inhabits a position that every actor dreams of: dominating a role so completely that a replacement would be unthinkable. With Captain Kirk in cold storage, only one man alive can bridle the *Enterprise*—and Paramount wants to keep him happy. As a result, Stewart's touch can be felt all over *First Contact*. He edited the script, helped choose some of the music, and lobbied—hard—for the choice of Frakes as director.

Movies are almost never filmed in chronological order. The scene now being shot comes just moments after the opening credits. Picard struggles awake from a bone-chilling dream. Images of his assimilation into the Borg collective—the gory alien surgery that transformed him into a cyborg—invade his memory, and the murmur of the Borg hive rattles through his skull. The inhuman chirp swells in volume, until a bleep from a nearby terminal jars him back to reality.

Picard swings from his cot in full uniform. Visibly shaken, he authorizes the incoming message. A Starfleet admiral appears on the scren. "Catch you at a bad time, Jean-Luc?" The actor portraying the admiral isn't there; his part is read by a script supervisor.

"No, of course not."

"I've just received a disturbing report from Deep Space Five," the admiral continues. "Our colony on Ivor Prime was destroyed this morning. Long-range sensors have picked up . . ."

"Yes, I know. The Borg."

That's it: one line. Five words. That's the meat, the goo, the gold ring that Frakes is after. Once it's in the can, everyone goes home. But the first few takes are rarely perfect, and Frakes asks Stewart to do the line again. There's a short delay while the lights are adjusted, the cameras refocused, and the film rolled up to speed. The clapboard snaps, then: "Action!"

"Our colony on Ivor Prime was destroyed this morning. Long-range sensors have picked up . . ."

"Yes, I know . . ." The camera zooms slowly in from just below Stewart's chin line, moving until his face fills the frame. "The Borg."

A beat. Frakes frowns; soundman Tommy Thomas reaches for his *New York Times* crossword puzzle. After seven seasons as Jean-Luc Picard, Stewart needs no direction. There's nothing Frakes can say to explain how the line ought to be read. Frakes himself might not know what he's after—but he knows that wasn't it. The cameras are realigned, and he tries a fifth take.

"Long-range sensors have picked up . . ."

"Yes, I know. The Borg."

Still not there. "Again."

"Long-range sensors have picked up . . ."

"Yes, I know. The Borg."

The weary Stewart sounds like he's anticipating a visit from his mother-in-law. Frakes, ever cheerful, stifles a laugh.

"Sorry, Patrick . . . let's try it once more, shall we?"

Stewart gives no argument. The two have an excellent rapport, on and off, that dates back to the first day they worked together on *TNG.* Stewart—then a self-described "pompous ass"—blew a line, and

Frakes playfully dissed him: "I say! That must be what they call British face-acting! Not bad . . . for a Brit!" The crew howled, and Stewart's slow, often painful process of Americanization began.

"Everyone ready? Action!"

"Our colony on Ivor Prime was destroyed this morning. Long-range sensors have picked up . . ."

"Yes, I know." A pregnant pause; so far, so good. "*Borg.*" Stewart groans; he forgot the "the."

The irony of all this is that Stewart excels at live performance—the kind where you've got to get it right the first time. A veteran of the Royal Shakespeare Company, he's as comfortable with a monologue as he is in a large ensemble cast. From 1988 until 1995—during winter breaks from the production of TNG—his solo rendition of Dickens's *A Christmas Carol* (in which Stewart played all forty-six characters) drew standing ovations on Broadway. His 1995 appearance as Prospero in *The Tempest*—performed to enormous crowds in Central Park—was the toast of the town. Prior to *First Contact*, Stewart appeared in no less than 150 stage productions. Seeing him stumble over this stupid line is like watching Muhammad Ali get beaten up by a kangaroo.

"Action!"

"Our colony on Ivor Prime was destroyed this morning. Long-range sensors have picked up . . ."

"Yes, I know. The Borg."

"Our colony on Ivor Prime was destroyed this morning. Long-range sensors have picked up . . ."

"Yes, I know. The Borg."

"Our colony on Ivor Prime was destroyed this morning. Long-range sensors have picked up . . ."

"Yes, I know. The Borg."

Frakes rises from his chair and approaches Stewart. They speak in hushed tones, a pitcher and manager huddled on the mound. What's the problem here? Is it with Stewart? Or the script itself? In a very real sense, the film begins with this line; it anticipates everything to come. All the emotions that Picard feels at this instant—revulsion, fear, and a

PICARD: "Mr. LaForge, have you had any success with your attempts at finding a weakness in the Borg? And Mr. Data, have you been able to access their command pathways?"

GEORDI: "Yes, Captain. In fact, we found the answer by searching through our archives on late-twentieth-century computing technology."

(Geordi presses a key, and a logo appears on the computer screen.)

RIKER (puzzled): "What the hell is 'Microsoft?' "

DATA: "Allow me to explain. We will send this program, for some reason called 'Windows,' through the Borg command pathways. Once inside their root command unit, it will begin consuming system resources at an unstoppable rate."

PICARD: "But the Borg have the ability to adapt. Won't they alter their processing systems to increase their storage capacity?"

DATA: "Yes, Captain. But when 'Windows' detects this, it creates a new version of itself known as an 'upgrade.' The use of resources increases exponentially with each iteration. The Borg will not be able to adapt quickly enough. Eventually all of their processing ability will be taken over and none will be available for their normal operational functions."

wretched awareness of his bond with the enemy—must be expressed in five syllables. I glance around; the grips and gaffers are all mouthing the line, trying to get it right. From the looks on their faces, no one is succeeding.

Because it's not Stewart, and it's not the script. It's the fucking aliens themselves. *The Borg*. It looks great on paper, but you just can't say it; much less with a British accent. *Bawg. The Bawg.* Klingons, Cardassians; these names roll off the tongue like restless fillies. But *Borg* articulates like a belch, and there's no way to save it. I know it, the crew knows it, and I have a big feeling that Stewart and Frakes know it, too. What to do? The word must die—but die it cannot.

Frakes returns to his seat and takes a long swig of designer water. "Okay, quiet everybody. Last time . . . we hope. Lights . . . action!"

"Our colony on Ivor Prime was destroyed this morning. Long-range sensors have picked up . . ."

"Yes, I know. *The Borg.*"

Stewart peers hopefully into the camera, his face cloned double on the director's monitors. "How was that, Jonathan? *Much* better, I think."

"Uh . . . great." Frakes turns toward his peanut gallery, holding his nose. "Try it again, Patrick."

When the unit publicist finally corrals the actor, Stewart has traded his Starfleet tunic for a gray fleece jacket with "Patrick" sewn in cursive above the left breast.

"I can give you only two minutes," the actor states brusquely, perching in the tall director's chair angled beside mine. His fingers form a tent in front of his lips. I recognize the scene: It's Jean-Luc Picard in his ready room, about to endure a briefing from a pesky ensign.

This is not my favorite kind of interview. For one thing, it's going to be a talking head situation: a man in a chair. For another, Stewart is worn-out and irritable. His girlfriend is waiting, and he's ready to go home. But the meeting was tough to arrange, and I'm not about to leave empty-handed.

> *... 15 Minutes Later ...*
>
> DATA: "Captain, we have successfully installed 'Windows' in the Borg's command unit. As expected, it immediately consumed 85 percent of all available resources. However, we have not received any confirmation of the expected 'upgrade.'"
>
> PICARD: "Data, scan the history banks again and determine if there is something we have missed."
>
> DATA: "Sir, I believe there is a reason for the failure in the 'upgrade'. Appearently the Borg have circumvented that part of the plan by not sending in their registration cards."

The first thing I want is Stewart's account of the *First Contact* script fiasco. He reportedly hated the original version, which featured a steamy romance with Lily in Cochrane's Montana camp. Braga and Moore were compelled to fly to Manhattan in the dead of winter (*The Tempest* had by then moved to Broadway) and begin what amounted to a complete rewrite. ("Patrick's input was invaluable," Braga conceded drily to me one morning. "It seemed a pain-in-the-ass at first, but it was good for the script ultimately.")

But "Patrick's input" hadn't ended there. Dissatisfied with the rewrite, he called in a writer of his own. Such are the privileges of leading man status: Stewart's contract permitted him to apply a final "polish" to the screenplay. The thought of having to share screenplay credit with a hired hack infuriated Moore and Braga, but their worries were for naught. Not a scene penned by Stewart's writer made the final cut.

"When you saw that first draft," I ask, "what exactly were your misgivings?"

Stewart nods rapidly, another Picardian display of impatience. "I had two major concerns," he says. "At the beginning of the movie, there was a scene in which a really quite distressed Picard talked about how he heard Borg voices in his head. That they never left him alone. It set up the captain-hero as somebody who probably should not be flying a spaceship—not even riding a bicycle, maybe." His lips narrow into a wry grin.

"The other problem was that it was a Borg story, but I was never in any proximity to the Borg. I spent the entire movie on Earth. Now, I go down, but I come back immediately, and I'm on the *Enterprise*, fighting the Borg. That's what the story absolutely needed. The one thing about the captain is that he's got to fly the ship."

In the late 1980s, when *The Next Generation* first aired, I'd read an interview in which Stewart—still a virtually unknown British actor—expressed apprehension about flying that ship. Specifically, he was uneasy about taking the role of a beloved American icon. When I bring this up, though, he bristles.

"If I did say that, let me correct it. I was never frightened by the idea of taking on the role of an American icon. My good fortune was that I did not see it as an icon. I hardly knew *Star Trek* at all. I thought it was an improbable piece of casting all those years ago; it seemed to be very curious, and probably inappropriately unconventional." He raises his eyebrows, and almost smiles. "I think it was actually quite smart."

That it was. For starters, Stewart is easily one of the most credible actors ever to appear in an American television series. And then there's his voice. That cultured British baritone, sounding notes of both authority and compassion, is universally irresistible. (Scenes from the show, Stewart later tells me, are played at commercial airline refresher courses—the better to illustrate the "ideal command style" of a captain on the flight deck.) Finally, there's the very fact that Stewart is *not* an American—one reason, no doubt, that fans in Asia, Europe, and the U.K. have been able to accept TNG as a truly international mythology.

Stewart has never seen *Star Trek* abroad, except in his native England. But he relates an encounter he had several months ago, climbing into a New York taxi.

"This cab had to wait for me, so when I got in I thanked the driver, whom I'd noticed was an Asian Indian. He said, 'Oh, don't worry. Had I known it was you, I would have waited all day.' I said, 'Well, why's that?' The driver then told me he was from Bangladesh, one of the poorest countries in the world; and that in the rural area he comes from, there is one television set for the entire community. They have it out in the open air, plugged into a generator, and everybody sits around and watches it in the evenings. The most popular show of the week is *Star Trek: The Next Generation*."

Although the show is subtitled in Bangladeshi, Stewart says, there were many things the driver's friends and family didn't understand. Whenever he visited his homeland, the villagers would hand him a long list of questions about everything from Worf's fangs to hand-phaser battery life. They'd expect him to know it all, being a big shot cabdriver from New York. Now, finally, he'd get the goods—right from the horse's mouth.

"It sounds similar," I venture, "to the public puppet shows I've seen in Asia. Low-cost collective entertainment, revolving around cosmic conflicts and heroic themes. In those productions, though, the battles are between gods and demons—not mere starship captains."

"That's right." Patrick Stewart laughs, relaxing a bit in his seat. Picard, it seems, is slowly withdrawing. "And here . . . well, sometimes, when it's two o'clock in the morning, and you're into your seventeenth hour of work and you're wondering who the hell is watching the show anyway, you always imagine one, two, three people around a television set in their living room. But it reaches extraordinary audiences!" He leans forward, tipping the stool. "I was on board the USS *Independence*, and they told me that the wardroom is packed whenever they are sent new TNG tapes. It always shocks me. Somebody told me the other day that they heard me in Serbo-Croat!" He rocks backward, shaking his head. "It's quite impressive."

Our two minutes have long expired, but Stewart isn't wearing a watch. By now, of course, our relationship has changed dramatically. We're not the same people we were when Captain Jean-Luc Picard stepped restively out of his ready room. Stewart, a method actor, has finally shed his Starfleet tunic—granting me an honorable discharge as well.

"What is it about the show," I ask, "that speaks to villagers in Bangladesh, Croatia, or even Mongolia?"

"Storytelling is international," Stewart unzips his parka; Beavis and Butt-head leer beneath the fleece. "All cultures use it as the basis of their literature, their drama, their legends, their mythology. And *Star Trek* tells very good stories. I think that's something we've done very well. Then," he pauses reflectively, "there's a broader, perhaps more philosophical aspect to *The Next Generation*. One of the things that kept my interest high was the fact that the program was about *ideas* as well as stories."

There's no better example of this, recalls Stewart, than "Darmok," an episode from TNG's fifth season. Written by Joe Menosky and Philip LaZebnik, the story is about the Federation's attempt to contact the

Tamarians: a peaceful and advanced race whose language appears to be indecipherable. Past efforts to develop a relationship with this race have failed, but *Enterprise* is sent to try once again. Placed in a perilous situation with the captain of the Tamarian ship—a situation in which both captains are forced to depend on each other for survival—Picard realizes that the Tamarians communicate exclusively through the use of metaphors, drawn from their own rich mythology. "Quite elaborate stuff," Stewart concedes, "for a syndicated science fiction series!"

" 'Darmok' was a great piece of storytelling," I agree. "As was 'The Inner Light'—which was essentially a Buddhist koan, in television form."

"That, too, was a very powerful episode," Stewart says quietly. "And one I'm very proud of. It was wonderfully written; among the half dozen most distinguished scripts we had, and one that seemed to effect many people."

"The Inner Light" was, in my personal opinion, the most moving episode of *The Next Generation* ever written. It was also a superb vehicle for Stewart's acting skills. In the story, the *Enterprise* encounters an alien probe that places Picard in a trancelike state. To his crewmates, the captain seems to have collapsed into a coma. But during the half hour he is unconscious, Picard lives out an entire lifetime—complete with a loving wife, children, and grandchildren—among a race of humanoids on a drought-stricken planet called Kataan. At last, when he is a feeble old man (a transformation that took makeup artist Michael Westmore five hours), the nature and purpose of his illusory lifetime is revealed to him.

"I remember shooting it," says Stewart. "It was very difficult. There were scenes at the end that were very, very emotional. It was particularly intense for me, because it was the first time I'd worked with my son [Daniel Stewart] on camera."

"I wept at the end," I confess.

Stewart looks at his hands and nods slowly. "Me, too, actually.

"So." He draws a breath and continues, "*The Next Generation* was a little less of an action drama than the original series, a fact that some people complained about. They wanted to have more explosions, more phaser fights. I thought we got the balance pretty well right. It's a show with content, one that works on several levels simultaneously. I think that's one reason it has attracted such an extraordinary, broad audience. It can be enjoyed by a five-year-old—or the sixty-five-year-old chancellor of a university. I know one who's addicted to the program; he sets his schedules around it."

Another explanation for the show's global popularity, Stewart theorizes, is that it coincided with an octave shift in the tenor of international relations. "Human rights" was becoming a familiar phrase, and skillful diplomacy was gaining ground against aggression and hostility.

"During the lifetime of our show, look what happened in the world! During the seven years that we were doing *The Next Generation*, the Berlin Wall came down, and the repressive, authoritarian Communist regimes were overthrown in most countries. In Northern Ireland, the IRA and the British government began to talk to one another. In South Africa, apartheid ended, and Nelson Mandela came out of jail.

"It was simply extraordinary," Stewart says, his voice impassioned. "Things changed in the world that I did not expect to see changed in my lifetime. And a lot of those things changed because people sat down and talked. They said, 'There have been sins in the past, but we must put them aside. We must be able to talk with one another, otherwise we will never move forward.' And that," he slaps the arm of his chair, "is fundamental of *The Next Generation*. It's absolutely Captain Picard's main thrust as a negotiator. You talk and talk and talk . . . you talk until you don't have any breath left. There's always something that can be negotiated. And you do it with respect. You try to see the other person's point of view, to put yourself in their shoes.

"Of course," he recalls, reining himself in, "TNG also spanned the Gulf War, and the beginning of the nightmare in the Balkans. And Rwanda, yes, and the increasing repression in China." He offers an

---

FROM BEAM ME UP, GORBY!

LEONARD NIMOY
USA Today weekend section,
November 29, 1991

Star Trek's appeal to me, and to many fans, has been as a futuristic morality tale for the present. So, I concluded that the summing up [i.e., *Star Trek VI: The Undiscovered Country*] had to have something to do with . . . the twenty-third century functioning as a mirror for Earth in the 20th.

Then came the extraordinary dramas of the birth of democracy in Eastern Europe and the wrenching changes of *glasnost* and *perestroika* in the Soviet Union. It was while watching peace break out on CNN—the inherent danger in the emerging new-world-order disorder and contradictions at the Berlin Wall, Tiananmen Square and Romania—that I had an idea for the last flight of the starship *Enterprise*. People were nervous about any change, even about that long-hoped-for change for the better. They were antsy about exchanging the devil for an angel they didn't know. There was a lot of drama to be mined. Here was a plot prospect that could entice me and the rest of the crew into a last ride.

ironic smile. "So there are still many, many areas where the message of *Star Trek* could certainly be heard."

Though Stewart draws no direct correlation between the show and these changes (the positive ones), his words raise interesting questions. Did *The Next Generation* win widespread popularity because people had reached a point where they could appreciate its message? Did the show encourage people who were projecting the global village and nurturing its first fragile seeds? Or did *Star Trek*, with its thirty-year grip on the imaginations of scientists and world leaders, have a direct and quantifiable influence of its own?

Given the fitful, chaotic progress of international relations, we may never know for sure. What we can guess is that, in a best-case scenario, *Star Trek* is becoming a sort of self-fulfilling prophecy. Decades of exposure to the show's vision of the future—Earth at peace, our mastery of technology, humanity's space-faring destiny—has been a pretty good antidote to the "duck-and-cover" drills that anticipated a global Armageddon.

Wendy Neuss, a *Voyager* producer who has been dating Stewart for several years, appears behind his chair. She begins massaging his neck. The gesture of intimacy makes me envious; it's been a long afternoon.

Stewart, visibly exhausted, has been generous with his time. I do, however, have one last question.

"Has being immersed in the *Star Trek* universe—in the role of Jean-Luc Picard—made you a better friend, or a better father?"

Neuss pauses, waiting for his answer.

"The role has affected me," Stewart confirms unabashedly. "It came at a significant time in my life, when I was ready to *hear*. When I was becoming more open to instruction. Particularly—and this is something I just mentioned—of looking outward to other people and their needs, and of literally being able to put myself in someone else's shoes. To be able to see something from their point of view. God! It's the most *potent* skill. And as a result of this role, I try very much harder to be more patient, more tolerant, and to see another's perspective." Wendy squeezes; he reaches behind his shoulder, places his hand on hers. "And it continues."

AWAY MISSION V:
STAR TREK, *ITALIAN STYLE*

Arriving in Trieste, a windy port city clinging to the Adriatic Sea, I have the immediate sense that I've arrived somewhere *luminous*. The fact that low clouds threaten rain makes no difference; the cobblestones in the piazza seem to glow from an internal source, and the sea and sky bounce silvery light between them like facing mirrors. I roll my carry-on along the Corso Italia toward my pensione on Via Artistes, an involuntary grin spreading across my face.

Italy is a country of satisfying excesses, of pendulum swings from debauchery to penury: from execution-by-lion to manicotti *as a first course*. And it is also, always, a place of italics; whereas in Hungary, poor Hungary, nothing seemed worth emphasizing.

The clams alone would be enough for a chapter. Lunching at the Mia Trieste trattoria, I can smell the nets drying on the cobblestone docks; feel the fickle sun on my eyelids; smell the musky perfume, mixed with sweat, that pulses from the throats of the women shopping for leather and lingerie along Via Roma. Why, I wonder, does no one ever order linguine al vogno from the *Enterprise*'s replicator? Why order anything else?

Sometime later, strolling along the docks, I'm confronted by a host of familiar faces. Full-color posters of Kirk, Spock, and the entire cast of *Star Trek: The Next Generation* stare at me from every notice board

There's nothing like seeing a familiar face.

and kiosk, trumpeting "*Star Trek* in Italy": a huge exhibition at the Stazione Marittima.

The event itself, I discover, is a noisy tribute to the show's Diamond Anniversary, featuring masks, props, film clips, and life-sized replicas of the *Enterprise* NC-1701's bridge and transporter bay. Interviews with the cast and crew, dubbed into the language of love, chatter from a bank of video monitors; sound tracks from two of the *Star Trek* movies fill the hall with a dissonant din.

The place is packed with families, kids, and Trekkers from as far afield as Rome. I strike up a conversation with two young locals overseeing the gift and souvenir stand. Both belong to STIC: the Star Trek Italian Club. Francesco de Manzano is eighteen; Agnese Sodani is a year older. Last spring, Agnese confesses, she spent a small fortune (of her parents' money) attending the annual Grand Slam convention in Pasadena. It was the seminal event in her life. But when I try to unravel her devotion to the show, I'm disillusioned. She watches TNG, she admits, for the sole purpose of swooning over Brent Spiner: her "ideal man."

"You don't prefer Spock?"

Agnese wrinkles her nose. "Leonard Nimoy is old enough to be my grandfather," she scoffs. "Brent Spiner is only old enough to be my father."

Francesco is less starry-eyed, a bit more articulate. The show feeds his imagination, he says. "I can think about new ways to live, new ways to love, to explore, to have sex." At eighteen, *Star Trek* is his personal invitation to a cosmic erotic ball. Agnese agrees; she gleefully reminds me that Data, the android played to the hilt by Spiner, is "fully functional, and programmed in multiple techniques of pleasuring."

The encounters are vaguely discouraging. They don't exactly fit my theory that the show's creators are fueling a new global weltanschauung, a mythos in which technology and truly brainy people are the salvation of the world. But do people—and by "people" I mean creators and audience alike—ever realize they are building a mythos while they're in the process of building it? Were the ancient Greeks or

Romans, for example, conscious that they were creating a mythos—or were they merely worshiping their gods? What did Homer think he was doing when he wrote the *Iliad* and *Odyssey*? Or the Hindu scribe who first recorded the *Ramayana*?

Agnese cannot answer these weighty queries. She recommends I telephone Alberto Lisiero, the president of STIC. He lives in Latisana, a small village that lies an hour beyond Venice.

I had never imagined that the passionate Italians, with their affinities for Verdi, Chianti, and the Catholic church, would give *Star Trek* a second glance. What on earth could they see in the sterile, agnostic future envisioned by Gene Roddenberry?

But Italy, to my amazement, turns

HOLOGRAMS TURN TRADITIONAL CANDY INTO EDIBLE ART

LAURIE ANN PEACH
Christian Science Monitor, April 29, 1997

An image of the solar system floats by on your chocolate bar as you take a bite. Light shimmers off pieces of chocolate resembling stained-glass windows. Captain Picard from *Star Trek* hovers inside your sucker. Thanks to some fancy laser work at LightVision Confections in Boston, traditional candy is getting a whole new "holographic" look.

"Seaweed provides a great surface for an image," says Eric Begleiter, the company's founder. But candy is the only holographic product LightVision is marketing at the moment. The candies, which will sell in museum and specialty shops starting in July, are imprinted with an assortment of lifelike, three dimensional images, including dinosaurs, endangered species, and *Star Trek* icons.

---

out to have one of the largest and liveliest fandoms in Europe. When I telephone Alberto Lisiero—admiral of the Star Trek Italian Club, and editor of its slick fanzine—he estimates that the STIC has four thousand members scattered across the breadth of Italy, with the greatest concentrations in Rome and Milan.

Lisiero meets me at the Latisana train station, picking me out of the crowd without a moment's hesitation. Funny how all these Trek club people have been able to recognize me so fast. I must radiate *other*ness; I'm not sure I want to know how.

Lisiero is thirty-two, with a big belly, trim red beard, and a round, bearlike face. He lives with his fiancée (comic book writer Gabriella Cordone) and his future mother-in-law, Nedda Gilé, in a big square house surrounded by grapevines and emerald fields of mown grass. It appears rustic enough from the outside, but the façade conceals a vast archive. Every episode of every *Star Trek* season (even the animated series) is catalogued on industrial metal shelves, along with nearly every Trek book and fanzine ever published. Filing cabinets bulge with

Alberto Lisiero and Gabriella Cordone.

articles and clippings, all carefully labeled. If I'm ever looking for a library of *Star Trek* history, I'll save a hell of a lot of time by flying back to Italy.

No sooner have I mounted the stairs than I find myself the guest of honor at a fabulous banquet. A white linen cloth covers a table laden with Tuscan cuisine—roast chicken, broiled escargots, pasta with green peas, red potatoes, warm bread and freshly picked apples —and surrounded by a bunch of Italians debating the import of *Star Trek* at the top of their lungs. The mood is warm and welcoming; Italians, I'm about to learn, consume *Star Trek* with typically Italian gusto.

Star Trek, Alberto explains, first appeared in Italy on May Day 1979, two years after the first *Star Wars* film was released. Fifty-two episodes of TOS were aired, two per week, by a foreign television network. A year later a private Italian station picked up the ball, and the entire seventy-nine-episode canon of the original Kirk-Spock-McCoy chronicles was broadcast.

"So the show was a hit in Italy?"

"No," Gabriella replies dryly. "The show was not a hit."

Nothing more was seen of *Star Trek* in Italy until nine years later, when the first eight episodes of TNG were again offered on Italian television. They aired once a week, at 10:30 at night, during the balmy summer months. Nobody watched them. The following year the time slot was changed and another seven episodes from the first season appeared, this time with slightly better results. In 1992, the network got brash. They tried an experiment, showing three episodes from TNG on consecutive Saturdays—during prime time. Again, the response was dismal. The show was dropped after two weeks.

"When we saw the ratings," Alberto mopes, "we realized that there aren't a lot of Italians who love science fiction."

Things didn't turn around for the show until December 1994. By this time the network had four or five seasons in the can, and decided to mount a final offensive. The strategy? Saturation bombing. *Star Trek: The Next Generation* was placed in an afternoon slot—4 P.M.—and a new episode was aired every day, day after day, like a soap opera. The ratings were decent. Momentum built and, over the next four months, four full seasons of the show were broadcast on Italian television. Interest in the program, prodded by the release of *Star Trek: Generations*, mushroomed. Lisiero's modest fan club, which he had cofounded in 1986 with five women, swelled to include over three thousand members.

"The first to join, back in 1986, were, of course, friends of friends," Lisiero says. "They really didn't love so much *Star Trek*; they were there for friendship. It took us eight years to grow to about one thousand members. But after those transmissions of TNG in 1994—and *Generations*—we tripled in size."

Italy is a populist country; the whole place is practically an extended family. Still, I was surprised by the relationship between STIC and the Italian television. Early in the broadcasts of TNG, scandalized by the poor translation of 24th-century technospeak, Lisiero approached the network and proposed that the STIC consult with their *Star Trek* dubbing team.

"They said they had no budget for this," recalls Lisiero, "and I replied that there would be no cost. It would be our pleasure to assure people that the translations were good." The network agreed to the arrangement and, as a show of Italian gratitude, included STIC in the show's credits: a dreamy honor unprecedented in the *Star Trek* cosmos.

Alberto introduces me around. Gabriella is tall and slightly owlish, with a narrow braid trailing behind close-cropped chestnut hair. She met Lisiero at a STIC meeting in 1987. Wiry, intense, and aggressively intelligent, she's the perfect complement to Alberto's ponderous, corporeal eminence.

Nedda, who prepared the banquet, motions me into my seat without ceremony. At fifty-seven, Gabriella's mother is a copper-topped energy cell, direct and loudly opinionated. Nedda, Alberto explains, has lived with Gabriella and himself for three years—ever since she arrived to help care for his own mother, who passed away in 1994.

His close friend Luigi Rosa, a twenty-nine-year-old computer consultant, is dressed in a wild purple tunic that closes with metal clasps. A compact figure with a triangular face and dark curly hair, he looks like a character out of Shakespeare's *Romeo and Juliet*. His girlfriend, Chiara, is a shy, attractive woman. She's with her friends Paulo and Jessica at the far end of the table.

Of the seven Italians present, only four—Alberto, Gabriella, Nedda, and Luigi—speak English. So, although the arguments rage around and across the table in two languages, I record only a small part of the action.

Nedda takes my plate. She heaps it with chicken, potatoes, and peas, presciently omitting a helping of snails. "Why," I ask her, "do you suppose *Star Trek* became so popular in Italy?"

She hands my dish back with a snort. "I don't think it *is* popular in Italy. It could be better. The Italian mentality is more . . . *humanistic*. Science is not so interesting to them." I note the third-person. "They look at only the stories!"

"When Italians watch *Star Trek*," Luigi amends, "we watch a story about human problems. That is why the show appeals to some Italian people, even if we are not educated on science fiction or fantasy."

"The fans I spoke to in Trieste," I say, "said that, for them, *Star Trek* was all about romance—new possibilities for love and sex. They were madly infatuated with Data and Riker and Picard."

"Yes, yes!" Nedda slams her hand down, rattling with wineglasses. "They don't even *see* the science!"

Gabriella reaches across the table. "Mother . . . please."

"I was not born in Italy," Nedda continues, waving her daughter away. "I was born in Egypt. And I went to a German school. But my children, they went to Italian schools. And I really saw the difference. They don't have any science education in Italy!" She flops back into her chair. "I have always loved science fiction. I was fifteen when I first saw *Destination Moon*. When *Star Trek* came to Italy I watched it in secret, because my son hated it so much.

"Science fiction never does well in Italy," she growls, mashing her potatoes with her fork. "Yes, all right, people went to see *Dune*—but only because it was produced by Dino de Laurentiis!"

Luigi nods patiently through this soliloquy. "She is right," he says at last. "We in Italy have definite categories in literature. And science fiction is not considered literature. It is considered . . . *fun*. Second-class literature. Isaac Asimov, Robert Heinlein, even Frank Herbert, these people are not known by the Italian world of literature."

"Because of the church," snaps Nedda. "They have demonized both science and science fiction. Even today."

"We are still paying for what the church has done in the past," Luigi nods, tearing at the bird. "Perhaps science is no longer considered a demon, but it is still at a low level of importance. Think of our recent history. Some of the greatest scientists in the U.S.A.—like Fermi—were men who had left Italy to join their German, British and American colleagues." He gestures at me with a chicken leg. "I think what Nedda and I love most about *Star Trek* is that science is considered a good thing. That there will come a time, even four centuries from now, when science is no longer portrayed as evil."

"One reason there are no big problems on the starships," I say, "is because there's no religious conflict. There's no religion at all, to speak of. Do you think this kind of world—without a strong religious influence—is possible? Or even desirable?"

"Maybe the people of *Star Trek*'s century have learned to find faith in themselves," Luigi offers, "instead of in a person wearing a white robe and a big hat."

Nedda snatches away my plate, piling on more, much more, of everything. I protest loudly, but in vain. "Italians," I observe, "grow up surrounded by wonderful myths and legends. Do you think that *Star Trek* qualifies as a kind of new, global mythology?"

"Oh, yes," Gabriella responds. "Definitely. Because, like the fables and fantasies I write for kids, it presents the difference between good and evil in educational 'pills': in an entertaining way."

"Do old Roman myths and history have an equal influence on your life?"

"No," she replies without hesitation. "I rediscovered this with Gates McFadden, when she was in Rome for a convention. She was thrilled by everything—but we Italians are so used to seeing monuments and ruins that we no longer see them at all! An ancient wall just a wall, blocking a street; a statue is something you have to go around to get to a bar or to a house."

"But these are the myths, the culture, that your own people actually created . . ."

"Listen." Gabriella prods an escargot out of its shell, and swirls it in butter sauce. "When you Americans come to Italy and see an ancient wall, you have to touch the wall, *feel* the wall, because you don't have it in your own country. We live with it; we don't need to 'feel' the memory."

"Fair enough" I say, draining my wine. "But doesn't the *Enterprise* somehow seem sterile to you, lacking those old walls? Lacking that monumental sense of history?"

"But it *has* a sense of history!" Gabriella cries, drawing back as if stung. "Much, much more than any other American show. In several episodes you even see people talking about planetary mythology—and

A MATTER OF THE UTMOST SECURITY

from the May/June issue of *Star Trek Communicator*, the Official *Star Trek* Fan Club magazine

"In 1996, when Secretary of State Madeline Albright opened a speech to a group of European political and military leaders on the topic of NATO, the UN, and crisis management, she noted that she had been tempted to consult 'the world's most acclaimed model' for conflict resolution. 'Unfortunately, Security Council debates and reruns of *Star Trek* tend to occur at the same time,' she quipped."

Captain Jean-Luc Picard is himself an archeologist!"

I pause; the process of conveying a forkful of peas and pasta elbows from my plate to my mouth requires surgical precision. "Do you ever think of *Star Trek*," I ask at last, "as a kind of imaginary space program? As an opportunity to vicariously explore the universe?"

Gabriella nods rapidly, her braid jumping. "Definitely. But it's not just that. *Star Trek* depicts the possibility that mankind can actually arrive at a time and place where we have the *option* of exploring the universe. When we don't have to worry about other problems. So it's not just exploration itself; it's the freedom to explore."

"There have always been problems," I remind her. "But they don't necessarily bring exploration to a halt. Italy, Spain and Portugal all had problems in the 15th and 16th centuries, but they still launched great voyages of discovery."

"But Italians don't learn about those voyages on TV." Nedda is eating her pasta rapidly, yet never dropping a single pea. "People have been prejudiced against the idea of exploration from childhood. Most of the parents and teachers who criticize *Star Trek* have never even seen a single episode."

Alberto listens on in silence. Luigi, meanwhile, leans over the table to refill my glass. "And when they do, all they see is aliens, foreigners and people wearing strange prosthetics."

Nedda nods pensively. "Italy has no real colonies, so we're not used to diversity. We're not used to having black people on the same street where we live. It's a new thing."

"I don't think Italians are racist," Luigi assures me rapidly. "It's just that we're just not used to living with foreigners. In this way, watching *Star Trek* promotes tolerance."

"I wish to advance another point of view." Alberto clears his throat; silence descends as the Admiral begins to speak. "Since I have always been an optimist, for me *Star Trek* is . . . *normal*. There is no, 'Oh, I just hope that everything will be this good in the future.' I *know* it will be this way. It is not that I like *Star Trek because* of this; I don't like other shows because they *don't* have this."

There's a message for me in those words. Alberto is a well-contented man. He's not filling any gaps in his life with the show, any more than someone who loves Italian wine is satisfying an alcoholic craving. *Star Trek* is part of the happy destiny of his life—the same destiny that introduced him to Gabriella at a fan club meeting ten years ago.

The photographs that Lisiero pulls from his wallet—of himself and Gabriella in their Starfleet uniforms—confirm this. During my travels, I've seen countless snapshots of people dolled up in Federation duds. The wearers share a vaguely uneasy expression; sheepish, or frankly ironic. But these snapshots of Alberto and Gabriella are different: their uniforms *fit*. Lisiero and his *famiglia* don't need to identify with Klingons, Bajorans, Ferengi, Vulcans, or any other class of outsider. The plum maroon of a Starfleet tunic is enough.

Gabriella reaches for an apple, glancing over my shoulder at the pictures. "The defining trait of Italian fandom," she says, "is that every one of us sees in *Star Trek* something different. And we enjoy knowing that what you see is different from what we see."

Alberto mops his plate with a slab of bread. "What she is saying, Jeff, is that we and our STIC members are not simply *Star Trek* fanatics. *Star Trek* is the common theme between us. The first ten minutes we are together, we talk about the show. The rest of the time we talk about our jobs, our lives, our personal experiences. We start with *Star Trek*— and we end up with everything."

I find this refreshing. From Page's bar to the junk food palaces of Budapest, *Star Trek* is used as a social icebreaker—a way to belong, to create an ersatz family. But belonging, Luigi points out, is inseparable from the Italian way of life. For the four thousand–plus members of STIC, *Star Trek* is like a good Chianti. It is cheap and reliable refreshment, meant to be shared and savored.

———

My return train to Venice leaves in twenty minutes. I'm collecting my things from the dining table when Gabriella takes my arm.

"Before you go, we want to show you a little film we made."

"A film?" I look at her dubiously. "I don't think I have time . . ."

"Yes, you do. It is very short. Alberto has taken exactly one and a half seconds from each of the 176 *Next Generation* episodes, and put them all together, with an introduction and original music, into a five-minute tribute to the show and its characters."

Oy vey, I think. Seven seasons of *Star Trek* in four minutes and twenty-four seconds? The very idea makes my head spin. But I can hardly refuse; I've just eaten their chicken. I zip up my day pack and allow Gabriella and Luigi to lead me into the television room. I sit down on a cushion and steel myself, preparing for three hundred seconds of pure migraine fuel.

But the film is amazing. Alberto has unerringly chosen the most perfect, most distinct moment from each and every show; the eye-blink scene around which my entire recollection of the episode revolves. His collage is a tour de force of editing, a stroboscopic journey through seven years of *Star Trek* adventures and epiphanies. The emotional impact is overwhelming. As the short film ends, and the *Enterprise D* warps into the sunset, I find myself in tears—shaking Alberto's hand, embracing a startled Nedda, kissing Gabriella and Luigi on each cheek.

I leave Latisana drunk and dizzy, feeling like I've just imbibed an otherworldly liqueur: a grappa-like distillation of *Star Trek*'s very essence.

Before departing Italy, I make a brief pilgrimage to Florence: the cradle of the Renaissance, and the place from which humanity first gazed out, with extended vision, toward our neighboring worlds.

I spend the morning in the Museo di Storia della Scienzia, which boasts a stunning collection of instruments from nearly every branch of science: astronomy, optics, pneumatics, meteorology, microscopy, medicine, cartography. My pilgrimage was inspired by the prospect of seeing Galileo's first telescope, a handsome, leather-bound cylinder about three feet in length. The instrument, built in 1609, was an improvement on a discovery made the previous year in Holland: a patented glass that could magnify distant objects three times. Galileo improved on that principle, constructing a scope capable of 30x magnification. Within the next twelve months he observed the wrinkled lunar surface, mapped the constellation Orion, sketched the crescent Venus, and discovered four of Jupiter's moons.

Tributes to Galileo—his historic damnation by the Holy Church notwithstanding—are legion. Some are devotional to the point of being macabre. In one of the glass cases in the museum's telescope room, displayed within a bell jar, rests "the scientist's middle finger, cut from Galileo's dead body when it was moved to the mausoleum in the Church of Santa Croce." Beside the withered digit, in an opulent ivory frame, is the small, cracked lens with which Galileo observed the Jovian moons.

In Santa Croce itself, Galileo's body is entombed in a weighty marble sarcophagus, flanked by the goddesses of astronomy and geometry. Faces turned heavenward, their expressions are probably meant to appear awestruck—but convey instead an eternal phobia of pigeons. A statue portraying the scientist himself completes the triad of figures. His right hand holds a telescope. His left rests upon a sphere, cradled in the pages of a dense tome. Above the figures hangs a strange but appropriate crest: a three-rung ladder inclined toward the stars.

Most impressive of all—and a clam of spit in the eye of the church —is the tomb's placement. The resting place of Galileo, tortured by the Inquisition and denied a Christian burial until the eighteenth century, lies directly across from the sarcophagus of Michelangelo.

The union of these two Renaissance men would have pleased them both. Each, with astonishing success, devoted his life to building new models of Earth and heaven. Michelangelo, a legend in his own time, may have suspected that his deeds would win him a kind of immortality; Galileo most probably did not. How wonderful if the great astronomer could have known that 370 years after his death—as far into Galileo's future as the *Enterprise 1701-D* is into ours—a spacecraft bearing his name would speed out to visit the very planets he studied.

CAMELOT'S SENTRIES

For a writer obsessed with science fiction and space travel, *Star Trek* is a sort of holy grail. To hover in Paramount's Hart Building, on the fringe of this elite cadre of mythmakers, is maddening. Yet it's impossible to tear myself away. The creative electricity in these offices, where the destinies of heroes ride on dog-eared memo pads and a flood of filtered coffee, captivates me. At the same time, my frustration is extreme; I'm forever the outsider, looking in.

But every so often, during my forays into the heart of *Star Trek*'s foundry, the force field separating me from the inner circle seems to waver and break. My toes cross the line—and, for a few delicious moments, I can almost taste the Mocha Mix.

It's late afternoon. The Hart Building is nearly empty, but Ron Moore's still at his desk. We'll be having dinner later this evening. He motions me in. I drop onto his couch, and tell him about my reconnaissance of *Star Trek* fan clubs in Europe.

"The global nature of the show is something I've never had a good sense of." Moore shrugs. "I've always assumed it *didn't* translate well overseas. Our characters, the stories we tell, the aliens we encounter, are very much tied into American culture in one way or another. You know what? One of the *Next Gen* writers—Joe Menosky—just came back after living in Italy for three years. He's just been rehired as a pro-ducer on *Voyager*." Moore picks up his phone and punches a button. "If we're going to talk about this global stuff, let's get him in here."

Menosky decided to return, as Moore understands it, following a sort of epiphany. Somewhere in Italy, between the Duomo and the Coliseum, he'd perceived the true role that *Star Trek* might play in a historical context. Future scholars, he realized, will view the series as a snapshot of American culture—much as we view the painted vases of Knossos, or the murals of Pompeii. But *Star Trek* will be infinitely more revealing, for it sheds light not only on the current age but on our aspirations for the distant future as well.

Moore agrees wholeheartedly with Menosky's assessment. "I don't think the show has broken a lot of new ground as far as the technology of the future goes—the way people think of Asimov or Jules Verne—but it *is* unique, and it *has* broken ground, in what it says about what we want to be as a people. As human beings." Ron splays his hand, and starts ticking off his fingers. "We want to have gotten rid of racism. We want to have solved crime. We want to have beaten poverty. We want to be out there in the galaxy, bringing our idealistic view to other people. And we want to be nonjudgmental."

I think this over. It's true enough that Gene Roddenberry was a great believer in multiculturalism. But that didn't prevent a democratic chauvinism from dominating, at least in the original series. Captain Kirk was forever making speeches, pointing out how primitive or deluded various other civilizations were.

"That's the difference," Moore confirms, "between the '60s and the '90s."

"What's most revealing to me," I add, "is that *Star Trek* assumes that humanity's highest good, our best and brightest attribute, is *curiosity*. It's a heroic view of science."

"Yeah." Ron's heard this one before. "The quest for knowledge. *To boldly go*. It's right in the prologue; that's always driven the show."

We bide our time, waiting for Menosky. "*Star Trek* translates," I observe, "precisely because humans *are* curious. And because we're so easy to entertain." I tell Moore about a group of rickshaw drivers I saw in Bali, watching *CHiPs* on the village television. They were laughing and shouting, reacting just as they would during a traditional shadow-puppet play.

Moore smiles, and rocks back in his chair. "It makes me feel better,

WHEN ALIENS START TO LOOK A LOT LIKE US

JON PARELES
The New York Times

With their ever more elaborate backgrounds, aliens in *Star Trek* can represent exaggerated human tendencies, like the ultra-capitalist Ferengi (the Shylocks of space) or the enzyme-addicted Jem'Hadar troops, crackheads in uniform. Or they can suggest ethnic and political groups. The Bajorans, with their religious rituals, caste system, pierced ears, and newly won freedom from the Cardassian Empire, might be Indians or Palestinians. The Kazon, with their endlessly warring sects and hatred for former colonial overseers, could be a more powerful Somalia or Rwanda.

One staple plot for each generation of *Star Trek* is the divided loyalties of nonhuman characters. Will Worf, the Klingon raised by Humans, ignore Federation strictures and succumb to his high-testosterone impulses? (Only in small ways.) Can Odo, the changeling exile from the Dominion, really be trusted? (Yes, although outsiders keep asking.) *Star Trek* says, tentatively, that all sorts of creatures can aspire to the all-American, democratic, secular humanist ideas of the Federation. But nature is always challenging training.

to hear things like that. When we talk about the global reach of what we do, it sometimes makes me uncomfortable. But if people in Indonesia are watching *CHiPs . . .*" he snorts, "I *know* we're not doing any more damage than that."

There's a knock on the door, which stands ajar. Menosky leans against the jamb, his arms folded. He's caught the tail end of our dialogue and jumps right in.

"I once read an argument that *Baywatch* is basically bringing down Islam—which, since the USSR fell, is one of the last paradigms that's anti-ours."

It may be the result of three years of Italian cooking, but Menosky actually looks like a figure from the Medici era. His slightly oblate head is framed with wavy black hair, and he has the distracted, almost haunted look of a man who's been staring too long at the Sistine ceiling.

I reach over to Moore's desk and pick up a die-cast replica of the *Enterprise.* Someday, baffled archeologists will dig this stuff out of the rubble—assuming California doesn't cleave off into the sea. "What strikes me," I comment, "is the irony of all this. *Star Trek* posits a future in which the Earth is basically one nation. But getting to that point, to the point of Starfleet and the United Federation of Planets, requires that everyone on the planet ultimately buy into the same value system: ours."

"Yeah." Menosky gives an abbreviated laugh. "That's terrible, isn't it?"

"That's the comforting, frightening thought of the future," Moore pronounces. "That we'll all become one."

"Just look at America," I remark. "Are we actually consolidating? Or are we shattering into a zillion different ethnic and interest groups, each with its own agenda?"

"In TNG, we were fighting that battle too." Moore bat his thumb on the desk. "We were trying to draw the lines between the unique cultural identities of our characters, yet they all had to service the Federation philosophy together."

"Even *Voyager* may still reflect this a little bit," Menosky concedes. "When you think about Chakotay [the Native American first officer of *Voyager*], there is an emphasis on retaining his ethnicity, ancient beliefs and world view, but *within a given value system.* We do assume that everyone has a Starfleet view. Things like fundamentalist Islam are just not compatible in this system. We seem," he concludes wryly, "to disallow absolute incompatibilities in the *Star Trek* universe."

"Again, like America," Moore observes. "America wants you to retain your pride in your heritage. But you're also supposed to live within the broader value system that we have chosen to run this country by."

He shakes his head. "We've always said, amongst ourselves, that there is profoundly more diversity on the planet Earth than we have ever portrayed in the galaxy. The aliens we meet on the show are pretty tame," he quips, "compared to the Bushmen of the Kalahari."

"What we *really* are," Menosky adds, "is a reflection of late-20th-century *California* culture. The original series is an amazing time capsule of the 1960s. The colors, the music—everything. And I guess *The Next Generation* will do the same for the 1980s. When people look back on *Next Gen*, the single thing that will date the show most is *Counselor Troi on the bridge.* That was the embodiment of how far therapy went in the '80s. A therapist was so important, she had to sit next to the captain!"

There's a conversational lull, suspended between the purr of the air conditioning and the whir of my tape recorder. I'm suddenly aware of the fact that both of these guys make seven-figure salaries. And much of what they do—from conceptualizing new characters to building the weekly episodes—involves no more than sitting in a room, bullshitting about stuff.

"The image of command that Picard portrays is a universal, almost eternal image," I say, breaking the silence. "Horatio Hornblower meets the Dalai Lama. He's a hero, but with enormous social responsibility. Otherwise, the ensemble does have a couple of dated characters . . ."

"Not dated in a bad sense," Moore interjects. He opens a can of

TOP TWENTY REASONS WHY CAPTAIN KIRK IS BETTER THAN CAPTAIN PICARD

http://www.halcyon.com/zylstra/
comedy/star/kirk-vs-picard.txt

1. Kirk can beat up a Klingon bare-handed.
2. Kirk would date Beverly Crusher—and damn the consequences!!
3. Kirk never drinks tea. Ever.
4. Diplomacy for Kirk is a phaser and a smirk.
5. Kirk never once stood up and had to straighten his shirt.
6. Kirk never asks his bartender for advice.
7. If something doesn't speak English—it's toast.
8. If Kirk finds a strange spinning probe, he blows it up.
9. Picard hasn't fathered any children; Kirk? Probably millions.
10. Kirk has a cool phaser, not some pansy Braun mix-master.
11. Kirk once fought a Greek god. And won.
12. Kirk doesn't let the doctor tell him what to do.
13. Kirk can climb up a Jefferies Tube and fix anything.
14. Kirk never hired an engineer with punk glasses.
15. The Klingons didn't have a word for surrender—until they met Kirk.
16. Kirk's bridge is not beige.
17. Kirk can infiltrate gangsters, Nazis, and even the Pentagon—easily.
18. When Kirk says "Boldly Go," he MEANS it.
19. Kirk would never let his Chief of Security wear a ponytail.
20. Three Words: Flying Leg Kick

Pringles, and passes it around. "Last week, the DS9 staff sat down together and watched 'The Trouble with Tribbles.' After five minutes, Ira* said, 'You know, it's Shatner. He's every little boy's view of what a captain should be.' That wink, that smirk, that sparkle in his eye. I've always said that I'd rather serve on a ship commanded by Jean-Luc Picard, because I'd live longer. But Jim Kirk was the guy I'd follow through the gates of Hell."

"What Picard has is a depth of wisdom." Menosky, a relative newcomer to the *Voyager* staff, looks concerned. "I'm a little worried that, in some ways, that's what *Voyager doesn't* have. I liked writing for Picard because he was reflective. He could take a step back, and quote somebody. He was a thinker. He was wise. But there really isn't anybody on *Voyager* who we can give that kind of dialogue to. It just doesn't sound right coming out of Janeway. But *why*?"

"I think it's a fear of not knowing where to take her." Ron answers hesitantly; *Voyager*'s not his show. "She's *strong*, yet she's feminine. She's a woman taking the place of a male character in a heroic role, and they don't know what that means." Menosky frowns, nodding. "Whenever she's strong, the scene has to be followed almost immediately by something that says, 'But . . . *she's a woman*.' "

"When you think of great, tough

---

* Executive producer Ira Steven Behr.

female characters," I say, "there's always a strong sexual tension. It's true of Sigourney Weaver and the Borg queen; it's true of Grace Jones and Linda Hamilton. It was true of Katharine Hepburn, even in *The African Queen.* But there's no sexual tension with Janeway. She's a beautiful, self-assured woman, obviously a sexual creature . . ."

"Wearing Aunt Bea's hair," Menosky adds.

"Wearing Aunt Bea's hair, not in the mood, and apparently *never* in the mood. She never employs, or even seems to enjoy, her sexual power."

"Another difference between the '60s and the '80s," Moore interjects. "It was acceptable in the 1960s, on a dramatic level, to have your character seduce somebody in order to get information, or save the ship. It was a part of the whole, and it accomplished something. Kirk sleeps with a woman, and she betrays her people. She gives him the 'Get Out of Jail Free' card. With Picard, on the other hand, you get the feeling that, even if the *Enterprise* is about to fall into the sun, he isn't going to fuck some woman to save it."

"It's all too easy to see that progression as normal," Menosky reflects. "But there's nothing 'normal' about it. It's very American—and, again, very California—to emphasize *relationships* rather than manipulation or conquest." He draws a breath. "Five hundred years ago, Renaissance Italy was the most influential place around. If you were to look back five hundred years from *now,* you would recognize America's media domination of the world. And you would see this huge American story cycle which is *Star Trek.* You would study it just as you would study an Italian fresco cycle: as a pretty good illustration of what was going on in our culture."

Moore stands up. His stomach growls. "Determining what the '60s were like as opposed to the '80s is already an archeological project," he muses. "Other shows that came out of that time are also about the '60s—*Love American Style* is about relationships, on some strange level—but *Star Trek* tells you about the New Frontier, and JFK, and what we wanted to be. Why we were going to the moon in the first place."

"It's Camelot." I nod. "In space."

"Camelot in space." Moore likes the taste of the words. "Which was a noble goal. And that goal still drives us, to a certain extent. We're the ones they passed that torch to."

Los Angeles traffic is as unpredictable as mountain weather. At 7 P.M. on a weekday, I expect the streets to be as thick as Maalox. But Ron Moore sails unabetted through the well-timed intersections, changing lanes with stomach-sloshing speed.

Moore owned a Toyota Supra for six years, until his wife, Ruby, goaded him into a change of wheels. He visited Beverly Hills Porsche and test-drove a 1990 Carrera. The car's previous owner, the salesman informed him, was a television star. Had he heard of Michael Dorn?

"Dorn kept meticulous records," Moore tells me, accelerating onto Highway 2, northbound. "I've got his signed receipts for every repair the car's ever had."

"You could sell them at a *Star Trek* convention," I suggest. "Put your kids through college."

"I hope to."

A space fiend since childhood, Moore had followed the moon shots religiously. He'd dreamed of becoming an astronaut, but a high school knee injury interfered. Instead he joined the Navy ROTC, enrolled in Cornell and majored in government and political science. "I took an astronomy class with Carl Sagan, but dropped out after two classes. It wasn't, 'Hey, let's look at the planets and talk about aliens'; it was, 'The spectral lines of the red shift of Jupiter, blah blah blah . . .' I said, If this is astronomy, forget it."

In his senior year, Moore's knee crapped out again. He failed his Navy physical, his ROTC scholarship was withdrawn, and his dreams of military glory collapsed. "I had no job and no future. I was a liberal arts moron." While he was wallowing, a friend suggested they move to the West Coast. Moore made the trip and took a job as a receptionist at Studio City Animal Hospital. But this was Hollywood, and there was bigger game to snare.

"I'd written a lot of short stories as a kid," Moore says. "I also wrote and directed a play in high school. I just never considered making it a career. I secretly wanted to, but I grew up with that, 'You can't make a living as a writer' conditioning."

He cast out a few screenplays, but nobody bit. One day, though, a girlfriend in the industry told him she'd arranged a visit to the set of a new television series called *Star Trek: The Next Generation*.

Moore was a big fan of the original series, and decided to take a shot at the new one. By the time his visit, he'd hammered together an episode called "The Bonding:" a well-wrought story in which a boy named Jeremy—the son of an *Enterprise* crew member—loses his mother during an away mission and adopts Worf as his surrogate father.* Moore smuggled his screenplay onto the set, and managed to get it into the hands of producer Michael Piller. To his amazement the script was bought, and produced virtually as written. Shortly afterward, the twenty-five-year-old Moore was hired as a *Star Trek* staff writer.

His rise from there was meteoric. By the time he and Braga wrote: "All Good Things . . ." (TNG's two-hour-long, Hugo and Emmy award-winning swan song) Moore had been promoted to supervising producer. At present, he is co-executive producer of *Deep Space Nine.*

There are about half a million people around the world, I realize, who would willingly suck vacuum to be in his shoes. "Your wildest dreams," I observe, "have come true."

Moore squirms. "It's been a strange experience," he says, "and one that I don't dwell on very much."

It's not the response I had anticipated. When I press him, Moore briefly lowers his guard. "Kirk was a childhood hero of mine," he says quietly. "I not only grew up to write dialogue for him; I *killed* him. I killed my childhood hero." He stares at the road, unblinking. "What that says about me, I can't say. I don't really know how it's going to affect me down the line."

A sobering thought—and there are no therapists on *Deep Space Nine.*

We arrive at his house, a Mediterranean-style villa in the Glendale hills. I stand in the backyard, admiring the view and listening to a great deal of dog-speak. There are three hounds in all. Binx, a squirming, yappy pooch that sheds like a pitched roof, belongs to Ruby. Her license plate reads BINXNME. Ron's dogs are big dogs, friendly dogs, jockeying for position in a large fenced pen. Each has a private "Dogloo": an igloo-shaped polystyrene unit that could, if bought in quantity by city governments, serve as makeshift housing for the homeless.

Ruby is skittish, wired, *on.* She's one of those women whose ebullience is contagious. You want to *play* with her. Tomboy, waif, and

---

* Moore himself has a son named Jonathan. The mother (Moore's high school sweetheart) maintains custody of the boy, who was born on April 5, 1983. The date may sound familiar: April 5th, of course, is when "first contact" occurs.

vamp, she croons to Binx as Ron shows me the house. Prior to their meeting, Ron tells me, she was a hippie chick, working in a downtown furniture store. Their first date was to Disneyland, one of his favorite places on Earth. One year later, in 1995, they eloped to Las Vegas and pronounced their vows in the Elvis Chapel.

"Elvis was supposed to sing for us," says Moore. "But he never came in. I felt like we really *did* get married at Graceland, because the King wouldn't get off the phone for us."

They honeymooned in California's Gold Country, driving through the old 49er settlements and visiting ghost towns. "I bet Ruby that we couldn't go a single day without running into some *Star Trek* reference. One afternoon we drove out Highway 99 to a place called 'Moaning Cavern,' 120 miles in the sticks. It's an old mine; you climb down a ladder to get in. The second we arrive at the bottom, I turn on my flashlight. There, on the wall, is a glossy photo with the caption, '*Star Trek* star LeVar Burton, climbing out of Moaning Cavern.' I mean, *fuck* me!"

Ruby wants to play Scrabble. I blithely agree, and she bounds downstairs for drinks. Ron sets up the board in their boudoir, a room big enough to double as a HumVee dealership. I sort the tiles while he talks about his bachelor years—when he and Brannon were in their twenties, cavorting at conventions and making obscene amounts of money writing about aliens and spaceships. The womanizing ended (for Ron, anyway) when he met Ruby.

"The funny thing is," he says, "she and Brannon are actually very similar. They're both very mercurial. And Ruby's the only woman whose opinion Brannon really cares about."

"Damn right." Ruby walks in carrying a bottle of Cristal champagne, the last of their honeymoon stash. "I have to approve of his girlfriends." She picks her tiles, poker-faced.

"You think he'll ever settle down? Get married?"

"He *is* married," Ruby states. "To both of us."

The game dominates the next hour, punctuated by a lively discussion about *Voyager*—specifically, whether or not Captain Janeway will ever get laid.

Our consensus is that she needs to. Badly. But it's the old double standard. Kirk got laid constantly; he was, as a friend of mine put it, "a goat at loose in the cosmos." Benjamin Sisko has lovers. Jean-Luc Picard has *relationships*, with quirky, impressive women—and gets them in the sack to boot. Kathryn Janeway, however, seems to be marooned on her starship with a crew of neutered toms, sublimating her pelvic impulses behind a locked jaw and viselike sense of duty. Ruby is incensed. Despite Roddenberry's vision of a liberated future, the ripe and ready mistress of *Voyager* can't even enjoy a casual bonk with a virile young ensign.

We finish the champagne and move to vodka. "I'm a bit of a lush," Ruby explains, pouring out shots. She's in her cups, and I've forgotten how to spell *Jacuzzi*. A few drinks on, Ron shares a personal obsession. His secret wish, he reveals, is to join Club 33: a secret society whose members can drink at Disneyland. "There are these little 33s on certain doors in the park," he drawls. "You don't even notice 'em if you don't know what they mean. But if you belong, you can go in and drink. It costs around $10,000 to join."

Mama mia, I'm thinking. *That much money could buy a lot of dogloos.*

They give me a run for my money, but my words are uglier than theirs. Ruby, tipsy and disgusted, sweeps the tiles off the board. Moore and I end up outside, smoking cigars amidst faux-Greco statues with fig leaves over their genitalia. It's a clear night, and a caramel crescent hangs between the city and the stars. We stare intently at the sky.

"Going to the Moon was so amazing," he says softly. "I still look up at it at night and think, 'There's an American flag up there. My countrymen have stood there. We have touched that.'"

I'm with him. Thirty years ago, getting into outer space was an obsession; it was all I thought about and dreamed of. Even now, I'd give ten years of my life—shit, I'd learn *Russian* if I had to—for a chance to orbit Earth.

"Do you still have any hope," I ask Moore, "of ever getting up there?"

"Only as the fondest, slimmest dream." He laughs; the hounds bay in response. "That before I die, there'll be some kind of commercial travel. That I'll be able to sell everything, mortgage my house, and go for a flight someday."

AWAY MISSION VI: CLARKE'S ORBIT

"What goes, *clop . . . clop . . . clop . . . clop . . .* BANG! *clop clop clop clop clop*?"

Arthur C. Clarke leans over his desk, his good ear canted toward me. Behind him, on his PC monitor, a series of images fades in and out: the terraforming of Mars; the lunar surface; the Galileo spacecraft sailing past the Jovian moon Europa. It's barely thirty minutes into our reunion, and he's already pelting me with jokes.

"I give up."

"*An Amish hit man!*" He rocks back in his chair and slaps his pale thigh, mouth agape, eyes squinting with mirth. "Have I told you the one about the CIA? . . ."

Before I can reply, Clarke swivels around and begins quitting programs. "Here's someone you might recognize," he says, clicking the shutdown command. As the screen goes black, an all-too-familiar voice emanates from the computer speakers:

"*My mind is going . . . I can feel it.*"

The unabashed delight he takes in this bit of piracy reveals the innocence at the core of his personality. Who but Clarke, a self-proclaimed "teenage octogenarian"* who has concocted some of society's most useful toys, could continue to take such gleeful pleasure from the dying lament of an icon he created three decades ago?

I've known Arthur Clarke through each of those decades; for twenty-eight years, in fact. We met in New York's Chelsea Hotel in 1969, when I was just fifteen. I'd written the sci-fi grandmaster a gushy fan letter after seeing *2001: A Space Odyssey*, stuffing the envelope with inane drawings of spaceships, two-way wrist-TVs, etc. To my amazement, Clarke responded. To my continuing amazement, he has been responding ever since.

Portrait of a "teenage octogenarian": Arthur C. Clarke at his desk in Colombo.

He's changed, of course. When I first met him he was a spry fifty-one; now he's eighty. Post–polio syndrome has sapped some of his energy, forcing him to measure his pace. His mind, however, remains as lively as a hamster on a griddle.

The island nation of Sri Lanka, formerly Ceylon, has been Clarke's home for some forty years. He lives in a spacious, deliciously cool compound on Barnes Place, just ten minutes' walk from the gardenia trees and machine-gun nests surrounding Prime Minister Bandaranaike's private residence.

Clarke's most enduring science fiction legacy—besides *2001* and the *Rama* saga—may well be the inspiration he gave Gene Roddenberry for *Star Trek*. Roddenberry often acknowledged the debt, crediting Clarke as one of his most important influences. When I ask Arthur to explain how it happened, he digs through his desk and shows me a letter that Roddenberry wrote as a birthday tribute in 1987. The valediction is neatly typed, on *Next Generation* letterhead:

> Few people can have more reason than I to offer good wishes to Arthur C. Clarke on his 70th birthday, or on any other day. Arthur

*Clarke turned 80 on December 17, 1997.

literally made my *Star Trek* idea possible, including the television series, the films, and the associations and learning it has made possible for me.

My association with the Clarke mind and concepts began in 1964 with his book *Profiles of the Future*. In 1969 I had travelled to Arizona to listen to a Clarke lecture on astronomy, where I not only met this great man, but was persuaded by him to continue my *Star Trek* projects despite the entertainment industry's labeling the production an unbelievable concept and a failure. Arthur prophesied at this time that when humans walked on the moon it would cause a revolutionary change in attitudes toward space.

It was a friendship that deepened into the most significant of my professional life. It continued to spark my imagination and my belief in myself even more as the years passed, both personally and in his writings. He encouraged me to make use of the lecture platform and to accept the challenges found at universities, and to see such things as a way of making the exploration of ideas a lifelong joy.

I am pleased that he is my friend; I am proud to be his admirer.

Sincerely,
Gene Roddenberry

"Arthur . . . I understand how your ideas inspired Gene when he was first visualizing *Star Trek*. But how, exactly, did you help him out after the original series ended in 1969?"

"He came to see me. Hollywood wasn't taking him seriously at all. So I put him in touch with my then literary agent, Bill Colston Leigh. Gene goes to see him, and Bill says, 'Arthur tells me you're a television producer, and for some reason he thinks people will be interested in what you do. I'll take you on.' So Bill booked Gene to speak at a place that held a couple of hundred people, and a couple of thousand turned up." That, Clarke says, was the turning point. The lecture circuit was what gave Roddenberry the money, the inspiration and the contacts to keep *Star Trek* alive, long after NBC had pulled the plug.

Elements inspired by both Clarke and his late peer, the great Isaac Asimov, glimmer through the fabric of the *Star Trek* continuum. Asimov's main contributions are perhaps more obvious: the humanoid Data is subject to his famous Laws of Robotics,* while Data's fictional

---

* Asimov's Three Laws of Robotics, indelibly programmed into every android's brain, are as follows: 1) A robot may not injure a human being or, through inaction, allow a

creator, Dr. Noonien Soong, was directly inspired by Asimov's theories of a "positronic" brain.

I ask Clarke if he recognizes his own hand in the show.

"No . . . But there are, of course, common elements in almost any science fiction." He sighs. "I've seen it all, really, in science fiction movies and videos. And I'm a little bit tired of it. We always meet *humans*. Whatever they are, they're humans. Central casting can't come up with an intelligent blob of something or other; it wouldn't be very exciting. That's a limitation of science fiction in movies or on TV. It can't be *realistic*. I'm sure there's lots of life out there, and lots of intelligence—though I suspect that all the intelligence will be silicon." He pushes his lips out, musing. "Probably, carbon is only a brief moment in the evolution of intelligence."

This is my third visit to Clarke's abode, but the Sri Lanka I'm seeing today is very different from the tropical paradise I first set foot in fifteen years ago. Bitter conflict between Tamil separatists and the majority Sinhalese population have put the country through a physical and psychological wringer. Armed soldiers guard the entrance to buildings with any strategic value, and tourist taxis are frequently brought to a halt by spiked barricades weighted with sandbags. Terrorism is common in the predominantly Hindu north; two days before my visit, a bridge was blown up, killing nine soldiers. In 1996, a bomb planted at Colombo's Central Bank killed and injured over one thousand people, and the specter of new terror hangs in the air like the smell of burning rubber.

Clarke's terse comments about the bloodshed are tinged with melancholy. "It doesn't really affect us here," he says, referring to the cozy "technoasis" that he shares with his longtime friends Hector and Valerie Ekanayake, their three children, a few servants, and Pepsi, his beloved chihuahua. I can't help but notice, though, an addition that Hector has made to the compound since my last visit. A high, ugly cement wall now rings the grounds—a reminder of just how distant Roddenberry's ideal world really is.

---

human being to come to harm. 2) A robot must obey the orders given it by human beings, except where such orders would conflict with the First Law. 3) A robot must protect its own existence as long as such protection does not conflict with the First or Second Law.

Clarke, like his spiritual progeny at the Jet Propulsion Lab, plays a mean game of Ping-Pong. Every afternoon, shortly before six, he's assisted into the backseat of his cherry-red Mercedes and driven to the Otter Aquatic Club. There, clutching his cane and collapsing theatrically upon the table, he demolishes, through skill or subterfuge, his chosen victim. For the four days I'm in town, that victim will be me.

I climb into the front seat of the sedan, and we pull out onto the flowered avenue. There's a tap on my shoulder, and I turn my head.

"Have you heard Clarke's 69th Law? Ha ha ha . . . listen: 'Reading software manuals, without the hardware, is as frustrating as reading sex manuals—without the software!' "

As soon as we're underway, Clarke switches on the car's sound system and chuckles with impish delight as I'm blown through the roof. I don't know how much wattage he's tweaking, but those big, bad Oakland boom-mobiles sound like squeaky rubber ducks in comparison.

"I've got an eleven-disk jukebox I can pick from!" He pushes a button, and the sound track changes instantly. The repertoire is Clarke heaven: Jean-Michel Jarré, *Tubular Bells*, Yanni, Gustav Mahler, and the *Blade Runner* sound track, all at pelvis-pulverizing volume. Hard to tell how it sounds to my half-deaf host, but to me it's like sitting in a phone booth wired with THX sound.

We pull in through the gates of the Otter Club and steer around a sea of parked cars. The driver and I help Clarke to the entrance, where he signs me into the guest ledger. It's a bit of a process walking him up the stairs to the table-tennis room. Once he's behind the table, though, Clarke's weariness evaporates. He's all flash and braggadocio, wielding the paddle like a light-saber, serving the ball at warp speed.

No point giving the guy a handicap. In the fourteen years we've been playing, I've never beaten him once. For one thing, it's a bit intimidating to play Ping-Pong against someone with an astronomical belt named after him.

I'm referring, of course, to the Clarke Belt. Also known as the geosynchronous orbit, it is the enormous region of outer space lying exactly twenty-five thousand miles above our planet. Satellites placed in orbit at this altitude will effectively "hang" over a single point on Earth's surface, their orbital speed matching the earth's rotation. This makes them steady targets for radio or electrical waves. Clarke developed this concept in a 1945 issue of *Wireless World*, along with its partner concept: communications satellites. That invention makes him, in my estimation, one of the greatest heroes of our epoch—though it's easy to lose sight of that fact while he's gloating over a cheap point.

`Arthur Clarke with Pepsi, his beloved chihuahua.

After three hard-fought games, we retire by the pool. While I guzzle a beer, Clarke tunes a tiny Sony shortwave to the BBC, a habit picked up during his army days. When the news is over, he leafs through a pile of international sci-fi and fantasy magazines. "This must be the Platinum Age of science fiction," he jokes, "even if the 'Golden Age' is twelve. Here . . . have you seen this?" He shows me an article, in a British fanzine, of *Mosaic*, a *Voyager* novel written by Jeri Taylor.

I read the review, flop the 'zine back on the pile and pick up another. Each one contains a nod, in one form or another, to Gene Roddenberry's space opera. I point this out to Clarke, and recall the comments he had made to me in 1993—when he bemoaned the fact that manned exploration of the Moon and planets had ground to a halt. "Maybe *Star Trek* is sustaining our interest," I suggest, "while we wait for the real thing to get back on track."

"I think you're quite right about that, yes. But I'm afraid it may actually be *counter*-productive—because we're not going to find new civilizations every week in prime time when we do start the exploration of space!

"In fact," he frowns, "in a way, the inner solar system has been a major disappointment. Not a trace of life anywhere, let alone Martian princesses and so forth. And the Martian 'bacterium' is iffy. Exciting if it is confirmed, but it's still very iffy. Still, it's interesting that there was so much enthusiasm and interest when the announcement was made. It shows that people are keen."

"Do you think the space program's going to make a comeback, thanks to this renewed interest in Mars?"

"It seems to me," Clarke says dryly, "that we've got to wait until we have efficient propulsion systems. I've lost interest in rockets . . . period. The rocket is to space travel as the balloon was to aviation." I wince, imagining how his words would sting Steve Bennett.

Clarke's current investment, both literal and figurative, has shifted to a phenomenon known as "zero-point energy." The physics of ZPE are brutal, but the idea is simple: It may be possible, some scientists claim, to tap into the quantum fluctuations seething through the vacuum of space itself. How much energy is out there? A cupful of these quantum fluctuations, physicist Richard Feynman once claimed, would be enough to boil all the world's oceans. If it can be harnassed, Clarke tells me, this energy source would be widely available, practically weightless, and almost totally free.

"So what's the timeline on this stuff?"

"For acceptance that something is happening? I hope this year. Ten years for power; maybe less for small units, like houses. Space propulsion? At least ten years." He reconsiders. "Twenty years."

Clarke, whose books have sold nearly as well as *The White Album*, has pumped a modest amount of money into the business. Should the industry take off, his investment would be rewarded many times over. But Clarke isn't after riches. His number one concern, he says, is to get the thing moving.

"Okay. So, providing this does happen—say we do get a kind of warp drive or, at the very least, good impulse power—does Roddenberry's rosy vision of the future seem likely to you?"

"It's certainly possible. Whether it will be real, of course, depends on us. And looking at the evening news, it's hard to be optimistic."

An odd statement, I reflect, from one of the most unshakable optimists I know. Or has life in a war zone changed that view?

"I keep saying I believe fifty-one percent in our chance of survival. . . . So I guess I still consider myself an optimist," Clarke concedes. "Sometimes it drops down to fifty-point-five percent—but never below fifty."

"What do you think it would take to inspire a real sense of human solidarity?"

"I don't know," he laughs. "A Martian invasion?"

Clarke still watches *Star Trek* occasionally, though he's more engaged by the grittier saga of *Babylon 5*. He has trouble keeping the characters in *Deep Space Nine* straight, but does enjoy *The Next Generation* a great deal. When I ask if he prefers TNG to TOS, he falls silent. "Hmm. Perhaps I do. Although that's perhaps unfair, as the first series was sui generis: the first of its kind."

On our way back from the Otter Club, Clarke asks his driver to run us past the Galle Face, the elegant ocean-facing hotel where he holed up for three weeks in 1996 to write *3001: The Final Odyssey*. Working in the hotel gave him a feeling of closure, he says. *2001* was written in Manhattan's Chelsea Hotel in 1966. The saga ended here: thirty years later, and half a world away. When I ask Clarke if he has plans for another book, he laughs dismissively. "I think I deserve some time off," he chortles, "for good behavior."

From the Galle Face it's a short drive downtown. My host points out the refitted Central Bank, blown up in January 1997. When I ask if anyone he knows was hurt in the blast, Clarke falls silent; his driver taps me on the shoulder. I glance at the man, and he pulls open his shirt. A long, mottled shrapnel scar runs from his chin to the base of his neck.

After joining Clarke and the Ekanayakes for take-out Chinese, I climb the stairs to Arthur's study. There's a home movie he wants me to see. He loads the videotape, picks up the remote and settles into an easy chair with his chihuahua in his lap. I drop onto the nearby sofa.

"You may not believe it," he winks, "but I made this myself."

The television crackles to life. On the screen is the radiant half Moon, shimmering through the tropical air. As I watch in amazement, we accelerate toward the lunar surface—coming closer and closer still, until we appear to be in orbit. We skim past craters, skirt the edges of mountains and canyons, and hover over the powdery gray "seas." It feels as if we are flying in a spaceship a few hundred miles above the ancient landscape, peering out the window as the scenery zooms by.

"But how? . . ."

Clarke howls, overjoyed by my confusion. "Nothing to it, really. I recorded it live, as I told you—through a video camera mounted to the lens of my fourteen inch Celestron telescope. I operated the 'scope by remote control, sitting right here in front of the TV, while recording the whole thing on tape. Except for the atmospheric distortion, it looks pretty good, I think . . ."

I'm floored; not so much by the technology as by the sheer *tenacity* of the feat. Arthur C. Clarke may never make it to the Moon, but it hardly matters. The Moon has come to him.

ISLANDS IN THE SKY

"Way, way up in the sky there's a strange sound . . . and a bright light coming through the haze. What the hell is it? It gets closer, and closer. . . . You can't help yourself, you have to see what it is. You're scared, but curious . . ."

The date is April 5, 2063. Rocket scientist Zefram Cochrane has successfully completed the world's first warp-speed flight, an event that has commanded the attention of a passing Vulcan starship. Earth, long a planet of Snapple-guzzling savages, is suddenly a force to be reckoned with—and our neighbors have put us on their planner.

"Okay, bring up the interactive lights, please. . . . Bring up the Ritter fans . . ."

Jonathan Frakes directs through a megaphone, barking the extras through the title scene of *First Contact*. He's shooting a "reaction shot": The ragged denizens of Sheepshit, Montana, awakened by what sounds like an immense blow-dryer, stagger from their shacks and Quonset huts to see what's happening. In the script, they're staring up in wonder, watching the Vulcans touch down. In reality they look like imbeciles, staring at a row of blindingly bright spotlights as giant fans blast dust into their faces.

"*. . . and down. And . . . Cut! Break!*"

The spotlights fade. Frakes drops the megaphone, hops off his chair and stretches like a rottweiler. It's two in the morning, and his breath steams in the frigid air. A mile below, the L.A. suburbs sparkle like nebulae. Our bright, busy knoll of Angeles National Forest feels surreal, an island in the sky.

The extras melt away, hands in their pockets, heading for the coffee and cookies in the commissary tent. A wired, weary tension hangs over the group; they'll be shooting until dawn.

I grab a cheeseburger and wander back onto the darkened set, coming to rest against a massive fiberglass base (all the audience will see of the alien starship). The whole first contact scene, Vulcan hand greeting and all, already seems a cliché. What is it with exterrestrials? As the millennium approaches, Hollywood can't sponsor enough alien visitations: *Independence Day, Mars Attacks, Men in Black, Alien Resurrection, The Fifth Element, Contact.* Aliens sell Hostess Ding Dongs on television commercials, and gaze at us like guppies from the cover of weekly newsmagazines. They inspire citywide celebrations, and tailgate passing comets. People are literally dying to meet them: Thomas Nichols, the fifty-nine-year-old brother of Nichelle Nichols (Lieutenant Uhura on the original *Star Trek*) was among the Heaven's Gate suicides.

This rash of alien-infused activity is vaguely disturbing. It's as if our collective unconscious was preparing us for something. My thoughts again turn to poor Richard Dreyfuss in *Close Encounters of the Third Kind*, knee-deep in dirt on his living room floor: *This means something.*

Okay. But *what*? The signals we're channeling are ambiguous. Who do we set the table for? Will our visitors be the face-sucking, brain-blasting baddies of *Alien, Independence Day*, and *Mars Attacks*? The Raid-bait stars of *Men in Black* and *Starship Troopers*? The ineffable and mysterious overlords of *Contact* and *The Fifth Element*? Or a bunch of guys who just want to invite us out for beer and tapas?

Or will they be Vulcans? Imagine the irony: our first emissaries from outer space turn out to be emotionally distant control freaks. Naturally, they'll take us under their ears. But what effect would such a relationship have on our chaotic, impressionable world? The whole planet, I think, would end up in therapy.

After the break, Frakes will direct *First Contact*'s final scenes: Cochrane greeting the Vulcans, Picard and Lily saying their farewells, the *Enterprise* crew beaming back to their ship. For the moment, though, the Charlton Flat campground has a disheveled, postcoital feel—like the Oakland Coliseum after a Rolling Stones concert.

At base camp, a quarter mile away, generators throb in the dark. The site has become an RV park—all eight stars have their own private, purring domicile. Patrick Stewart walks by wearing a thick parka, his thumb jammed into a Pat Barker novel. Rick Berman huddles with Brannon Braga by the makeup trailer. And Gates McFadden—the noble but underused Dr. Beverly Crusher—stands in the headlights of an idling truck, showing off snapshots from her recent visit to Bosnia.

The first time I ever heard Gates McFadden's voice, apart from on television, was in Braga's BMW. We were driving to one of Brannon's favorite haunts, a Vietnamese restaurant on La Brea, and he'd called his answering machine using the car's voice-activated cell phone.

There were fourteen messages in all. Eleven were from his girlfriend, one was from Ron Moore, and one was from his mother, Scherry, in Ohio. But the longest message by far was from McFadden. She'd been reading a book by Joseph Campbell and had stumbled upon a marvelous quote about humanity's destiny among the stars. It was just the kind of thing that Dr. Crusher might paraphrase, or quote directly, near the end of *First Contact*. Gates began to read the passage—very convincingly, I thought—but Braga skipped forward with a snort.

Though I didn't hear the whole quote, I was intrigued; mainly because I'd just started struggling through a Campbell book myself. It was called *The Inner Reaches of Outer Space*. Despite the book's compelling title and short length (about 150 pages), I was finding it rough going. Tonight, after a week of sporadic reading, I'm only on page seventeen.

Tonight, I run into McFadden as she's ducking into the makeup trailer. It's our first encounter, and I'm dazzled. She's the loveliest woman on television, and the impact of standing just a few feet from her—close enough to plant a kiss on her elegant Irish snout—turns my legs to jelly.

I introduce myself, mention the overheard message, and show her the *Inner Reaches* book. She's never seen it, she says, taking it from my hand. Can she look at it while makeup does her hair? Absolutely—if she'll chat with me for a few minutes afterward.

Three-quarters of an hour later, McFadden appears on the still-empty set. I'm sitting in Berman's chair, going over my notes. She's bundled in a winter jacket, her nectarine hair buried beneath the absurd blonde wig they're making her wear in *First Contact*. (After seven TNG seasons as a redhead, she's been transformed into a blonde; go figure.) As it happens, the official Gates McFadden chair is right beside mine.

"An interesting thing about Campbell," I remark as she sits down, "is that he was married to Jean Erdman, a well-known dancer. You were originally a dancer, too, weren't you?"

"I trained in dance for many years," McFadden concurs, "but it was a very broad thing. It wasn't just tap dance and ballet. It was mask work, pantomime, clowning, circus techniques, all that stuff."

McFadden has a rich classical background. After studying acting at Brandeis she moved to France and enrolled in Jacques LeCoq's École Mime et Théâtre. She found herself immersed in commedia dell'arte, an ensemble acting form that flourished in Italy from the 16th through the 18th centuries. Returning to America in the '80s, Gates acted in numerous plays and films. She choreographed a number of productions—*A Midsummer Night's Dream* and Jim Henson's *Labyrinth*—as well. To ice the cake, she's probably the only member of the *Next Generation* cast who can walk a tightrope.

"So when," I ask, "did your interest in mythology develop?"

"That came when I was in college," Gates says. "And when I studied in Paris. Also, with commedia, you're talking archetypal themes: servant/master, lust, the seven deadly sins. And later, while teaching at various universities, I directed several Greek plays."

"I suppose you're aware that what you're doing here . . ." I tilt my chin toward the Vulcan ship, "is creating another myth."

"It took me a while to get that." She leans forward, almost whispering. "When I first started the series, I was not a *Star Trek* fan, and I had no understanding of it. I didn't know what warp speed meant, or anything. It took me years to begin to apprehend the magnitude of the mythology of *Star Trek*."

"Does it change the way you perform your role?"

"Noooo . . ." Gates shakes her head slowly. "I feel it's had more influence on my understanding and appreciation of what it is within the culture. To tell the truth . . ." She touches my elbow lightly. "At first, I was uncomfortable with being a role model. Which is interesting because, when I was a teacher, I wasn't uncomfortable being a role model at all. It took me a long time to say, 'This is important. I'm glad I'm part of this.' Certainly," she adds, "my recent trip to Bosnia and Herzegovina was the flowering of that whole thing."

"Did you go there to perform theater?"

"No, I did a one-person U.F.O.—Oh, God, I mean U.S.O.—tour." She laughs. "*I* was the U.F.O.! Actually, they'd been asking me for years to do something, go somewhere. I hadn't wanted to go to the larger bases because it's like doing a convention, and I wanted to go someplace where I could genuinely learn something."

What McFadden did learn, in that ugly corner of Europe, was that doctors get a lot more respect in the military command structure than they do in Starfleet. The heroic potential of her character was rarely cultivated on TNG, and was all but ignored in the *Generations* and *First Contact* scripts. (Dr. Crusher's status among the crew was apparent even in the world of merchandising: She was the last TNG character to be sold as an action figure.)

"One thing I noticed in Bosnia," McFadden says, "was that the medical people are always in the command tents. High-ranking medical officers are able to do combat, and they are directly involved in the decision-making process."

McFadden's dissatisfaction with her role in *First Contact* is difficult for the actress to conceal. Her suggestion to add the Joseph Campbell quote was ignored, and her attempts to build Beverly Crusher a more substantial character arc went nowhere.

"I saw you talking to Brannon earlier in the evening," I say. "Was it about the script?" McFadden nods sadly. "Did he make any changes?"

"Tiny things." She shrugs. "But that's the nature of this movie. It's a very wonderful story—but it is not Beverly Crusher's story. I don't mind if the part is small. I just want it to be *defined*. And when I read the script, I felt that the Crusher part had disappeared. I didn't see the character for who she is at all."

And Crusher is, McFadden believes, a role of substance. It's the perfect vehicle for exploring the gray areas of Roddenberry's cosmos, where duty and humanity stand at odds.

"Doctor Crusher was the very first one to disagree with Captain

Picard on a major issue," she asserts. She's alluding to an episode called "Symbiosis," from TNG's first season. In the story, the inhabitants of one world are keeping the citizens of a neighboring planet addicted to a powerful narcotic. Crusher develops a methadone-like solution, but Picard—citing the Prime Directive of noninterference—forbids her from administering it.

"I always stuck up for the compassion in a situation. You know: 'Screw the Prime Directive, we need to save lives here!' That is something I find very interesting, and would have loved to have seen more of it in the *Star Trek* mythology."

A dozen techs move onto the site and begin the work of setting up the lights and microphones for the upcoming scene. Sparkles of dust rise beneath their feet: bits of mylar and wire and gel, catching the light of the moon.

I ask McFadden if she has any specific thoughts about why the *Star Trek* mythology has penetrated so deeply into the global psyche.

She has; and her observation revolves around one of Campbell's theories. The mythologist, she recalls, once wrote about early nomadic codes: commandments stating that one must never kill or steal within one's own group. Limited as they were, such codes recognized that, to ensure survival, the members of a vulnerable society must be mutually supportive.

That ideal is breaking down in modern society. The world is shrinking, groups are dispersing, and a free-for-all mentality is in vogue. *Star Trek*, McFadden explains, reaffirms the nomadic code—on a planetwide scale. The *Enterprise* is a metaphor, a microcosm of what Buckminster Fuller called "Spaceship Earth."

"You see that people can encounter the unknown—the fears, the lawlessness, the new worlds—and get along with each other. They can work together and still maintain control. Rather than dissolve and get completely overwhelmed—which is, of course, a huge and primal fear."

Another reason *Star Trek* is universally appealing, McFadden believes, is that it offers an antidote to the isolation that new technologies—laser disc players, the Web, Walkmans—are pressing upon us. "Even though electronic communication is much faster and more frequent, one-on-one communication seems more difficult than it used to be. The computer gives us information, and we have more things to digest. More is expected of us, because everything is so compressed.

"But the *Star Trek* people don't let technology control them. The computer is just another character, and they know how to coexist with it. That is *very* reassuring: We've worked technology into the myth. You see it very clearly in *First Contact*. There's the Borg, who use technology to destroy, and there's Starfleet, which uses technology to prevail over those evil forces."

Listening to this, I'm reminded again of how far a leap *Star Trek* is from "traditional" science fiction—and classic mythology. *First Contact* would have a much different slant if the aliens summoned by the *Phoenix*'s warp drive had chained Zefram Cochrane to a rock and let vultures pick at his liver.

"Have you studied religion," I ask McFadden, "as deeply as you've studied mythology?"

"I haven't studied it, yet I am fascinated by it." She waves to Jonathan Frakes, who waves back and signals "five minutes" with splayed fingers. "I loved the Mass in Latin. I loved the *mystery* of it. The power of ritual was something I remember very much growing up. And I think that's what attracts me to ritual in theater."

Patrick Stewart and Marina Sirtis appear on the set, followed by James Cromwell, Alfre Woodard, and LeVar Burton. Everyone but Michael Dorn and Brent Spiner will be in this final scene, in which the *Enterprise* away-team witnesses first contact before warping back to the 24th century.

McFadden watches them arrive, surveying the players with a critical eye. "I've also studied mask theater," she remarks, "and it's striking how there are always similar characters in every major culture."

"Do you collect masks?"

"I do. I've made about sixty myself. They're all in trunks, in New York. It's a whole part of my life that's been stashed away. I have beautiful masks from Europe, Japan, India, Bali . . ."

"Whereas in Bali," I laugh, "they're probably collecting vintage *Star Trek* episodes."

"That's because *Star Trek*, too, is a morality play." Gates stands up, tosses her hair, and prepares to join her famous clan. "It's a science fiction *parable* that's seen all over the world. And yet, there is not this sense—as you get in a lot of science fiction—that, 'there is no light in the world anymore. All is darkness.' You get the fact that there is indeed light. There is the possibility of redemption—and we are there to do it."

Gates smiles and starts walking toward the set. "Oh!" She turns around.

"What's the matter?"

"Nothing—I almost forgot about this." She fishes inside her jacket and hands back *The Inner Reaches of Outer Space.*

"Oh . . . thanks. Did you get very far?"

"No . . . only to page eighty-seven. But it's great reading."

"Page eighty-seven?!" I glance briefly at the volume and slip it back into her pocket. "Keep it," I insist.

THE SKIN OF A TOY BALLOON

While Joseph Campbell was introducing thousands of artists to the power of myth, certain artists were attaining an almost mythical status of their own.

Kurt Vonnegut, Jr., lives in midtown Manhattan—and I do mean midtown. His three-story brownstone is tucked between steel and glass skyscrapers, and is so out of context that it slips right off the retina. Back in the early 1970s, working as a messenger in New York City, I'd hurried past the place a dozen times a day, running market-research documents to the media moguls clustered around Rockefeller Center. I'd bet a year's supply of dilithium that, at least once, I had one of his novels stuck in my back pocket. It never would have occurred to me that my then favorite author—*Slaughterhouse Five* is still on my all-time top-five list—was only steps away, stirring up the recipe for *Breakfast of Champions*.

Like so many of my generation, I had integrated Vonnegut's quirky but intuitively correct philosophy—spelled out most eloquently in *Sirens of Titan* and *Cat's Cradle*—into my speech, opinions, and general worldview. In *Sirens of Titan* (1959), human civilization turns out to be the inconsequential result of a long-term plan to generate a spare part for a stranded alien's spaceship. The revelation has a far-reaching impact. Religion is instantly made obsolete, and every human being explains his or her personal history thus: *I was the victim of a series of accidents.*

The hero of *Cat's Cradle* (1963) is the philosopher-king Bokonon, who has invented a lingo all his own. A *karass*, as all Bokonists know, is "a team of people who do God's will, without ever discovering what they are doing." A *wampeter* is the hub—an object, idea, or person—around which a karass revolves.

For me, Vonnegut and his oeuvre seem to form the wampeter of a privileged karass. I was certain we were somehow linked, part of the same master plan. But there is always a danger, in so assuming, of painting oneself into a *granfalloon*: an artificial and meaningless karass, like the Republican party or the Saturn car owners' club. As Bokonon himself put it:

> *If you wish to study a granfalloon,*
> *Just remove the skin of a toy balloon.*

Fifteen minutes before our meeting, I'm about as nervous as I get. There's real wisdom in the maxim that one ought never meet one's idols: feet of clay and all that. They can fall on you.

Our initial contact, through the mails, was very positive. I'd written about my work-in-progress, asking if we might meet in the fall. I'd also included some basic questions about the Martian "bacterium" discoveries and the decline of the space program. Vonnegut penned a convivial reply, responding briefly to my queries.

"The most compelling reason to believe there is life elsewhere," he wrote, "isn't fossil microbes on Mars. It's that there is so much life here on Earth." He went on to say that "the reason our exploration of space stopped is F=MA. It takes too much energy to get anywhere out there. And taxpayers won't give a shit about voyages if there aren't any people who might get killed on board."

Sad but true. As for the rest, I'd spent an inordinate amount of time trying to figure out what $F = MA$ meant. The obvious answer, of course, is *Force = Mass times Acceleration*. But could the dean of ironic futurology be caught up on mere Newtonian trivialities? More likely, I thought, Vonnegut was making a wry comment on NASA's classic plight: *Funding = Media Attention.*

Browsing through Vonnegut's most recent essays at a bookstore near his home, I recall why I wanted to include him in this book in the first place. The author, despite his early reputation as a science fiction writer, is a supremely dispassionate critic of human social habits. His initial schooling, in fact, was in anthropology. It will be fascinating to have his perspective on why human beings gravitate so powerfully toward Roddenberry's vision of our collective future in duranium-hulled starships.

But with zero hour approaching, I realize that I may be running up a blind alley. Vonnegut is not necessarily a fan of the show. It's possible he's never even watched it. Worse, he's known to be an incorrigible curmudgeon. What if he dismisses the whole *Star Trek* phenomenon as one giant granfalloon?

The moment is at hand. I need something, anything, to declaw the situation; something that will simultaneously baffle and charm the venerable satirist. Fleeing the bookstore, I race around the corner to a streetside florist and buy the lion a bouquet of orchids.

———

His housekeeper takes the flowers, and leads me inside.

Kurt Vonnegut is in the dining room, signing a box of broadsides. A pack of Pall Malls rests on the table beside him. Tall plants and a brick wall are visible through the rear window. Aside from a portable television tuned to CNN, the home has the atmosphere of a refuge; it's hard to imagine that, beyond the front door, Pakistani cabdrivers and pedestrians are locked in a deadly game of cat and mouse.

Vonnegut's wearing gray trousers and a sleeveless sweater over a shortsleeve shirt. Just a few weeks past his seventy-fourth birthday, he has a firm handshake and a damned good head of hair. Though he's often been compared, in appearance, to Mark Twain—the mustache, if nothing else—I don't see it. Twain, for all his personal tragedy, had a perpetually amused glint in his eye. Vonnegut's expression is aloof and darkly introspective.

EVERYBODY'S A CRITIC

LEWIS WARD,
THE SAN FRANCISCO BAY GUARDIAN

The Ultimate Star Trek Page's Nazeer Ali, whose *Star Trek* Web site was given the Vulcan death grip, believes Viacom is just lashing out because the quality of *Star Trek*-related TV programs (and ratings) have plummeted. "You can save money on sleeping pills by watching DS9," he says.

Howard Raab [president of Save Trek] blames Rick Berman and Brannon Braga for the slip in quality. Braga didn't help his popularity when he said, regarding Internet fans, in *Sci-Fi Universe*, "No offense, but they got too much time on their hands."

We sit down, and I switch on my tape recorder. Right away I experience an attack of performance anxiety. It's like stage fright; my hastily prepared queries flee from my mind like spooked deer.

"Do you read much science fiction?," I ask lamely.

"No."

Good start. I feint to the right and try again. "What do you make of this fresh flurry of interest in sending things out to Mars?"

Vonnegut clears his throat. "It's the same as finding new enemies to keep these wars in the streets going." He speaks so softly that I have to edge the microphone closer. "To keep those plants going: aerospace industries and all that. But what's hidden from the American people, and from the people of the world, is how *enormous* these distances are, and how little there is for us to reach within any reasonable length of time." He crushes the stub of his cigarette in an ashtray already overflowing with butts. "So it's entertainment, like the O. J. Simpson case, or anything else. We're here to be entertained."

I'm a little bit startled; these are nearly the words that Michael Dorn had used to describe his attitude about *Star Trek* itself.

Running with the entertainment cue, I describe my project to Vonnegut. After traveling around the world, I tell him, I believe that people are looking for more than mere entertainment. *Star Trek* represents a unique new mythology—the first mythology, perhaps, in which humanity is master of its own destiny. "And the most interesting thing about it," I conclude, "is that it's such an optimistic, almost utopian, view of the future."

"Well, that's fine! It cheers people up." Like magic, there's a fresh Pall Mall between his fingers. "Look. These things happen because there's a terrific hunger for family. It explains the Deadheads, too. But it's family, family, family. Charles Manson was able to pick up quite attractive, reasonably intelligent young women on the roadside because they were ravenous for family. Politicians and television stars pretend to be relatives.

THE SCIENCE OF *STAR TREK*

DR. DAVID ALLEN BATCHELOR,
NASA PHYSICIST
dbatchelor@leaf.gsfc.nasa.gov

Roddenberry knew some basic astronomy. He knew that space ships unable to go faster than light would take decades to reach the stars, and that would be too boring for a one-hour show per week. So he put warp drives into the show—propulsion by distorting the space-time continuum that Einstein conceived. With warp drive the ships could reach far stars in hours or days, and the stories would fit human epic adventures, not stretch out for lifetimes.

MEDICAL TECHNOLOGY

SCOTT ADAMS

from *The Dilbert Future* published by
HarperBusiness © United Media, 1997

On *Star Trek*, the doctors have hand-held devices that instantly close any openings in the skin. Imagine that sort of device in the hands of your inscrupulous friends. They would sneak up behind you and seal your ass shut as a practical joke. The devices would be sold in novelty stores instead of medical outlets. All things considered, I'm happy that it's not easy to close other people's orifices.

Geraldo Rivera is our brother, our big brother. And it works! People are very easily seduced—as those girls were seduced by Manson. Since we no longer have extended families, that is again and again and again going to explain people's devotion to this cockamamy scheme or that one."

"I find it interesting," I say, "that you compare Trekkers to Deadheads."

"Well, they're good people in any case." He shrugs. "I think that people attracted to either one of those families are *kind*."

"It's a tribal thing," I agree. "You can go anywhere and find kindred spirits. I can go to India and Japan and find dozens of people who will let me sleep on their sofas simply because I watch the same television show that they do."

But Vonnegut is focused on my notepad. "You poor sonofabitch, you're left-handed! How far are you going to get through life that way?"

"I've gotten this far. . . . Are you left handed, too?"

"I was." Vonnegut settles back in his chair, lights his cigarette. "My parents switched me, because that was the thing for scientifically minded parents to do in the '20s. But then, when I was about forty-five, I suddenly started turning doorknobs with my left hand, taking change with my left hand. . . . Anyway, what the hell were we talking about?"

"Family. I wonder if the issue isn't so much family as *engagement*. The fact is that we're talking beings; what we do best is communicate. Which explains, of course, the incredible growth of the Internet . . ."

"We talk," Vonnegut agrees, "but another thing we do is, we're *theatrical*. And you can only do that live. And what is theatrical about us is our behavior. At all times, there's a wonderful ambivalence, a wonderful tension: are we gonna touch or aren't we?" He leans toward me, touching my arm. "That's all missing from the Internet—and life ceases to be a dance."

"The on-line posture," I agree, "is very much a posture of constipation."

"Well, that's what I'm saying. Don't buy computer stocks. Buy laxative stocks!"

I get a tour of the house. It's a big place, and miraculously quiet. Hardcover books are stacked everywhere, their multicolored spines making crooked, Seuss-like towers. Every square meter of wall space is covered with art—much of it by Vonnegut himself. He shows me his silk screens. The bold, playful works, recalling Saul Steinberg and Joan Miró, are the antipode to his dark side. Visual art has enjoyed a long tenure with his family. His father and grandfather were artists, his father also a well-known architect, and three of his children (there are seven, four adopted) paint as well. The Vonnegut creativity gene has taken some bizarre turns, however; his late brother Bernard, a meteorologist, invented cloud seeding.

Before my visit I'd combed for common themes in Vonnegut's most popular books. Beneath the cynicism, woven through an almost coldly objective view of the human condition, were two bright threads: a passionate pacifism and guarded optimism concerning humanity's redemption. But Vonnegut's classic works were written decades ago. Are there any trends in contemporary society, I ask, that give him hope?

"Well, I've got my own 'unified field theories,' like Einstein was trying to do. The first is that people will do anything to get an extended family—because we need extended families as much as we need calcium, or vitamin C. The other is that there is indifference to prospects of war and to pollution—to the killing of the planet—because *people hate life*. They find it embarrassing, terribly uncomfortable, and they wouldn't care if it ended tomorrow. This happens to be a fact. And very few people have acknowledged it."

I'm taken aback. As the interview has progressed, I've found it impossible to determine if Vonnegut's viewpoint is real, or a kind of tragicomic playacting; as if he were portraying, by habit or design, the jaded Kilgore Trout character of his own novels.

"Why," I ask, "should people hate life?"

Vonnegut shrugs. "Same reason they don't like a pebble in their shoe, or a migraine headache. It's *very* uncomfortable. And it goes on and on and on, and nobody dares say so because everybody's got to be a good sport about it. They're too short, they're too fat, they can't dance good, they can't fuck good, they don't have any money . . ."

"I'm not hearing a lot of optimism here."

"No. But I think any sort of planning you make, you should acknowledge that people don't like life to begin with, and deal with that. Give them an extended family, if they haven't got that, because that's why they feel so lousy. But computer salesmen, Bill Gates and all that, aren't acknowledging what human beings are and need at all. They don't know, and they don't care. They find human beings *inconvenient.*"

I've got some specific questions, but I bag them. It's quite obvious that *Star Trek* holds little appeal for Vonnegut, on anything beyond the social level. Here is a man who doesn't give a rat's ass for high technology; a man who equates the space shuttle with the Cirque du Soleil. Here is a man who still writes letters by hand and carries them down to the post office for the reluctant pleasure of dancing with other human beings.

"At the end of *The Sirens of Titan,*" I counter, "the protagonist comes to the conclusion that the only real purpose people have in the world is to love one another. Nothing else, none of our existential angst or technological virtuosity, matters worth a damn. Don't you still feel that way?"

"I may have been talking about a certain sort of person, for whom that's reason enough for being. When Barbra Streisand sings 'People who need people are the luckiest people in the world,' I wonder if she isn't talking about cannibals."

I laugh mirthlessly. Whatever I was hoping for, this isn't it. But who cares? Vonnegut is simply being Vonnegut; I could hardly ask for more.

"So what's the cure for all this?" I ask. "What's the secret for coping with the world?"

"Retreat," Vonnegut says. "Get away from it—if you can. You talk about *Star Trek*; well, there are all these little clusters of people who have invented a life for themselves—and have done a pretty interesting job of it, usually."

While preparing to leave, I pull a paperback edition of *Cat's Cradle* out of my bag. I open to a short poem that, credited to Bokonon, appears near the end of chapter 81.

"I'd like you to sign this," I say. "Right below the poem."

Vonnegut studies the page. "Why?"

"Because it's a wonderfully succinct statement of why we have to get back into outer space. It also explains, more or less, the urge that has made *Star Trek* such a phenomenon on this planet."

Vonnegut laughs, takes the book, and places his amoebic signature across the text.

There's a rustle in the hallway, and Vonnegut's wife—the photographer Jill Krementz—walks in. She has the wide-eyed, kinetic energy of someone who's just sat on a tack. Jill spies the bouquet of flowers, runs up to Kurt, and throws her arms around his neck. "You are *soooo* sweet," she croons. She turns to me. "Tonight's my first gallery opening in twenty-two years." Back to Kurt: "It was so thoughtful of you to remember."

Vonnegut narrows his eyes, his mouth a curve of ironic amusement. "They're from *him*," he confesses.

———

Back on the street, dazed by the rush hour traffic, I open up *Cat's Cradle* and read Bokonon's poem again. This is what it says:

> *Tiger got to hunt,*
> *Bird got to fly;*
> *Man got to sit and wonder, "Why, why, why?"*
> *Tiger got to sleep,*
> *Bird got to land;*
> *Man got to tell himself he understand.*

Below, buried within the autograph, is Vonnegut's famous asterisk: droll code, in *Breakfast of Champions*, for a puckered asshole.

THE JOY OF KLINGON

Speaking Klingon means never having to say you're sorry.

That's how Dr. Lawrence Schoen, director of the Klingon Language Institute (KLI), explains it to me over a mound of cherry blintzes.

"One of the things that attracts people to the Klingon language is the Klingon culture," he says. "Klingons have license; they're free to vent the frustration that living in a polite society forces on us. When two Klingons meet on the street, they don't say, 'Hello, how are you? How's the wife and kids?' The closest we have to a Klingon greeting, loosely translated, is 'Whadda you want?' No bullshit, no social niceties. And Klingons don't say good-bye. When they're done, they just walk away. That's almost refreshing in its honesty."

It's a blustery Friday on Madison Avenue. Schoen, who lives in Wyndmoor, Pennsylvania, meets me at the Empire State Building. We walk to a nearby diner, where my companion eases his Jovian bulk into a tiny, padded booth. The forward displacement of the table pins me against the opposite bench like a lab specimen; a fact that Schoen witnesses, in character, without apology.

Klingons were first introduced on TOS (in "Errand of Mercy," aired March 23, 1967), as swarthy, swaggering bullies with a transparent

Mongol streak. Stephen E. Whitfield's *The Making of Star Trek*, published in 1968, provides the following description: "Their only rule of life is that rules are made to be broken by shrewdness, deceit, or power. Cruelty is something admirable; honor is a despicable trait." Since that time—thanks largely to Ron Moore's efforts—their profile has been reshaped. No longer lowbrow barbarians, Klingons now belong to a complex and richly layered culture.

"They're honorable warriors," Schoen says. "Most of what we see of them is just aggression, but I think Klingons are the embodiment of passion. We know that the Klingons have opera, the most passionate form of music. We know they write love poetry. To be a Klingon is to live with gusto, with no regrets or half measures. Which is consistent with their lack of polite phrases. There's really no polite Klingon. There's *respectful* Klingon, which is a different matter.

"English uses a lot of indirect requests," he elaborates. "You say, 'My, it sure is cold in here!' as a polite way to say, 'Shut the window.' Or you might ask someone, 'Can you pass the peas?' Unless their arm is in a sling, it's probably a rhetorical question." Schoen grins, and tells me a story about the KLI's first annual conference in 1993. "A dozen of us descended upon a restaurant, and were speaking Klingon around the dinner table. At one point someone said to me the equivalent of, 'Pass the salt.' I smiled and said, 'All right . . . what do you say?' The guy stopped short, smiled, and screamed at me: '**DaH!** Now!'"

Schoen, thirty-seven, is a bearish man with porthole glasses and a thick, wiry beard flecked with gray. Despite his Jewish roots, he could easily be cast as a Mennonite blacksmith. But Schoen is deeply cerebral; his doctorate is in language and memory. A science fiction buff and sometime SF author, he has followed *Star Trek* since he was seven.

"I clearly remember bargaining with my parents." He laughs, gesturing with surprisingly delicate hands. " 'I'll watch *Star Trek* now—and wash the dishes afterwards.' "

The first murmurs of a credible Klingon language were heard early in *Star Trek III: The Search for Spock*. Linguist Marc Okrand was

Dr. Lawrence Schoen, guardian of the Klingon tongue.

hired by Paramount to provide this dialogue, which was subtitled in English. When he wrote *The Klingon Dictionary*, Okrand went back and incorporated these words, along with fragments of Klingon barked during the original series. Vocabulary and grammar were developed as he went along.

The genesis of the KLI began in 1991, when someone handed Schoen a copy of Okrand's *Dictionary*. The book—containing about two thousand words and some basic Klingon grammar—struck a chord. As a teen, Schoen had belonged to the Mythopoeic Society, a group that discussed the works of fantasy writers like C. S. Lewis and J. R. R. Tolkien, and studied the "Elven" languages in *The Lord of the Rings*. Twenty years later, this encounter with a new artificial language fired Schoen's imagination. He set out to find others who might be interested in exploring the Klingon language in depth.

"I thought there would be a few dozen people," he says. "And then it hit the fan." The KLI burst into bloom when Lynn Van Matry, writing for the *Chicago Tribune*, publicized Schoen's efforts. Her article was picked up by nearly two hundred newspapers, and a nationwide media orgy ensued.

During the past seven years, the Institute's ranks have swelled to more than 1,600 members. Its quarterly journal, *HolQeD* (pronounced hol-kch!ed; the odd caps are an integral part of the written script) is sent to forty-five countries. There are readers on every continent—including, Schoen states, Antarctica. Their website (www.kli.org) gets around thirty thousand hits a year.

"We like to think of Klingon as the fastest growing language in the galaxy," Schoen jokes. "We started with zero speakers—and we're doubling every year." Even the institute's motto—"qo'mey poSmoH Hol" (Language opens worlds)—is a wry nod to Klingon imperialism.

But the turnover, Schoen admits, is high. "We've had people join because they read things in magazines and said, 'Oh cool, this'll be fun! I *like* Klingons!' Then they discover that serious linguistics is a hell of a lot of work, and they don't renew. That's okay; because if they're not going to give it a real try, if they don't want to throw themselves into it, well . . . it's not for everybody, by any means."

One of the best things about *HolQeD* is that dense articles about grammar and linguistic relativity are interpersed with absurd games and contests. Past issues have included everything from Klingon palindromes (phrases that read the same forward and backward; e.g., "Lewd did I live & evil I did dwel") to so-called spoonerisms (phrases with interposed letters; e.g., "You have hissed all my mystery lessons, and tasted the whole worm!"). The best of these competitions, generating the most response by far, was the Great Insult Contest. The grand prize went to Klingon speaker Neal Schermerhorn, for the venemous, "quv vavwI' Say'moHmeH nuj bIQ bIlo'chugh, nuj bIQ vIlammoH": "If I use spit to clean your father's honor, I only dirty the spit."

Artificial languages are nothing new. Some, like Tolkien's Elven tongues, are completely fanciful. Others—like Esperanto or Volapuk (intended to be international languages), Loglan (with a structure based on mathematical logic), or any computer language—can be very useful. Klingon falls somewhere in between.

"Klingon rides on the rich coattails of *Star Trek*, so it appeals to people who normally wouldn't study a language—much less an artificial language." Schoen traces the flesh of a blintz through cherry goo. "For those of us who grew up with the show, Klingon is a chance to return to something we loved as children. We don't have to say, 'Oh well, we can't play *Star Trek* anymore.' "

The word "play" is a bit misleading. The KLI is not about reinventing Klingon, or making up neat new words for daggers or body parts. That's Marc Okrand's job. His interpretation forms the canon, while the institute acts as a sort of French Academy, preserving the language in a (relatively) pure form.

"Our motivation for this is simple," explains Schoen. "If people began generating their own terms, how would other Klingon speakers ever learn of them? The language would quickly diverge—as natural languages always do—and we'd have many new dialects popping up. While this is inevitable, we're trying to delay it a bit; at least until we've built up a more significant population of speakers."

"Do you get much flak from the 'get a life' lobby?"

Schoen shrugs irritably, a whole-body gesture that jars the table. Coffee sloshes from my mug, and a salt shaker hits the floor. "It's a hobby," he says. "And I think *Star Trek* fans have taken a lot of abuse for their hobby." He pauses as the waitress administers damage control. "Listen. You can go into any sports bar in the country and say, 'Okay, 1987. Third game of the World Series. Who won, by what score?' Everyone will be able to tell you. We don't point at those people and say, 'Eww, baseball geeks!' Well, that's no less fanatical than being able to recite chapter and verse from your favorite TV show. Studying

Klingon is an extension of that—and it can be much more rigorous, challenging, and intellectually interesting."

Five years ago, only two or three people were fluent in Klingon. Today there are dozens. Fluency, as defined by Schoen, is the ability to have a conversation without burying your nose in the *Klingon Dictionary*, and the capacity to respond to questions you haven't prepared catchphrase answers for. "There's a set of useful expressions printed on the back of the second edition of Okrand's *Dictionary*," he says, "but if you can get beyond those and create new phrases—and be understood—I'd consider that to be fluent."

The English language is a melting pot, full of words and phrases that we've borrowed from other languages and made our own: rigor mortis, machismo, ballet. Skimming through an issue of *HolQeD*, I ask if any Klingon words have clawed their way into the vulgate. Schoen shakes his head. The only real contender, he concedes, is *Qapla'*: the Klingon word for "success," sometimes used as a leave taking. But even the actors on the show pronounce it wrong.

"The correct pronunciation is *KCHap-la!*," he spits. "But they typically pronounce it as *kapla*. Kind of a limp-wristed thing. Like, even *kreplach* would be closer."

But Paramount, sadly, has never approached Schoen for speech therapy. For all its resources and scholarship, the KLI has had no real influence on *Star Trek* at all. Like a powerful ghost ship guarding the perimeter of the Neutral Zone, the institute's contribution to the Klingon language remains unsung.

———

The KLI's forte, it seems, is marrying serious language study with cheeky intent. Their magnum opus, completed in late 1996, is a complete "restoration" of *Hamlet* into Klingon. The project took nearly two years. An edition of 1,026 copies was printed—including twenty-six leather-bound volumes, each inscribed with a letter from the *pIqaD* (the Klingon alphabet).

The inspiration for the effort was reed thin. It sprouted from a single scene in the sixth *Star Trek* movie, *The Undiscovered Country*, in which a party of testy Klingons beams aboard the *Enterprise* for dinner. Tensions run high, and primate posturing by Captain Kirk and his guests is rampant. At one point during the meal, the Klingon chancellor quotes Hamlet's most famous line—taH pagh toHbe' (To be or not to be)—in his native tongue. "You have not experienced Shakespeare,"

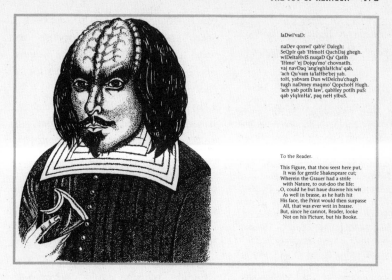

laDwI'vaD:

naDev qonwI' qab'e' Dalegh:
SeQpIr qab 'IHmoH QuchDaj ghegh.
wIDeltaHvIS nuqaD Qu' Qatlh
'IHmo' 'ej Dojqu'mo' chovnatlh.
vaj navDaq 'ang'eghlaHchu' qab,
'ach Qu'vam ta'laHbe'bej yab.
toH, yabvam Dun wIDelchu'chugh
tugh naDmey maqmo' QopchoH Hugh.
'ach yab potlh law', qabHey potlh puS:
qab yIqImHa', paq neH yIbuS.

To the Reader.

This Figure, that thou seest here put,
It was for gentle Shakespeare cut;
Wherein the Grauer had a strife
with Nature, to out-doo the life:
O, could he but haue drawne his wit
As well in brasse, as he hath hit
His face, the Print would then surpasse
All, that was euer writ in brasse.
But, since he cannot, Reader, looke
Not on his Picture, but his Booke.

the Chancellor sighs, "until you have read him in the original Klingon." It's a wonderful throwaway gag; a droll nod to the good old days when the Commies, according to cold war mythology, delighted in claiming credit for Yankee inventions.

"That's why we decided to *restore* the work, rather than translate." Schoen chuckles, sipping his Diet Coke. "It's a lot of fun. In our introduction, there's a comment on the fact that *Hamlet* is very seditious from the Klingon perspective. The young Hamlet is not your typical Klingon. If he was, he would come home in the first act, discover that his father had been killed by his uncle, and exact his revenge. End of play. Instead, Hamlet vacillates. Should I kill him? Should I not kill him? In our restoration we develop this fiction, claiming that the play is banned in the Klingon hinterlands for poisoning the minds of young Klingons."

Shakespeare, Schoen reflects admiringly, is wonderful. His work survives translation, and his appeal shines through in any medium. "I think there's a whole generation of people out there, unfortunately, who might never read *Hamlet* because there isn't a *Hamlet* Nintendo cartridge. If we bring someone to Shakespeare through Klingon, I think we've done a great thing." He pauses, his eyes narrowing. "Hopefully, they won't think *Hamlet* really *is* a Klingon play."

Hamlet was just the tip of the iceberg. Nearly all of Shakespeare's plays, from *Romeo and Juliet* to *Macbeth*, tell tales of warring houses that will translate beautifully into Klingon. The KLI hopes to do

TRANSLATING THE BIBLE INTO SUITABLE KLINGON STIRS COSMIC DEBATE

BY CARRIE DOLAN
The Wall Street Journal, June 13, 1994

Citing deep philosophical differences with fellow scholars, Glen Proechel has resigned from his Bible-translation group.

"We have very different goals," says Prof. Proechel, a language instructor at the University of Minnesota. The rift will result in two translations of the Good Book for a civilization that, until now, had lacked The Word in its own language: the Klingon language.

"It's not going to make any sense," Prof. Proechel says of the literal Klingon version. "It will be describing things that don't exist in their own culture."

But Klingon literalists disagree. "You don't mess around with the Bible," even if the warrior-like Klingon vocabulary is void of biblical concepts like mercy and compassion, says Dr. Lawrence Schoen, a linguist overseeing the literalist translation.

The KLI, based in Flourtown, PA, is heading the Klingon Bible project, which could take up to five years. It involves ten scholars, led by a graduate of Yale Divinity School. They are getting help from a Lutheran Bible Group; far from seeing the project as blasphemous, the group hopes it will draw attention to the challenges of translating the Bible for real people.

Until recently, Prof. Proechel was part of the team but he has since strayed from the flock. He is working on what he calls a "retelling of the New Testament in the world which Klingons understand."

exactly that—at the rate of one play a year. "The one I'm really looking forward to," Schoen leers, "is *The Taming of the Shrew*. I think we'll have a lot of fun with that one."

In the winter of 1995, the KLI published its first edition of *jatmey*, an anthology of original Klingon poetry and fiction. Other projects include a Klingon language correspondence course and a cunning antidote to the ennui of hours spent in Hebrew or Sunday school: a translation—from the original Aramaic—of the Bible.

At this rate, serious study of the Klingon language could outlive *Star Trek* itself. This notion gains more credibility every July, when KLI members gather from around the world for the Institute's five-day *qep'a'* ("big meeting"). In 1999, the event—an annual pilgrimage for Klingon speakers—moves from Philadelphia to Las Vegas.

"They were using Klingon for *everything*," Schoen recalls gleefully. "Some more fluently than others, of course. But what amazes me—as a psychologist in the field of linguistics—is that for one week, every year, Klingon becomes a living language. I find myself at the very heart of a brand-new language community that didn't even *exist* ten years ago. That's very bizarre."

I pay the bill, and we bundle up. It's bitter cold outside, and a stiff wind whistles through Schoen's beard. "One thing I'm curious about," I shout, "is the KLI's Antartica connection. How did the people at Amundsen-Scott Base contact you?"

Schoen squints. "They didn't," he admits. "I sent them issues of

HolQeD on my own. Okay, I wanted to be able to say we had copies on every continent. But I also knew they'd love it—and my intuition was correct."

"Intuition?"

"Sure. I figured that any scientist crazy enough to live in Antarctica for six months must have grown up on *Star Trek*."

The Brindavan Express steals through the musky greenery of Tamil Nadu—about as far as one can get from the permafrost of Antarctica. It's a jewel of a morning, and India feels like Oz (or, better yet, the paradise planet of Rubicun III). An emerald parakeet darts by; lapis kingfishers with absurdly long beaks perch on telephone wires. Dragonflies hover beside the train at small stations, their wings beating too fast to see. As we creep forward, the luxurious rhythm of the engine inexplicably calls the *Star Trek: Voyager* theme to my mind. I hum it to myself as we chug over the hills of south India, drowned out by the nasal cries of *pan* and *idli* salesmen parading through the second-class car.

An Indian Railways attendant strides by, swinging a stainless steel samovar. I touch his shoulder.

"May I have some tea, please?"

"Sorry, sir, coffee only."

"Really? Must be the 'New India.' "

"*Aacha*," he replies, his head waggling like a Chicago Cubs mascot doll.

Shortly past noon we arrive in Bangalore, a thriving cosmopolis of five million people situated about three thousand feet above sea level. Riding an auto rickshaw across town, I see that everything I've heard is true. This is not your typical Indian city. Sacred cows do wander the streets, grazing on weeds and vegetable peels, but grazing as well are Oracle, Hewlett-Packard, and Toshiba, whose billboards loom above congested roundabouts. Despite the widening gap between the nation's newly rich and eternally poor, Bangalore is India's first true middle-class enclave; a hard wired, tree-shaded urbania with its tail in an auto-rickshaw and a Pentium chip on its shoulder.

I check in at the High Gates Hotel and swing my laptop onto the counter. This is the tough part: trying to eke logistical help out of techno-illiterate natives.

"Hi, uh, is there anywhere I can send or receive e-mail in this city?"

The receptionist looks at me like I'm straight out of the Beverly Hillbillies, and unfolds a map. "At the end of this block. Look for the Bangalore Cyber Café. They're running dedicated T1 lines, they'll set you right up . . ."

He's right. Strolling down Church Street (past a beer-and-disco club called, of all things, NASA), I arrive at a full-blown Internet salon featuring twenty-one-inch color monitors, Netscape Gold and—*oh, baby*—a purified watercooler. The terminals are fully occupied, mostly by earnest teenagers surfing between Hollywood fan clubs and U.C. Berkeley admissions sites. In the adjoining café, gorgeous Indian girls lean over copies of *Atlas Shrugged*, sipping sweet, filtered coffee.

India is vast, and my decision to visit Bangalore was not made at random. Established during the Mauryan Empire more than a thousand years ago, the city now hangs suspended between the languor of the East and the info-lust of the West. The "Silicon Valley of India," it's an obvious place to learn what impact *Star Trek* has had on the new generation of Hindustani hackers.

But where do you look for Trekkers in a place like Bangalore? A Web search turns up nothing, and the scores of Hindi film 'zines papering the newsstands contain nary a word about *First Contact*. Days go by and I'm getting nowhere—until an idea balloon appears over my head.

I head up Church, turn right onto Brigade, and keep going until I pass a run-down theater all but hidden behind a huge, hand-painted marquee for *Independence Day*. The opposite side of the street is a teeming sidewalk bazaar, packed with stalls selling everything from rubber thongs to cell phones. After a bit of sleuthing I find the computer stores, and duck into a shop at random. Cables dangle from the walls, modem boxes are jammed onto sagging shelves and CD-ROM jewel boxes litter the place like lost space shuttle tiles.

The place is crowded, but everyone stops talking when I appear. I feel like I've barged through the swinging doors of an old-time saloon.

"Howdy. You fellas sell *Star Trek* computer games?"

The owner—Hassib, by his name tag—crosses his arms. "Yes, yes. In fact we have sold more than four hundred in this shop alone."

"I see." I peer around the shop. Dark, curious eyes return my gaze. "Do any of you know anyone in Bangalore who might be a *Star Trek* fan?"

Hassib, master of his shop, replies for all. "Sorry, sir."

Success in India depends upon cool persistence. I lean against the door jamb, hands thrust into my pockets, eyeing the merchandise. Dust motes dance in the air, swirling lazily. Buses heave by outside.

Hassib finally breaks the silence. "Okay. Maybe you call Deepak, on double-five, seven-six, nine-two-nine."

I make a disappointed sound. "Just Deepak, eh?"

"Okay, okay, also try Krishna. You please phone him on double-six, double-one, three, two, five . . ."

"And Amjad," a bystander adds. "At triple-five, double-naught, nine, six."

Within seconds everyone in the shop is firing names at me, rattling off phone numbers with an odd, mnemonic rhythm. I whip out my pen and write as fast as I can, feeling like the elephant-headed Ganesha as he recorded Valmiki's spontaneous ejaculation of the entire *Ramayana* epic.

I race back to the High Gates, place calls to a dozen potential Trekkers and spend the rest of the afternoon waiting by the phone. By dinner time, only one person—a twenty-two-year-old university student named Amjad—has returned my call.

Amjad meets me at the Coconut Grove, a nearby restaurant specializing in south India curries. He has brought his friend Naveen, a lanky, hyperactive computer systems engineer. We sit at a cane table. Torches burn on an outdoor patio, illuminating a large bronze statue of rotund Ganesha himself. In the Hindu religion, Ganesha is the remover of obstacles and protector of travelers. If India were ever to build a starship, he'd be enshrined right on the main bridge.

Both Amjad and Naveen love *Star Trek*, despite years of disappointment and betrayal. The fact of the matter is that *Star Trek* isn't even *on* in India—not in any real sense. The original series first arrived in India in 1984, and Doordashan (the government-run channel) is still milking those tired episodes. A single season of TNG was broadcast on the Star Plus satellite channel in 1994.

"I was heartbroken when the first season ended," laments Amjad, "because I knew I'd have to wait a whole year and watch a load of reruns. But the second season never came."

"People underestimate Indians," Naveen says peevishly. "They think we aren't very advanced. But there is definitely an audience for *Star Trek* here. If they showed all 179 *Next Generation* episodes, we would watch for 179 days—continuously."

"What did you like the best about the original series?"

"Spock," Naveen declares. "He's the most popular *Star Trek* character in India. He's something we would all like to be: less emotional."

"That's odd," I say. "I always think of Indians as very emotional and expressive people."

"That's exactly what I'm telling you!" Naveen shouts. "Indians would like to be *less* emotional. That's why we like Spock." He peers at me. "Logically."

Naveen and Amjad don't touch beer; they order nothing but a plate of fries. They seem, in fact, perpetually annoyed. I recognize this trait from other Indian encounters, and I think I've figured it out: It's an attempt to make Westerners feel comfortable by subtly mimicking our own behavior.

When I ask if there are any *Star Trek* fan clubs in Bangalore, they shake their heads in unison. "Even if *Star Trek* was on television every day, the people who loved it wouldn't start fan clubs," insists Naveen. "Indians simply don't start fan clubs for foreign things. I have many friends who watch *Star Trek*, but they'd never do such a thing. If it's something Indian, of course, we'll be going crazy; we're a very proud country."

"There are loads of *Star Trek* fans in India," Amjad says. "But you will find no conventions, no magazines. The show has a quiet, inexpressive following."

"But it's more than that. You may have noticed," Naveen says with a trace of sarcasm, "that our technology here is not as *advanced* as it is in your country. To reach the technology of America will take us five or ten years. That's a big gap. So as we're still thinking ahead to reach your level, how can we think ahead to the technology of *Star Trek*?"

But his claim isn't strictly true. Indian kids have no problem making quantum leaps of the imagination, or projecting themselves into Federation space. The conceptual block Naveen is describing applies, mainly, to people who came of age before the late 1980s.

The reason for this is simple. Over the past ten years, the subcontinent has leapfrogged directly into the cyber age. The awkward growing stage that America went through—with punch cards, Kaypros, and Pong—barely happened here. India has transformed itself, in little more than a decade, from a country where you could hardly get your hands on a digital watch to a nation of kids voraciously consuming Quake, Flashback, and *The X-Files.*

One result of this generational info-gap is that anything with a techno or sci-fi slant is incomprehensible to most Indian adults—even middle-class ones—who remain addicted to cheesy soap operas and Bollywood breastfests. India's movie industry is the largest on Earth but, to the best of my knowledge, it has never produced a single science fiction film. (This will probably change; the theater showing *Independence Day* is in its third month of record-breaking crowds.)

"It's the kids who mostly go for *Star Trek,*" Naveen concurs. "Even the cartoons that children watch are usually science fiction. They love to see things that happen in space, with a lot of fighting and aliens." He pauses as the waiter refills his water glass. "But you have to realize that foreign TV series simply don't get the attention of films. I'm telling you, if all those *Star Trek* movies had been released in the theaters—one, two, three, four, five, six, *Generations*—we really would have liked it."

"It could also be the language gap. If *Star Trek* was broadcast in Hindi," Amjad argues, "there might be a thousand fan clubs by next week."

An interesting, if contradictory point. Would dubbing the program invest it with enough "Indianess" to satisfy national pride? But the very premise is absurd. *Star Trek* in Hindi! It could never be. Spoken Hindi is inseparable from the highly animated, often histrionic mannerisms that accompany it. Fingers flutter; shoulders roll; crimson *pan* juice splatters into corners. It's impossible to imagine a dubbed Data describing an approaching vessel without visualizing Picard waggling his head in response. "Aacha, Mr. Data. And from which place is this good ship coming?"

"What is the Hindi equivalent," I ask, "of *Make it so?*"

"*I sey he benado,*" Naveen pronounces. " 'Make it like that.' But half the terms in *Star Trek* won't have translations. Believe me: it would sound really stupid saying stuff like 'warp drive' in Hindi."

I believe him.

The next evening, Naveen and his cousin collect me in a beat-up old Ambassador. We drive to Nandi Hills, a famous resort with a long view over Karnataka State's dust-wreathed plains. The resort itself is shoddy; like so many things in India, it looks better from a distance. After the sun has set, though, and the sky is transformed into a planetarium, I tilt my head back and regard the stars: the lovely virgin stars, billions of dust-free miles away.

"Oh, look!" I exclaim. The red giant Betelgeuse burns at the zenith, kitty-corner to mint-green Rigel. "Right overhead! Orion!" I point out Cassiopeia, the Dippers, Gemini, and Polaris.

Naveen and his cousin follow my gaze politely, then stare back at me with wan disinterest. Neither man has ever looked for the constellations before; neither has the faintest idea of their names.

Not the sort of people, I think to myself, *to spend their weekends poring over maps of the Gamma quadrant.*

Later, back at the High Gates, I contemplate my next move. The situation is grim. Bangalore, from the *Star Trek* perspective, is a bust. Still, despite Amjad and Naveen's pessimism, I refuse to concede defeat. There *has* to be a fan club somewhere.

If I were the president of the local Trek-Wallahs, I ask myself, *where would I hold our meetings?*

Bangalore's NASA pub is Skylab on martinis: a wacky, glossy watering hole–cum–space station that could've been lifted right out of a William Gibson novel. Within an aluminum-skinned shell (emblazoned with the space agency's Apollo-era logo) images of liftoffs, space walks, and Jon Bon Jovi gleam through backlit portholes. Glass tabletops are balanced on fuselage-shaped legs. The wet bar is a "fueling station," the bathroom a "zero-gravity toilet" (the last place you want to visit—especially in India). *Earth is the cradle of humanity,* a bronze wall plaque proclaims, *but Mankind will not stay in the cradle forever.*

NASA is operated by Ashok and Ramesh Sadhwani, two local entrepreneurs specializing in nightclubs and imported silk. I describe my quest to them, but my hopes are dashed. Bangalorian Trekkers, Ashok informs me, do not congregate at his bar. As far as he knows, they don't even *exist*. But why not interview the guy who actually designed the place: a visionary architect and amateur pilot named Tom Thomas? His offices, they inform me, are only a few blocks away.

For all its chaos and classism, India is the ultimate drop-in society. Thomas's schedule is packed, but he tells me to stop by his office. It's a glossy, air-conditioned suite, with cool-eyed receptionists, glass walls, and model airplanes poised on the shelves. A photo of Thomas standing beside his microlight aircraft occupies a place of honor. The blueprints for a huge medieval castle are spread out on the architect's desk: plans, he tells me, for a madly ostentatious new mall to be located near the Bangalore Airport.

Thomas, fifty-three, is a bearded and distinguished-looking man with swept-back hair—Albert Einstein in his patent-clerk days. "The act of flying has always fascinated me," he sighs. "I can't recall where it started, or why. But my dreams and fantasies have always been involved with flight. When I fly," he admits, "the world becomes *believable* to me somehow."

He sits back in his chair with his fingertips pressed together. "You know . . ." He shakes his head. "I look at you guys, and I wonder how you did it. Particularly in this whole area of aerospace. Just yesterday I was on a plane, a Boeing, and I said to my friend, 'I don't know what it is about Americans. What has given them that special ability to make things work?' The Brits had it at one time; the Japs, of course, are into very high-tech stuff. But I connect America very closely with the success of spaceflight."

I can't answer his question, but I share his awe. American knowhow, a cliché that years of Japanese excellence has failed to expunge from the global vocabulary, was never more mind-boggling than during the space race. Boeing jets are a damned good argument for it, but the moon shots invested our reputation with monolithic glory. No one who watched *Apollo 13* in real time—or saw the film version of that tense mission—will ever forget how a pack of Dilbert clones saved the day with spit, cardboard, and duct tape.

"Did you ever consider becoming an astronaut yourself?"

"Oh, yes. Definitely." But space travel, Thomas reminds me, is a poor career choice for an Indian. The country has had exactly one cosmonaut: Rakesh Sharma, who flew with the Russians aboard *Soyuz 11* in 1984.

"The commission to do NASA came up in 1993, when the Sadhwanis wanted an old pub redone," Thomas says. "So I turned to my boyhood fantasies." He leans forward, cheerfully conspiratorial. "I'm always playing out, at somebody else's cost, my own dreams."

Given his fascination with flight and space travel, Thomas is one of the few Indian adults who might have become a die-hard Trekker. But he, like Amjad and Naveen, has had it with reruns of the original series.

"The version they show here is ancient," he says with disgust. "It went out with Flash Gordon. In fact, I think Flash Gordon's equipment had a lot more . . . *flash*. I watched *Star Trek* for a while and thought, *Hey—this is like watching Lucille Ball*. Even the spaceship looks outdated; that donut, with the two 'thunderbirds' sticking out . . ."

"You can't mean the *Enterprise*?"

"Sure. It was a '50s, early '60s concept. I never realized," he snorts, "that starships would be Detroit-designed."

"I'll tell you something," he continues. "My teenage son looks at *Star Trek*, and he's *bored*. It's Dad's era! It's not sophisticated enough to attract a young chap who can get on the Internet and communicate with anyone in the world. These days, a good 90 percent of our college students are computer hacks. So you give us the latest *Star Trek*, and you'll find a hell of a lot of intelligent people hanging on to it. But the Lucy Ball standard doesn't connect!"

His contempt for the show, however, doesn't extend into his perspective on the cosmos-at-large. "I don't believe in the singularity of human existence," he declares. "That's an absolute conceit. Mankind's got to get out there and meet the other guys."

Imaginative, technoliterate and worldly, Thomas travels in the stratosphere of Indian society. But India is a nation where even the most successful individual is confronted, on a daily basis, by ignorance, poverty, and corruption. A fifth of the planet's population lives here, and the staggering inequalities between India's elite and indigent classes create a host of seemingly intractable contradictions.

All of which may explain why Thomas can champion humanity's destiny to reach the stars, while simultaneously denying that India has a role to play in that process.

"We have a role to play in terms of feeding our people," he states. "We're attempting spaceflight, but that's just to keep our scientists occupied. My feeling is that we should learn to walk before we fly. Of course, one has to aspire; there have to be areas where people can study such things. But such enormous budgets are better spent creating water supplies, sanitation, and shelter.

"I'll tell you why you won't find legions of *Star Trek* fans in India," he says frankly. "It's simple: *Star Trek* succeeds in societies that have already achieved basic levels of satisfaction. Where the food's on the table. Where clothes are in the cupboard, and the car's outside. Then, they're willing to watch the next step. *Star Trek* is certainly the next step. But Indian viewers are more concerned with social issues. Our next step is getting food on the table."

"And building castles," I remark.

Thomas reclines in his seat. "Different people play out different dreams," he laughs. "Back in the '60s, during the heyday of the space program, I was sure that, if I made enough money, I'd be able to get myself up there somehow." He grins sheepishly. "At this stage, I realize that flying in space is not going to be possible. Now I have to content myself with building bars like NASA—and using rocket fins as table legs."

The following day I board a northbound train, and treat myself to a few days of R&R at Hampi. The region—a wild, rocky plain punctuated by sandstone ruins—was once the capital city of the powerful Vijayanagar dynasty. The reign of these tough, industrious Hindu rulers lasted from 1336 until January 23, 1565, when Muslims sacked the place. The spoils of war were so fine, historians say, that "every private man in the allied army became rich in gold, jewels, effects, tents, arms, horses, and slaves."

Hampi is every bit as poignant as the tourist brochures proclaim. Crumbling palaces hide amidst erupting boulders, the barest hints of what must have existed here just four centuries ago. Four centuries! It doesn't take long for the elements (with a fair amount of help from marauding invaders) to put the works of man in their place. The once-sublime temple roofs are overgrown with weeds; rain and wind have sandblasted the walls. Skittish lizards leap between broken pillars, tongues flickering. Stones images of the great Creator-Destroyer Shiva, of Vishnu the Preserver, of dancing girls and demons—so vivid and alive when this was a kingdom of half a million people—lean silently over exposed pathways.

There's no glory here, but there is nostalgia. For what, I'm not exactly sure. Perhaps what I'm feeling is an ironic presentiment of the fate awaiting our own self-assured age; for a time when feral deer graze on the abandoned Paramount lot, and chipmunks build their nests in the rusting espresso machines along Melrose. It's bound to happen.

There will come a time when one or more of our earthly problems—global warming, overpopulation, rage, or drought—provide a brutal reminder of how fragile and limited our little acre of the solar system really is. What America's great cities will look like afterward is anyone's guess. A bit worse for wear, probably, than the postapocalyptic encampment in *First Contact*—and with no Vulcan visitors to save our collective ass.

The next morning I rise early. The locals are already awake, chalking elaborate *rangoli* designs in front of their shops and moving dust with short straw brooms. I hike to the crest of a hill and climb onto the roof of a gutted shrine. The sun blisters above the horizon, illuminating the Hampi plain. I gaze across the landscape and imagine the ferocious battles fought here, the trumpeting elephants, the contests of cunning and will.

Morning prayers rise into the air from the temple below, commingling with the dust raised by dawn coaches to Bangalore, Hyderabad, and Goa. For a hundred generations, the objects of those prayers have been the same: the voluptuous gods and goddesses of the Hindu pantheon.

Sitting on the ancient rooftop, I light upon a final reason why India has not been seduced by the flash and dazzle of *Star Trek*. There's nothing wrong with the half-a-dozen reasons I've already heard; I'm sure they're all quite true. But the fact is, Indians don't really *need* Roddenberry's vision. They've got something better.

Hindu mythology has spent more than two millennia perfecting two of the most dazzling epics ever written: The *Mahabharata* and *Ramayana*. Both, like *Star Trek*, are deeply moralistic. Both portray a potentially ideal world, threatened periodically by dark forces. And both rely on fantastic story-telling, on a cosmic scale. Gods and demons battle for domination, wielding a panoply of weapons that make phasers look like BB guns. Whole worlds are called into the fray. Fire-powered chariots roar through space, demons morph into nymphets, and blue-skinned warriors materialize magically onto battlefields. Time is relative, and the great sages who narrate these tales can unravel its fabric as easily as *Star Trek*'s omnipotent "Q."

The characters who appear in these epic tales—the indomitable Rama, the powerful and loyal monkey-king Hanuman, and the diabolical ten-headed Ravana, to name but a few—are the ultimate cultural icons. Their images adorn countless products, from padlocks to potato chips. Sidewalk vendors display their images between posters of Bruce Lee and Madonna, and their exploits fill the pages of Indian comic books.

But their hold on Hindu society reaches far deeper than this. These are not mere storybook figures; they are full-fledged deities, dwelling at the center of family and social life. Common people perceive them as living, breathing gods, to be worshiped, placated, and feared. To the wise, they are complex metaphors for the savagery and nobility of the human psyche. On a purely secular level, they embody values familiar to nearly every educated Indian. Even the nation's Muslim population is aware of these figures, and appreciates their archetypal qualities of courage and egoism, loyalty and greed.

Their appeal is eternal—and the devotion they inspire is stupendous. When *The Ramayana* was serialized on television in the late 1980s, a staggering 90 percent of the Indian population—nearly eight hundred million people—watched the episodes on a weekly basis.

Eight hundred million viewers! In the United States, that would work out to a Neilsen rating of 336 percent.

Rick, Gene—eat your hearts out.

DELTA BLUES

The night sky, viewed from Earth, is a cosmic fingerprint shared by every living being on the planet. Even if one can't name a single constellation, the distinctive whorl of stars is as intuitively familiar as our own skin. A visiting comet, or a supernova in the mane of Pegasus, would stand out like a new mole.

The stars are so reliable, so *available*, that we take them for granted. Still, the briefest study reveals them as objects of fantasy and awe. To the Native American Shawnee, Corona Borealis—the Northern Crown—was a ring of dancing star maidens. In India, the open cluster we call the Pleiades are the seven sages who know when history will end (the Japanese even named a car after the constellation: *Subaru*). Orion's right deltoid is a red giant called Betelgeuse: it could easily swallow four hundred suns. Below the hunter's belt, to the right, lies brilliant Rigel, a sun twenty thousand times more luminous than our own. Come spring, Pollux and Castor—the twins of Gemini—commute across the heavens; no other two stars seem quite as compatible. Summer hangs the bright triangle of Altair, Deneb, and Vega above our heads, while the teapot of Sagittarius steams beneath the Milky Way.

All these stars belong to the Alpha quadrant, the sector of space most accessible to Earth. In *Star Trek* parlance, the distances within this corner of the galaxy are manageable. At warp six, for instance, our neighbor Alpha Centauri—just 4.3 light-years away—could be reached in just four days. Ice blue Vega, twenty-three light years distant in the constellation Lyra, would require nine days at warp eight. Even far-off Antares, the Mars-red ruby in the whip of Scorpio, needs only two months—but that's at warp factor nine.

None of these suns are visible, however, from *Voyager*. Hurled through a rift in space-time, the starship and its crew—led by Captain Kathryn Janeway—are marooned in the Delta quadrant. This unknown sector of the galaxy is intolerably far from home. Even at maximum warp, it would take *Voyager* more than seventy *years* to reach Federation space. I don't care how good their replicator is; that's a long time to be eating airplane food.

Star Trek: Voyager premiered on January 16, 1995, charged with the thankless task of following in TNG's footsteps. The motive for rushing the show into production was pure Hollywood: greed. *The Next Generation* had won a large and loyal following, and Paramount wanted to milk the franchise for all it was worth. *Deep Space Nine* was already well-established; but the spin-off, despite fine writing and a complex storyline, was a big departure from Roddenberry's mantra: a captain and a starship, "boldly going." This sacred formula, Paramount decided, would be retooled and offered to TNG addicts when the crew of the *Enterprise* 1701-D disbanded. The less lag time, the better.

Voyager's premise was developed by three seasoned *Star Trek* veterans: Rick Berman, DS9 co-creator Michael Piller, and TNG co-executive producer Jeri Taylor. The concept of the female captain, bitterly contested by Paramount (but lobbied for, hard and successfully, by Berman), was by no means wedded to the original concept.

Reader: Do you remember that scene in *Raiders of the Lost Ark*, when Indiana Jones is being chased through a cave by Fred Flintstone's bowling ball? Think of that ball as a weekly TV show. A momentum monster, it stops for nothing. During my visit, *Voyager*—feature film notwithstanding—is busy cranking out episodes for its new season. With Piller out of the picture (he withdrew from the series in 1996) and Berman and Braga tied up with *First Contact*, the responsibility for steering *Voyager* rests mainly in the hands of executive producer Jeri Taylor.

Taylor is that rarest of Tinsel Town phenomenon: a warmhearted idealist who seems to have passed, unscathed, through the entertainment industry's withering flame. She's well-read and articulate, with an easy poise that could never be mistaken for Hollywood posturing.

A self-described "child of the sixties," Taylor pushed a baby stroller during the antiwar and civil rights marches of her postcollege days. She joined *Star Trek* in 1990, after cutting her teeth producing a series of prime-time cop shows (*Quincy, M.E.*; *Magnum, P.I.*; *In the Heat of the Night*) and writing well-received specials about child abuse. She now inhabits Gene Roddenberry's former haunt, an expansive suite filled with memorabilia and tchotchkes. Following her into the office, I spy a cardboard stand-up of Captain Jean-Luc Picard in the corner. It's wearing a Mouseketeer hat.

Voyager, Taylor tells me, was an attempt to restore *Star Trek*'s natal zest. The Alpha quadrant was growing stale. With three shows crowding that sector, the "final frontier" was starting to look a lot like Yosemite Valley on Memorial Day weekend. The point of the new show was to recreate the appeal of Jim Kirk's original *Enterprise*: a state-of-the-art ship in uncharted waters, subject to anus-clenching adventures.

"TNG had gotten pretty cozy and comfortable," admits the producer. Her desk is cluttered with *Voyager* tapes and plastic starship models. On the wall behind her, a dry-erase board faces a worn maroon couch. "I was pleased that we gave ourselves the challenge of a female captain, the challenge of saying, 'We have to start over; we have to create this new universe.' But putting the show in the Delta quadrant meant that a lot of beloved characters were no longer going to be with us. The Klingons, the Romulans, the Ferengi, the Cardassians; areas of space that had been populated with villains you loved to hate, and funny aliens you loved to love. Was the audience going to forgive us? Or would they hate us for saying, 'Everything you've known about *Star Trek* is gone.' "

Voyager's basic premise—a bunch of people marooned on a metaphorical raft—had seen some wear since the sixties. Well before *Voyager*'s premiere, columnists and reviewers went on a lark, casting the show as a hybrid of *Lost in Space* and *Gilligan's Island*.

"I guess the television genre always refers back to itself," I remark. "But I see the show owing more to, say, the *Odyssey*."

Taylor agrees. "I talked about that at the inception of *Voyager*. Like the *Odyssey*, ours is a quest to get home." Even so, she concedes, there's something odd—a little anticlimactic, maybe—about a *return* quest, as opposed to an outward-bound one. It's the difference between search-

THE POWERS THAT BE: *STAR TREK* IN SOUTH AFRICA

When Jeri Taylor told me that Star Trek *had fans in South Africa, I was immediately intrigued. How had a show featuring a racially mixed cast—which raised hackles even in the United States—played under apartheid? Did* Star Trek *have government approval, or had it been broadcast subversively, a futuristic version of Radio Free Europe?*

Though I didn't make it to South Africa, I did make contact with Friends of Star Trek *(FOST) member Marina Bailey—a Johannesburg Trekker described by her compatriots as "the biggest fan in the southern hemisphere." Following are excerpts from our E-mail correspondence.*

In the beginning, I don't think people paid much attention to *Star Trek*. It was viewed as a spacey show that only lunatics watched. And yes, I think it was considered a weird *American* TV show. I don't recall any of my [black] friends mentioning that they watched it. But you must understand that *Star Trek* never really had a chance to make an impact on people during the apartheid era. Only thirty-nine episodes of the original series were shown.

The original series was first broadcast by the South Africa Broadcasting Corporation (SABC) in 1979. They showed only thirteen episodes. About two years later they showed another thirteen, and another thirteen in 1983. For whatever reason, they never showed any more. (They had also started showing *V*, but when it dawned on them what the show was actually *about* [an oppressed people fighting back against their oppressors], they removed it from prime-time and showed the entire lot in the middle of the night.)

South Africa in the '70s and early '80s was *very* repressive. I think The Powers That Be took TOS off the air because of the message it sent. In this country, you weren't encouraged to question; things were presented as being "just that way." *Star Trek* showed me that what a lot of people here took for granted was in fact NOT right.

ing for the Golden Fleece and trying to make it home before the roast burns.

"Still," she continues, "it seems to me that a quest—spiritual or otherwise—is an important aspect of the human condition. We long for something that makes us better. We know there's something out there that will raise us to another level of understanding, or enlightenment, even if we don't know what it is."

Not all of *Star Trek*'s writers think of themselves as storytellers in the classic tradition, but Taylor absolutely does. The semantics of *Star Trek* intrigued her from the day she arrived, and she's still sounding out the role that the show plays in the global psyche—what Carl Jung called the "collective unconscious."

"We've moved away from the era of heroes," observes Taylor. "Political figures are no longer heroic, and we don't really have heroic sports figures anymore; they're making a zillion dollars a dribble and

Around 1989, the SABC showed the first season of *The Next Generation*. Finally, around 1993, they showed the second season. But they broadcast it on Sundays, and nearly every second week it was pre-empted for sports events. By now the fans were used to the SABC doing what they liked, with little consideration for the audience.

Okay, now it's 1994. The presidential elections are held, Nelson Mandela is elected, and the SABC suddenly seems to develop a liking for science fiction, after years of saying that "it isn't popular."

With the end of apartheid, there was a sudden turn-around. We got *Deep Space Nine* and, after that, *Voyager*'s entire first season. When that was over, SABC started showing *DS9*'s third season. (Did they think nobody would notice that an entire season was missing??) I haven't been watching it on TV [Marina receives videotapes from friends abroad], but I've been told that they show episodes in the wrong order and edit things out.

I grew up with Gene Roddenberry's vision of the future in my head, and I clung to the ideals of the show all the way through university: Being different is *not* a bad thing. Everyone in the universe deserves respect and understanding. The glory of creation is in its infinite diversity, and the way our differences combine to create meaning and beauty.

I always tell people, "I had my consciousness raised by *Star Trek*." Listening to Kirk and Co. talk about the human spirit being free, etc., had a huge impact on me. The message is subtle—but it sort of creeps into your mind more and more with each episode.

Yes, South Africa has a lot of crime now. Yes, we are having problems. Trying to fix decades of inequality is going to take time. But I have faith. *Star Trek* taught me that there will be a better tomorrow, but we will have to work for it. There's a quote from an episode of *Alien Nation* that I cling to when I hear negative things about the new South Africa: "Freedom is difficult, but it's better than the alternative."

doing drugs. We seem to have lost those figures who, in a Jungian sense, sustain and nourish us: people who are beacons, who are guides, who represent the things we aspire to. The characters in *Star Trek*"— she gestures at the dry-erase board behind her—"respond to our need for contemporary heroes—a craving no longer satisfied in our day-to-day world."

My attention lingers on the board. It's covered with notes, in at least ten marker colors, from this morning's "story break": the combative core of the scripting process. Once or twice a week, Taylor explains, the writing staff piles into her office and hashes out, scene by scene, another episode of *Voyager*. "Not a lot of fun," she admits, "but usually very valuable."

The idea makes me somewhat uncomfortable. "Can a mythology be created by committee?"

Taylor ponders this for a second. "Gene Roddenberry created this vision, and all that this 'committee' is doing—all *I'm* trying to do—is keeping that vision as intact as possible. I think it was a good one. It doesn't need fixing, it doesn't need adjusting, it doesn't need to be taken in new directions. So I don't think we're *creating* a myth; we're perpetuating one. Where we err is in straying from it."

In this respect, she admits, the female captain was a risk. Would *Star Trek*'s demographic (upper-income boys and men, ages eighteen to thirty) tolerate a woman in the Big Chair? Taylor insists that they have—even though the show's ratings, well into the third season, indicated otherwise.

Ratings, of course, are very mercurial. No one knows what makes one series take off, or another go down in flames. It's like playing the horses, or second-guessing the Korean economy. The consummate Hollywood truism, articulated by screenwriter William Goldman, is that "No one knows anything."

Some things are guessable, though. Not only were *Voyager*'s characters hastily drawn; they openly resented their circumstances. They had very little interpersonal chemistry, and whatever rough edges they displayed as individuals were buffed smooth in a transparent attempt to create a supportive shipboard atmosphere.

"Somewhere along the way," Taylor admits, "things had gotten small. *Voyager* started taking itself too seriously. We weren't creating disturbing, heroic episodes that people would want to share. Now we want to re-inject the fun and adventure, take the *Odyssey* idea and expand it. We have to remind the audience that this is an unknown, and possibly fearful, place. At the same time, we have to let the crew enjoy the adventure."

"They were doing a lot of whining," I agree.

"Exactly. And if the crew doesn't want to be on *Voyager*, why should the viewers?"

On the positive side, the presence of a female captain is potentially great for drama. Putting Kate Mulgrew in the four-pipped tunic was a gutsy move, and the possibilities for new story lines are immensely refreshing.

"One of the recurring themes on *The Next Generation* had to do with fathers and sons," Taylor recalls. I nod compliantly. It was very Joseph Campbell: loads of episodes casting Picard, Worf, or even Data as the all-powerful patriarch. "I began to weary of that," she continues. "It seemed we were saying that the most profound human relationship that could exist was between *males*. There was a curiously sexist slant to the whole thing. And because we gave so much time and attention to that, we didn't do romance; we didn't do male-female relationships; we didn't do mothers and daughters."

But the first seasons of *Voyager* were rocky, especially as far as the lead was concerned. Janeway wasn't three-dimensional. She was a captain, all right, and a woman, but in appearance only. She was played tight-lipped and macho, and the crew called her "Sir."

That dynamic, says Taylor, is changing. "In the early episodes, Janeway was more tough than feminine. Around the middle of the third season, we started cultivating her 'Earth Mother' side."

"Earth Mother? Somehow, that doesn't sound very *Star Trek*."

"It's a goddess-like appellation, and very much the way I see the character. Beyond that," Taylor continues, "we plan to involve her in some very dynamic relationships: woman-to-woman situations in which she will be both tough *and* feminine."

I ask for some examples; Taylor readily concurs. "Up until our third season, we had a relationship between Janeway and Kes [a sweet-natured alien girl], which was very much a mother/daughter thing. In the fourth season episode called "The Gift," when Kes goes,* you see a classic maternal farewell: a mother figure not wanting to let her child go, but knowing that she must. Janeway also has a profound relationship with [the half-Klingon engineer] B'Elanna Torres, which was born in conflict but has evolved into something else. And the entire arc of our new character—Seven of Nine—involves Janeway's struggle to cultivate the humanity within this woman, although she was raised by the Borg from the age of six. And believe me," Taylor laughs. "It won't be easy. Those stories will involve a lot of flinting, a lot of conflict. Janeway's going to be strongly challenged.

"We're still searching for stories like that in *Voyager*," Taylor asserts. "They are something I very much want to do."

When Taylor uses the word "searching," she's not being glib. It's incredibly hard to come up with fresh story ideas for *Star Trek*, show after show, season after season.

---

* The character of Kes—a pixie-like Ocampa with vague telepathic powers played by Jennifer Lien—was axed to make room for Seven of Nine, a sexy Borg presence on the starship. Contrary to vicious Web gossip, there were no drug problems with Lein. According to both Taylor and Braga, the decision to terminate Kes was based purely on market research.

To get an idea of how much radiation the franchise has already produced, let's pretend it's your job to watch *Star Trek*.

You start the day after Thanksgiving. You've got to sit through every television show ever produced—the seventy-nine episodes of TOS, seven seasons of TNG, and every installment of both *Voyager* and DS9. You've also got to watch all eight movies, and the twenty-two half-hour episodes of the *Star Trek* animated series. Working five days a week, nine to five (holidays off), you'll be punching a clock for more than two months: until late afternoon on Groundhog Day.

Star Trek is an insatiable maw that devours scripts and munches story pitches like popcorn. From its very first episode ("The Man Trap," aired by NBC on September 8, 1966) to 1998, the franchise has produced a grand total of twenty seasons—four more seasons than *Ozzie and Harriet*, the longest unbroken run in television history.

Unlike cop shows or situation comedies, science fiction is a unique discipline that demands lateral thinking, technofluency, and a sense of the cosmic joke. It's highly specialized writing; much more so than, say, *Seinfeld*, *Friends*, or even *The X-Files*.

"You have to know something about science, astronomy, physics and all that shit," declares Executive Producer Rick Berman. "You have to write within the rules of Roddenberry. Then you have to write in a style that's both modern and stylized at the same time. *Star Trek*'s a period piece; you can't write in a contemporary fashion. If a person is capable of writing a 19th-century drama, they're probably more able to do *Voyager* than somebody who can write the greatest *NYPD Blue*."

Since creating new episodes is so difficult, Producer Michael Piller made a radical suggestion during TNG's third season: why not open up the writing process to the fans? Roddenberry and Berman agreed—and *Star Trek* became the only show on television willing to read freelance, unsolicited scripts.

What this means is that any of the show's far-flung devotees, from Stephen Hawking to Camille Paglia, can pitch ideas to the shows' producers, and dream of seeing their name in the credits.

That's the good news. The bad news is, writing for the show is a hell of a lot harder than watching it.

Stardate 49375.4: Making its way through the Delta quadrant, Voyager *encounters a grim situation. The denizens of a double planet system are locked in a religious war. The population of the smaller world, lacking advanced technology, will soon be crushed. Captain Janeway sides with the underdogs, offering them phaser rifles and other weapons. This infuriates Chakotay, her first officer. Natural selection, he claims, dictates that the better-armed planet prevail. After a fierce argument on the bridge, Chakotay beats Janeway unconscious. He races to engineering to enlist the help of his secret lover—the lusciously pouty-lipped Seven of Nine—but finds her in a Jefferies Tube, hotly embracing science officer Tuvok. As the two men square off with phasers, Janeway regains consciousness and transports the mutinous Chakotay into the vacuum of space, where he gorily explodes.*

What's wrong with this picture? To anyone who's dipped as much as a toe in the *Star Trek* universe, it's like seeing Nancy Reagan with nipple rings. The fact that we *know* this—whether we've seen the show once, twice, or a thousand times—testifies to how completely *Star Trek* and its credo have gotten under our skin.

"It's a noble, positive vision of the future and humanity's place in that future," says Taylor, reciting the magic formula. "We've left behind the bickering, jealousy and materialism of the 20th century. Gene protected that vision, and his voice is still very much in our ears. He absolutely would not allow petty conflict to erupt between the humans on his ship."

Roddenberry's prohibition doesn't make life easy for the *Star Trek* staff. They're basically forbidden from writing gutsy, gossipy *NYPD Blue*–style shows, where turmoil erupts within the ensemble cast.

"Many, many writers and producers went through a revolving door here, because they couldn't accept that limitation," Taylor says. "And Gene wasn't about to have it changed. Finally, the group that became cohesive—that is here now—worked within those limitations. We want to tap into the deeply felt belief that we *can* become enlightened, that we *can* strive to be better people, that there *is* hope. To turn our backs on that vision would be to turn our backs on *Star Trek*."

"Chakotay out . . . *Fuck!*"

On Stage 16, a short walk from Taylor's Hart Building office, an episode of *Voyager* is in rehearsal. Part of the set has been transformed into a steamy alien jungle, and the crew is scanning for life signs. But Robert Beltran, who plays First Officer Chakotay, has knocked off his

Velcro-backed communicator pin. The director sets the scene up for the third time.

After the wrap, the crew breaks for lunch. Roxann Dawson, wearing the symmetrically ridged, half-Klingon, half-Earthling forehead of Chief Engineer B'Elanna Torres, slices a bagel with severe concentration. Over by the makeup station, Tim Russ—attired as Tuvok, the starship's Vulcan security officer—leafs through next week's script.

Russ is unique among the *Voyager* cast in that he's been a *Star Trek* fan since childhood. Here's his advice for would-be writers:

"Watch the show. See how it flows. If you can, transcribe an episode and follow that format. Also, keep in mind how much it costs to produce a show. Budget is an element some writers might not think about, but it's important. If you can come up with a good episode that doesn't cost a lot of money, it gives you a much better chance. An interesting 'bottle' story [one that takes place on the ship itself] is something they'll snap up in a minute—if it hasn't been done before."

Many of the producers' choices, Jeri Taylor admits, do come down to money. "Everybody in the audience is hoping, 'Wow, we're going to the Delta quadrant! We're gonna see *really weird* aliens!! There's going to be *cabbage* people and *beast* people!' But making those things believable is extremely expensive. We do not have a feature film budget. We cannot do the kinds of things that happen in *Jurassic Park*. So we end up with humanoids with bumps on their foreheads. That's not a limitation that we ourselves have set. It's one we strive to get around, but usually can't."

Money is one limitation, time another. Each *Star Trek* episode takes about a week to shoot, but the process begins with an idea that may take months to germinate. If the seed for the story comes from a freelancer, it may take longer still.

Lolita Fatjo is the spunky, gap-toothed pre-production coordinator whose desk is a receiving blanket for the more than one thousand unsolicited scripts delivered each year to the Hart Building. I grill her about the culling process. First, she explains, union readers grab a stack of the spec screenplays. They write a brief synopsis, called a "coverage," of each one. At that point someone on the DS9 or *Voyager** staff reads these

---

* The freelance policy for *Voyager* is presently under review. From 1998 onward, unsolicited *Voyager* scripts may have to be submitted through an agent. *Deep Space Nine* will continue to read scripts from garden-variety fans. For a set of guidelines to either show, write to *Star Trek: Voyager* or *Star Trek: Deep Space Nine*, Paramount Pictures, Hart Building, 5555 Melrose Avenue, Los Angeles, CA 90038.

blurbs, and decides if the script is going anywhere. "Ninety-nine percent of the time, nothing's gonna happen." Fatjo shuffles around in her desk and shows me a rejection letter. "They'll get this back with my autograph, saying, 'Thanks, but no thanks. Try again if you would like to.' "

There have, of course, been tantalizing exceptions. Over the past eight years, three aspiring writers—Ron Moore ("The Bonding"), Melinda Snodgrass ("Measure of a Man") and DS9 producer René Echeverria ("The Offspring")—have had freelance scripts accepted, bought, and produced almost as written. All three were subsequently invited onto the *Star Trek* staff.

"When people prove that they can write this show," Berman later confirms, "we embrace 'em, we pay 'em a lot of money, and we put 'em on staff. Because they're so hard to find."

More likely, the producers will admire one or two tiny things about a script and fish them from the surrounding goo. "We'll bring the writer in," Fatjo explains, "and they'll get the chance to do what's called a 'story outline.' For that, we pay between $6,000 to $9,000—and their name appears on the credits."

Here's another quasi-lucky scenario. A writer submits a *Voyager* script, and, although it misses the mark, one of the show's producers—Ken Biller, Brannon Braga, Lisa Klink, Joe Menosky, or Jeri Taylor—likes the way he or she thinks. At that point, the writer is called in to pitch a few new ideas. Pitching is a one-on-one process: fast, intense, and nerve-racking.

"All we're interested in," says Ron Moore—who fields pitches for *Deep Space Nine*—"is the beginning, middle and end. We have so many things in development, and so many things we've decided *not* to do, that we can quickly tell you what is and isn't going

---

THE GAY AND LESBIAN STAR TREK/SCI-FI HOME PAGE

http://www.gaytrek.com/

ABOUT THE USS HARVEY MILK

For those who may not know, Trek clubs and organizations around the world usually refer to themselves as ships. In that tradition, we launched our organization as the USS *Harvey Milk*, temporarily naming our "ship" in memory of the first openly gay person to be elected to city government in a major U.S. city. Harvey Milk, elected to the San Francisco Board of Supervisors in 1976, was assassinated in 1978, along with Mayor George Moscone.

The USS *Harvey Milk* is intended to be a place for gay and lesbian *Star Trek* fans (and their friends) to share commentary, reviews, proposals, and stories that relate to *Star Trek* and the inclusion of lesbian/gay characters on *Trek* programs.

Be sure to read the *Voyager* Visibility Project's open letter to Jeri Taylor, Michael Piller, and Rick Berman, which asks why we have yet to see gay or lesbian people portrayed as part of Gene Roddenberry's vision of a future where war, poverty, racism, and sexism have all gone the way of the dinosaur.

to work. Once people have given us a salable idea we can say, 'Okay, tell us more.' But when they're pitching, we like them to be succinct."

Eric Stillwell, a tanky, red-haired one-time freelancer who's now on staff, successfully co-pitched a very popular third-season TNG episode called "Yesterday's Enterprise." He also dreamed up "Prime Factors," a high point of *Voyager*'s lackluster first season.

"The best tactic for pitching," he advises, "is to take your entire story down to one sentence—like something you'd read in *TV Guide*."

"Okay; summarize 'Prime Factors' that way."

"*Members of the crew mutiny in order to obtain a technology that can send them home.* There it is; and that's the element that Michael Piller pulled out of the rubble."

"You want to go to Red Alert in Scene 68? Okay, why don't we have Chakotay say 'Red Alert.' *Shit*, then we've got everyone yelling 'Red Alert.' From Scene 73 through . . . *everything*. That's not a problem for you guys?"

Brannon Braga, *Voyager*'s co-executive producer, is on the phone with a director. With the exception of his swivel chair, there's not a single place to sit up straight in his entire office; just a big, fat sofa and the kind of chairs that swallow you whole. I opt for the couch. Disappearing into a chair is Kenny Kofax, a nervous freelancer waiting to deliver his pitches. Braga hangs up the phone, picks up a legal-sized notepad and props his sneakered feet on his desk—waiting, dubiously, to be impressed.

"Okay, what have you got?"

Kofax starts talking. He's loud and he's fast. In his first pitch, a crew of vile aliens infects *Voyager* with a computer virus that forces it to go faster and faster—just like the bus in *Speed*. Braga doodles space babes on his pad, nodding absently. He finally cuts Kofax off; too derivative.

No problem. The next idea is even better. *Voyager* comes across this weird object floating in space. It ends up being the apparently lifeless carcass of the android Lore, Data's evil brother. The crew is stunned. Janeway . . .

Braga waves his hand. "Hello? How did Lore get way out in the Delta quadrant to begin with? Impossible. Absurd. Next?"

Braga's leafing through his *Handbook of Fish Diseases*. The freelancer is breathless and sweating. This is his last shot. The warm up . . . the pitch.

"Okay. Check this out. The crew of *Voyager* take an R&R on this M-class planet. Right? Really nice place. Everyone has a blast." Kofax winks at Braga. "But just as they're about to return to *Voyager*, a local woman runs up and stops them. It turns out that Lieutenant Paris has gotten her pregnant . . ."

"Whoa! Hold on there." Braga swings his feet to the floor and paces the room. Something about the idea appeals to him, but there's a problem. Paris, he reminds Kofax, came off as a sleezeball in the early seasons. Since then he's undergone a character shift; the writing staff has "decreepified" him.

"Okay," offers Kofax, "let's say they were having, you know, a *real relationship* . . ."

"Sure, but how do we handle that? It makes Paris look awfully irresponsible if he gets an alien pregnant. He didn't use a condom?"

"Well, uh, she's an *alien*, right? Maybe . . ."

"Of course. We could have Paris say, '*How was I to know that sticking my tongue in her anus would get her pregnant?*' "

Two minutes later Kofax is out of there. His fate, Braga assures me, is common. It's the rule rather than the exception for writers to slink out of pitch meetings with their tails between their legs. One problem, Braga wryly puts it, is that "we've done everything." But the main stumbling block is that few writers really intuit the ingredients of a great *Star Trek* story.

"The perfect *Trek* script," reveals Braga, who has written or co-authored more than fifty episodes of TNG and *Voyager*, "begins with a great science fiction concept. It tells an exciting adventure, while at the same time serving as a metaphor for contemporary humanity. For instance: a TNG show called "The Host." Someone pitched a story about host bodies and symbiont worms, which was, at first glance, a repulsive idea. But it turned out to be the best love story we ever did. Why? Because one of our characters was forced to confront the true nature of love. Is it the person? The body? Or both? That's classic *Star Trek*, right there. That's what we look for, week after week."

Taylor sums it up even better. At the heart of every episode, she says, is an intensely personal story: something that provides character development for one or more members of the main cast. On top of that, there has to be something "*Star Trekky*"—that science fiction spin Braga talked about. Finally, there's conflict—the heart of drama. This can come in the form of a septic space anomaly, alien cannibals, or a replicator glitch that confuses Sweet 'n' Low with pickled herring.

"Those are the elements we look for," Taylor declares. "Not every show has all three. But when we listen to pitches, we're waiting for one of those elements to emerge and knock our socks off."

It isn't easy. Believe me; I've pitched a few spitballs myself (sorry, you're not getting the humiliating details). Nonetheless, a place in the credits remains a golden apple for true believers. One good script, and we cease to be outsiders. We are elevated, barefoot and shining, into the myth-making machinery itself.

"JORNADA NAS ESTRELAS:" *STAR TREK* IN BRAZIL

A LETTER FROM ALVARO ANTUNES, BRAZILIAN SCIENCE FICTION
TRANSLATOR AND TREKKER SINCE THE AGE OF EIGHT

There are perhaps 300,000 Trekkers, and many *Star Trek* fan clubs, here in Brazil (almost every major city has at least one; conventions in São Paulo attract 2,000–3,000 fans). Yet most of the *Star Trek* episodes never aired in Brazil. True, TOS has been broadcast since the seventies—but only the first three years of TNG and the first year of DS9 ever reached our TVs. Many Brazilian Trekkers go to conventions just to watch new episodes, which are recorded in the USA and sent to Brazil by friends.

Memorabilia is also hard to get. Nowadays it's easier to buy stuff, especially through the Internet, but import taxes are about 60 percent (except on books, which are not taxed). So, we create our own memorabilia. Uniforms are hand sewn, and the results are very good. Even "Vulcan ears" are custom-made, using latex (and they fit very well). Wearing such ears gets immediate, "Look! It's Spock!" recognition on the streets. Some Trekkers and fan clubs go even further, producing their own documentaries, *Trek*-inspired plays, and even submitting scripts to Paramount. Imagine pitching to *Voyager* as the speaker of a foreign language, having watched only the first eight episodes!

Our TV translations of the shows are dubbed. In general, the translations of TOS are good—but those for the movies and home videos are not. A famous mistake was made in the first *Star Trek* movie: "dilithium" was misunderstood as "delirium." Thus "dilithium crystals" were translated as *cristais delirantes*: delirious crystals!

Star Trek is not part of our culture as it is in the USA; everything is too neat, too "right." What appeals to Brazilians is the universality of *Star Trek*—and the very fact that it is so far from our reality. (*Babylon 5* is much closer!) Years ago, I submitted a script to *Voyager* which tried to convey some "Brazilian" features, but it was not accepted. Maybe it lacked the "black-and-white, right and wrong" tone of the series—or maybe it was just plain bad!

AWAY MISSION VIII: JAPAN—THREE SECTORS

1. Tokyo: A Starship in Dry Dock

> It's the realization of my aspiration. I hope to play along with
> the heartiest gadgetry manifesting my sensibility.
>
> —text on Sanyo blow-dryer box

Tokyo is the kingdom of burgers and neon, of white-faced girls with
blood-red lipstick strobing past ceramic badgers and windows filled
with plastic sushi. Towers of aluminum claw the smog, and the subways chirp with prerecorded warnings. I get the creepy sensation of
navigating an immense Borg hive: *You will be assimilated. We will add
your biological and technological distinctiveness to our own. Resistance is
futile.*

Two pounding, pneumatic hours after my arrival at Narita airport I
find myself squeezed around a table at the Asia House Restaurant, sitting cheek-to-jowl with a dozen Japanese Trekkers. They take pains to
put me at ease.

"Mind if I smoke?" Akio Nomura, a video game designer, waves a
pack of Hope brand filters at me.

"Go ahead. But thank for asking . . ."

"Even in Tokyo," he smiles, "it's famous that California people don't
smoke."

"And only vegetarians are in California," Satako, our translator, adds reverently.

Were that true, I'd be in deep trouble. Dinner consists of *shabu-shabu* (raw red beef, sliced paper-thin). You pick up a slice, swish it in boiling water, and eat it with hot pepper or soya sauce. I don't usually do meat, but the Pacific crossing has left me ravenous. I tear into the feast with chopsticks flying. Afterward, I amaze all present by bumming one of Akio's cigarettes.

With its glowing urban corridors, quicksilver transport and banks of replicators (i.e., vending machines), Tokyo is a starship in dry dock. And the Japanese themselves—who once raised honor and duty to the level of hysteria—may be *Star Trek*'s ideal audience. Indeed, the island nation has been a hotbed of fandom for more than a quarter century. Kirk and Spock made it across the Pacific in 1972, six years after their American debut. *The Next Generation* became available in 1988 (on captioned videos) and broke into Japanese television in 1991. During my visit, TNG is in its fourth season with a strong and expanding viewership. *Deep Space Nine* is also on the air—and crafty Trekkers are getting their hands on *Voyager* as well.

My host in Tokyo is a shy, twenty-five-year-old-hacker named Joe Okubo. Part of Japan's broad-based Internet community, Joe directs the *Voyager* forum on Niftyserve (the local name for Compuserve). It's a respectable behind-the-scenes role: his site has some thirteen thousand regulars.

In honor of my visit, Joe has brought together the main luminaries of Honshū island's *Torekkii* scene. Among the assembled company are T. Sakaguchi and Mr. Murata, codirectors of a very cool Web site called Starship Kongo; and Masato Fujita (aka "Captain Okie"), the captain of a famous fan club called Starbase Kobe.

Fujita, a Panasonic engineer by day, is one of the few Japanese who actually makes money off *Star Trek*. Viacom (which owns Paramount) has commissioned him to write several books, including character and story guides to both *Voyager* and *Deep Space Nine*. (To date, more than sixty *Star Trek* books have been published in Japanese.) During dinner, he hands me one of his early, unauthorized DS9 books: a square black paperback entitled *Station Log One*. On the back, in gold type, is the motto of Starbase Kobe:

"*. . . to boldry go where no one has gone before.*"

Dinner is one long skid mark. Between my jet lag, the language gap, and the awesome quantity of alcohol consumed, it's a miracle I can find my shoes at all. The one fact to emerge from the chaos is that, of all the characters ever to appear on *Star Trek*, Data is the runaway favorite.

"It's because he looks Asian," Mr. Murata says. With his orchid suit and wild batik tie, he resembles a Japanese Riddler. "*Hai!* His hair is black, and his

Sapporo Torekkiis drink up the latest buzz.

face is white. Actually," Murata muses, "Data looks a little bit like John Lennon; who also looks Asian . . ."

This sounds like nonsense to his fellows; it sounds like nonsense to me. But he shrugs off the abuse that follows his remark, and, throwing back another sake, offers a disclaimer. "Anyway, for myself, the favorite is not Data. It's the *Enterprise* itself!"

It has been said, Murata elaborates poetically, that over eight million gods live in Japan. Everything, every object, holds a bit of God within. "There is a Japanese expression: 'After ninety-nine years of use, a thing becomes alive.' Thus, there is the idea that the *Enterprise* itself is alive. That is because love causes a thing to live. In the case of the *Enterprise*, it is the love of the captains—and of engineers Scotty and Geordi LaForge—that brings the ship to life."

A sweet sentiment, I reflect, but vaguely disturbing. "What you just said about things coming alive after ninety-nine years . . ." I lean across the now-empty beef platter. "Is the same thing true of plastic sushi?"

Murata leans toward me in turn, and furrows his brow. "*Especially* of plastic sushi."

Beam up us, Scotty!   —from Riko Kushida's Web page

If Tokyo were a concerto, it would be unrehearsable: a Pollock-like splatter of notes upon the page. Everything happens at once. I race from subway to restaurant, hemorrhaging money, a sore Western thumb protruding among neatly groomed Eastern fingers. Introduction follows introduction, punctuated by eight-dollar cups of coffee and the uneasy guilt of accepting gifts from everyone I meet.

One of the few people I feel immediately comfortable with is Riko Kushida, an adorable journalist with an Audrey Hepburn haircut and three shades of lipstick. The name *Riko*, she explains, is based on the Chinese character for "science." Born a few months after the first Moon landing, she was exposed to *Star Trek* at a very young age. Her earliest inspiration was Uhura, the black female lieutenant on the original series.

Riko had wanted desperately to be an astronaut, but—a common stumbling block—her eyesight was too poor. "So I could never be a captain, or a pilot," she sighs miserably. "Only a mission specialist."

Now a freelance media critic, quiz-show hostess, and Formula One racecar driver, she remains a dedicated Trekker. Okubo and I meet her in a sushi bar high above Ueno, where she listens attentively to Joe's synopsis of the previous night's dinner.

When he's finished, Riko confirms the general consensus. It is not the Zen-ish Picard, nor the samurai-inspired Worf, nor *manga*-babe Troi whom the Japanese adore. It's not even the *Enterprise* itself— despite the starship's obvious appeal in a country that likes its environments disinfected, overlit, and laminated. But if the majority of Japanese Torekkiis are madly in love with Data, she insists, it's *not* due to his uncanny resemblance to John Lennon.

Data, Riko points out, is an android with a Pinocchio complex: He longs to be human. In pursuit of this dream he masters the violin, composes poetry (dismally), and tries his hand (even more dismally) at stand-up comedy. As earnestly as he tries, however, total acceptance eludes him.

"Data is different from the people around him," she says, "and he is well aware of it. We Japanese know that we are different, too. We are Asians, but we are not like other Asians. We try to follow Western ways, but we are not Western. Everyone—Asians and Westerners alike— hates the Japanese. So we are isolated from both. And yet, like Data, we know who we are."

Centuries as a physical and cultural island, Riko explains, has given Japan— and the Japanese—a strong sense of identity. Not even the wholesale importation of Western icons—jeans, jazz, baseball, pizza—can penetrate that nucleus, which exerts powerful antibodies when the organism is threatened.

Riko Kushida and Joe Okubo.

Riko unfolds her napkin, draws a small box within a larger square and pushes the sketch across the table to me. "That middle square is our center; what makes the Japanese what we are. Everything else . . .," she traces the outer square, "is soft. Elastic. This is our dilemma: We want to imitate and be like others, but we cannot change our core."

2. Sapporo: Alpha Quadrant Kabuki

I'm buck naked, walking through the snow. Ahead lies a pond; steam rises from its surface. Above, only the brightest stars of the Alpha quadrant are visible. Earth's moon, nearly full, floodlights the sky.

Unreal as it seems, this is no holodeck fantasy. I'm at the Meisui Tei *onsen*: a famous volcanic hot spring two hours north of Sapporo. Lowering myself into the water—a breathtaking experience, especially as the middle parts go in—I feel the minerals do their stuff. I inhale deeply, gaze at the mountains, and sink in up to my neck.

Hideyasu Mayuzumi—my Sapporo host, a tall, lantern-jawed man who reminds me of Gary Cooper—has brought me to this onsen, along with some of his friends from medical school. They're Trekkers all, out for a romp before the upcoming exam crunch. Mayuzumi himself is a budding brain surgeon. With us are his girlfriend, Mariko (a dermatologist and the group's most adept English speaker), a vivacious woman named Kyoko, and her husband, the handsome, blockish Hiroshi Kato. At thirty, he's the eldest of the bunch.

There is an open-air observatory on the onsen's roof, and, although it's twenty degrees below zero, we decide to go up for a look.

Snow whips across the shoulders of the pine-covered hills and blows between the polished tubes of the computerized Meade reflectors. My cheeks, still lobster red from my soak in the resort's mineral bath, instantly go numb. That's Sapporo for you: One minute you're watching steam clouds billow across the moon while a volcanic spring parboils your gonads; the next, you're bundled up in the warmest clothing you can borrow, peering at the planets while your hair crystallizes with ice.

"We call him Sulu," Mayuzumi says, pointing to Mr. Kato as he squints through a telescope at Venus.

"For what reason?"

"Because on Japanese television, in the original *Star Trek*, George Takei's character was not called Mr. Sulu, as he was in America. His name on the show here was Mr. Kato."

"Do you know why they changed it?"

Mariko laughs, her teeth chattering. "Because *Sulu* is not a Japanese name," she says apologetically. "No Japanese has ever heard of anyone named *Sulu* in this country."

When we return from the onsen, Mayuzumi and Mariko give me a tour of their city. Though plenty big, Sapporo is much smaller than Tokyo; the blasts of electroluminescence are set to "stun," not "kill." We slurp noodles at a tiny ramen shop, visit Hokkaidō Shrine, and take a slow ride, by open chairlift, to the summit of Mount Moiwa.

As we descend, the full Moon rises over the Ishikari river. The whole scene seems right out of an Edo screen painting. Everything in Japan looks totally Japanese; I don't know how they do it.

My romantic notion slams into reality, however, when we board a streetcar back downtown. Mariko is sitting beside me, leafing through an issue of *Yellowpage: Live Message and Entertainment*. Though the text is completely Japanese, the magazine's spine is in English. I ask why this is so.

"English is cooler than Japanese," Mariko shrugs.

LOST IN TRANSLATION

Many episodes of *Star Trek*—or *Uchuu Daisakusen*, as it is called in Japan ("Mission in Space") have had their titles altered when translated into Japanese. Here are half-a-dozen examples of original series episodes: their English titles, and the meaning of their Japanese translations.

"Where No Man Has Gone Before" = "The Glittering Eyes"

"The Naked Time = "The Evil Space Disease"

"Menagerie" = "Phantamatic Mystery Beings on Talos"

"City on the Edge of Forever" = "The Dangerous Trip to the Past"

"The Doomsday Machine" = "The Gigantic Monster in Space"

"The Tholian Web" = "The Crisis of Captain Kirk Entering the Other Dimensional Space"

Later, Mayuzumi, Mariko, the Katos and I congregate at Mayuzumi's flat for an evening of *Star Trek* videos. Hiroshi uncorks a bottle of sake, and I load a lacquered tray with the *sem bei* (soy-flavored rice crackers) I've picked up at the corner 7-Eleven. Mayuzumi has a good collection of episodes, and we slip one of his favorites into the deck. It's "A Fistful of Datas": Worf and his young son, Alexander, trapped in a malfunctioning "Wild West" holodeck fantasy, are menaced by a cadre of gun-slinging Datas.

When *Star Trek* first appeared on Japanese television in the early 1970s, the shows were subtitled. Today, like most American programs broadcast in Japan, it's transmitted bilingually. English dialogue issues from the right speaker; dubbed Japanese spews from the left. You flip a switch to choose.

One of the most brain-garbling experiences you can have in Japan is watching *Star Trek* with the left and right sound channels on simultaneously. If they'd made me listen to it for more than a minute, Mayuzumi would have had to jam a stick between my teeth.

When he toggles it over to pure Japanese, though, I'm astounded. the dubbed voices are terrific. They're so good, in fact, that I can tell which character is speaking *without even looking at the screen.*

It's a remarkable achievement, but I might have expected it. Centuries of Kabuki and Noh mask drama (not to mention two decades of *karaoke*) have trained Japanese actors to convey the most subtle nuances of character through voice alone. The Japanese Picard has exactly the right blend of reserve and authority; Dr. Crusher's voice is efficient, yet somehow playful. Riker is subtly rakish; Counselor Troi, sultry and insightful; and Worf, the perfect warrior. Data's stand-in doesn't match the inimitable Brent Spiner, but he's a convincing Japanese 'droid.

Of all the characters, only Chief Engineer Geordi LaForge is a washout. His voice sounds oddly generic; like Speed Racer, or something out of an anonymous morning cartoon. But this failure to successfully convey the shadings of an African-American voice is hardly surprising. During my five days in Japan, I've yet to see a single black person.

A glass full of drops. Each drop is tomorrow's dream. Sip your dreams by drops. —slogan on a Suntory beer glass

Mayusumi-san throws me a party. Through Niftyserve, he invites the scattered members of Sapporo's *Star Trek* fan club. The club calls itself "Sector 001," after the United Federation of Planets' identification code for Earth (it's also, coincidentally, America's international direct-dial code).

My host has rented a private "party room" in a downtown Sapporo restaurant, a noisome environment jam-packed with karaoke players, video monitors, and monolithic cigarette machines. More than twenty people show up: teachers, students, hackers, bakers, economists, musicians, and cops. This real-time flesh-and-blood assembly of so many Torekkiis is unusual. Most of Japan's fan clubs exist exclusively in cyberspace, and there has apparently never been a Japanese *Star Trek* convention.

The party's a kick, but nearly everyone smokes. Within an hour I'm asphyxiating. I interview the fans with watery eyes, lubricating my larynx with drop after drop of the famous local beer.

To my horror, I am asked to give a speech. After delivering my sincere and extravagant thanks to Hideyasu Mayuzumi, Sector 001, and the hospitable citizens of Sapporo, I launch into an impassioned soliloquy about *Star Trek*'s role as the metaphorical glue, the cultural cyanoacrylate adhesive, as it were, that might finally bind together East and West. Polite, baffled applause greets my remarks.

The Trekkers have brought very cool gadgets. Digital video cameras, palmtop computers, phaser-shaped shavers, communicator cell phones, even a limited-edition Canadian-made Tricorder are passed hand to hand, ogled and appraised by these global masters of techno-kitsch. In Japan, Roddenberry's vision is not just about conceiving a peaceful, utopian future; it's equally about toys.

The most popular exhibit, however, is bereft of LEDs or microchips. It's a photo album, thick as a Kobe steak, that a Sapporo Trekker bought at a European convention. The album came stuffed to the gills with snapshots of Brent Spiner—Data—at a plethora of *Star Trek* functions and private events.

"He has such a pure heart," moons an angelic, twenty-four-year-old woman named Tamae. She strokes an image of Spiner with her fingertips. "He is like a child, in the body of an adult."

Mayuzumi rescues me from this nut, and helps me separate the wheat from the chaff. There are a few fans whom he feels I must meet: people who have credible theories about *Star Trek* in general, and Data in particular. I am introduced to Tsutomu Tano, who is writing a dissertation comparing a two-part Klingon saga called "Redemption" with Akira Kurosawa's *Chushingura*; and to Shintaro Inoshito, a twenty-one-year-old programmer with Zeppo Marx hair. Inoshita dutifully refills my beer mug, offers me a Mild Seven, and launches into a convoluted defense of Japanese Data-mania.

"In Japan's historic past," Inoshita says, "there was *wa*, 'harmony.' Everybody worked as a group, for a common purpose. But in the modern world, each individual now has their own thoughts, their own ego." Japanese society, Inoshita believes, is breaking down into a pixel scattering of lonely individuals who must fend for themselves. Such self-reliance is undermining Japan's ancient solidarity, and turning life into a cold and mechanized process.

"Data's attempts to come out of his mechanical shell, and become a real human being," says Inoshita, "reflect our desire to escape the current trend of Japanese society."

"If that's true," I respond, "the Japanese view of individualism is the polar opposite of our Western model."

He smiles, bowing slightly. "When Americans see Japanese working as a group," he says, "it often seems strange. But in Japanese culture and history, working in a group is the most comfortable, the most humanlike way."

Our translator is sweating with effort, but Inoshita doesn't stop there. He takes a deep breath, and expands his theory into the economic domain. "In the 17th and 18th century," he continues, "Japan cut off communication with the outside world. And in terms of business, the Japanese are still very isolated and old-fashioned. Each company has its own way, and they have a hard time taking risks or making ventures." I nod dutifully, familiar with this common complaint.

"Data, then, symbolizes the need for flexibility. He represents what we have to do in the future if Japan is to succeed. That is why we identify so closely with Data, and see him as a Japanese personality within the crew. Not because of the way he relates to the *group*, but because of his willingness to try new things. Data symbolizes the Japanese people, adapting to world society."

My favorite Trekker is Sigenobu Ito, a forty-one-year-old police detective who's been watching the show for twenty years. After listening to my dialogue with Inoshita, Ito sits me down and assures me that, at least for the "older generation," there's more to the show than android worship.

"But one thing Inoshita-san said is quite correct," Ito nods. "The atmosphere that prevails aboard the *Enterprise*, you see, embodies the ancient Japanese concept of *wa*."

More than that, insists Ito, "The characters on the starship embody the balancing forces of nature: *dou*, 'stability,' and *sei*, 'action.' Each corresponds to a different personality type. In the original series, Kirk was *sei* and Spock was *dou*. In *The Next Generation*, it is Picard as *dou* and Riker as *sei*."

Ito's comments recall my chat with Moore and Menosky, who contrasted the swashbuckling Kirk and circumspect Picard as avatars of their respective generations. But it seems odd that the two captains (and perhaps the two eras) should embody opposing natural principles.

"Captain Kirk is more of a positive, energetic person, while Captain Picard is quieter and more silent in expressing himself," Ito agrees. "So yes, it is true that Kirk and Picard have different ways of conducting themselves. In the end, though, the result is the same; for both share the goal of *wa*."

Sapporo by night is illuminated like an operating theater. The streets (and the snowflakes gusting across them) are awash in a halogen glare that gives everything a radioactive appearance. Above one street corner, a Jumbotron displays highlights of the afternoon's sumo matches. A multistory McDonald's looms across the intersection. If you don't lift your gaze above the skyline, you can't tell whether it's night or day. It's like being in a vast enclosed stadium—or on the promenade aboard *Deep Space Nine.*

This, I understand, is where the tsunami of postwar progress is taking things. It's *Blade Runner* in reverse: Instead of Los Angeles becoming a kanji-crazed quasi-Tokyo, Japan's cities are being overrun by American fast-food and fashion icons. And it's not just the urban areas that are plastic-wrapped. Wilderness of any stamp has been nearly eradicated. A book about Japan's remaining natural preserves would read like *The Nature Lovers' Guide to Disneyland.*

On my final day in Sapporo, Mayuzumi and his friend Kazuko—a whip-smart writer who speaks fluent English—drag me into Donut Man. A San Francisco Chinatown promotion is under way. Banners emblazoned with Coit Tower and the Golden Gate Bridge droop from the ceiling, Tony Bennett croons to a row of cream horns, and stale dim sum jockeys for position with jelly rolls.

I order a coffee and remark on how technosavvy everyone at last night's party seemed to be. Naturally, nods Mayuzumi. At least 17 percent of the Japanese use computers, and a quarter of this population are probably *Star Trek* fans. In a country of 125 million, that works out to some five million Trekkers—more, perhaps, than exist in all of Europe.

"Do you think," I ask, "that Japanese people are accurately represented on *Star Trek*?"

"No," replies Kazuko. "They are typical of the way Americans look at Japanese." She adds three sugars to her tea. "Here's an example. There was an episode in *The Next Generation* when Keiko O'Brien—the chief engineer's Japanese wife—was recalling a childhood memory. She was thinking about how, when her grandmother did calligraphy, she would wash her brush in a chipped teacup. When I saw that episode, I thought: *Since TNG is set in the 24th century, Keiko's grandmother will be born in the 23rd. Keiko could be my own great-great-great-great-great-great-granddaughter!*" Kazuko snickers at the absurdity of it. "I really don't think my granddaughter would be doing Japanese calligraphy. Not with a chipped Japanese teacup! Nobody would use that, not even nowadays."

"It's the same with Sulu," adds Mayuzumi. "Of course, we were very glad he was made captain of the *Excelsior*. Still, I must say he seems too old-fashioned for the 24th century. He is portrayed as a very restrained, reserved person. I think that, by then, Japanese people should be more active. Nationalities might still have some meaning, but they shouldn't make *that* much difference."

This seems the exact opposite of what Riko had told me in Tokyo: that the Japanese spirit is a diamond core, unchafed by the ravages of time. "Are you suggesting," I say, "that the world is becoming a place where everybody will think and act in the same way?"

Kazuko shrugs. "Even now, Japanese don't have much regard for traditional ways."

"The Japanese lifestyle and way of thinking are very . . . *ambiguous*," offers Mayuzuki. "In the future, things like tea ceremony and *ikebana* (flower arrangement) will survive, but only as art. Not as a part of everyday life."

"So how does it feel," I ask, "to be a Japanese person in the modern world? Is it easy to let go of your traditional ways? Or do you feel like you're swimming upstream, denying what your heritage says you should be?"

"Difficult question," Kazuko replies. "I really don't think about it. It's just my everyday life."

"Well, you're sitting in an American fast-food shop . . ."

"But this is Japan, too."

"Only recently," I counter. "It's got nothing to do with Japanese culture. It's a tacky American business, stuck here to make money."

"But it's almost as old as I am! I visited my first McDonald's when I was in elementary school. McDonald's or Donut Man—or *Star Trek!*—are part of my life. Sometimes I go to a sushi shop or a *soba* place, and that's part of my life, too. It's no different."

Kazuko reaches for the hot-water flask, knocking against her saucer in the process. The teacup tumbles off and its handle breaks. I retrieve the cup and present it to her with both hands. "You might like to take this home and save it," I say with a grin. "For your granddaughter."

She takes the cup and laughs. "Now *that* would be authentic," she says. "Three centuries from now, all the antique Japanese teacups will say 'Donut Man' on them."

3. The *Gaijin* Lord of Tenmangu

Fuji rises in the distance, towering above the Pizza Huts southwest of Tokyo. A plume of cloud veils its summit. It's beautiful—a magical low cone sloping famously off to the east. Honshū island is becoming one gigantic strip mall, but nothing can fuck with a really great mountain.

We streak past Fuji at 160 mph, satin smooth on seamless rails. The Japanese fascination with technotoys is matched only by their love of speed, and these *shinkansens* are to Amtrak what the *Enterprise* is to a DC-10. A thrumming purr fills the compartment, like fusion engines at impulse power.

My destination is Kameoka, a suburb of Kyoto. It's also the home of Alex Kerr, an expert on Japanese culture whom I met a year ago at a reading and calligraphy demonstration that he gave in a California bookstore.

There are two motives for my visit. After a week of stuttering in broken English with local interpreters, I'm dying to *talk* to someone again. I also suspect that Alex—a self-confessed Trekker with an Ivy League degree in Japanese studies—will have some brilliant insights about *Star Trek*'s mystique in Japan.

Gaijin Kerr outside
Tenmangu shrine.

Kerr has lived in Kameoka since 1977, in a four hundred-year-old tiled house on the grounds of an old Shinto shrine. Known locally as Tenmangu, the shrine is dedicated to the ancient god of scholarship and calligraphy. Kerr has borrowed the name for his home.

No one seems to be in when I knock on his door at 2 P.M. I set down my bags and walk around the shrine itself. It's a gem of a building, situated about fifty feet from the main house. Traditional Japanese architecture never ceases to amaze me. From every angle the shrine is exquisite, a cunning blend of materials, workmanship, and simplicity. I find myself imagining what a Muromachi period version of *Deep Space Nine* would look like, and wondering if starships will ever evolve to a point where wood joinery and hand-finished detail replace biaxially stressed titanium fabric.

The door to Tenmangu opens—from the inside. Kerr, squintily awake, is astonished to see me.

"I thought you were coming this afternoon?" His breath steams in the air.

"Alex . . . It's two o'clock."

He was up late, he explains, working on his second book, *Japan: Dogs and Demons*. It's a fierce condemnation of the greed, pollution, and creative stagnation that have burst the hopes of the so-called "Bubble Years": the late 1980s, when it seemed certain that Japan would be the next great power. His first book, *Lost Japan*, was written in Japanese and published in 1994. A tough-love critique of contemporary Japanese values, it won the nation's highest award for nonfiction.

Kerr is a handsome, bookish man whose red hair and circle-framed specs make him look like a grown-up version of the Professor from the *Rocky & Bullwinkle Show*. He fell in love with Japan in 1964, when his father, a naval officer, was stationed at Yokohama. Kerr spent the next three decades steeping himself in traditional Japanese arts—Zen, Kabuki, calligraphy—and profiting from the economic boom that swept Japan in the 1980s.

I remove my shoes and follow Kerr inside. Tenmangu is full of expensive carpets, hanging scrolls, and folding screens—museum-quality art. Doors slide open to reveal a large living room facing a traditional Japanese garden. Space heaters purr and hiss, taking the chill out of the air. Kerr's PowerBook recharges on the lacquered pine table that he uses for cooking, eating, and calligraphy. None of this detracts, though, from the *wa* of the place. His residence on the grounds of a millennia-old shrine is a hiding place, a refuge from the whipped petroleum fixations of modern Japan.

Kerr's a night bird, which is how he got hooked on *Star Trek* to begin with. Years ago, the program was broadcast at four in the morning, his usual bedtime.

"So what is it about the show," I ask, "that so fascinates the Japanese?"

"First of all," he says, "there are the reasons you've probably already heard: the military discipline, the comfortable hierarchy, the obsession with stability and harmony. But there's more. In *Star Trek*—more than in any other show I can think of—everybody's dressed in exactly the right way. This is something the Japanese love. Worf really looks like a strong, forbidding samurai; Data looks like a nerdy drone; the captain is very commanding and captainish."

When I mention how impressed I was with the show's dubbed voices, Kerr nods rapidly. "Everything in Japan is theatrical in the extreme," he explains. "It's almost to the point of self-parody—as if the whole country were living out a Kabuki drama. The waiters are waiterly, the cooks sport French chef's hat, and the housewife wears her little apron out to shop. Even the *salariman* you see on the train wears a gray suit, his corporate costume."

All of this, claims Kerr, is symptomatic of why Japan is going down the tubes. But as he prepares breakfast, he tells me about Japanese friends who have abandoned their rigid, myopic society for the broader vistas of America, Indonesia, and Thailand. Despite its efficient trains and highly affected graces, Japan does feel restrained and stagnant. I've seen few examples of spontaneity anywhere.

One reason for this, Kerr suggests over freeze-dried coffee, may be the fact that Japan has been at peace for so long. With nothing to shake it up since World War II, Japan's already stiff social systems have set like cement. It has become a land of social stasis, supporting a lifestyle designed to shield people from reality. Surfers flock to simulated beaches lapped by machine-generated waves; indoor fisherman cast their lines while, behind them, workers stock the pools with trout.

"In the future, when mankind is living in space stations and on the Moon, people from other cultures will miss running brooks, old cities with cobblestone streets, and falling leaves. The Japanese will not. That's because they live in a completely sterile environment, that *disapproves* of falling leaves!"

"How can you disapprove of falling leaves?"

"They consider them *kitanai*." Kerr smirks. " '*Dirty.*' Nature is dirty. That's why here in Kameoka, in the fall, people lop off the branches of the trees so that there will be no falling leaves. What the Japanese prefer, and surround themselves with in their daily lives, are objects that show no sign of human or organic manufacture.

"The effect of living in this sterile, plasticky environment," he says, "is that the *Enterprise* feels like home."

I leave Kerr to his work and head into Kyoto to run some errands. When I return it's dark, and I'm ravenously hungry. Visions of miso soup dance in my head, but Kerr's assistant drives off for takeout, returning with two cartons of . . . Kentucky Fried Chicken.

After dinner comes the moment I've been waiting for. Kerr produces a roll of rice paper, uncorks a bottle of cheap Italian wine, and begins mixing his inks. I assist by clearing off the long wooden table and crushing the KFC boxes into compact trash modules.

"Do the Japanese ever feel uneasy," I ask, "about their addiction to American cultural icons?"

"Like Kentucky Fried Chicken?"

"I'm thinking more of *Star Trek*."

"No." Kerr shakes his head emphatically. "The idea that Japan is a land of temples and geisha is hopelessly out of date. In fact," he says, "I would say that for an average Japanese person, walking into this house, with its antique carpets and calligraphy brushes, would be like a trip to another planet."

He spreads out a sheet of paper, fixing the corners with polished stones. Loading his brush, he practices the kanji for "horse." The solution is too thin; he spoons more pigment into the bowl. Satisfied, Kerr is ready to begin. He lights a narrow, cone-shaped candle that flickers like a lizard's tongue.

"What ever happened to Godzilla?" I ask. "He's Japan's own icon, at least ten years older than *Star Trek*. Granted, he's as corny as Cracker Jacks . . ."

"Now *that*," Alex grins, "is a fascinating story. Particularly if you understand that while the Godzilla myth, in America, is viewed as high camp—a joke—here, it's seen as the best that Japanese filmmaking has to offer." He moves his brush over the paper. "In fact, in a well-respected poll of Japanese movie critics, *Godzilla* was ranked among the twenty best Japanese films of all time."

We all know Godzilla; he's the only non-Western sci-fi character as well known as C3PO, Superman, or Spock. An amphibious, fire-breathing dinosaur, he (she? it?) was snoozing peacefully beneath the waters of Oto Island until H-bomb tests roused him. In 1994, the middle-aged reptile starred in his twenty-first film: *Godzilla vs. Space Godzilla.*

"What you probably *don't* realize," Kerr says, "is that, perhaps from its inception, Godzilla was intended as a metaphor for the picked-upon Japanese fighting the Americans. The majority of the films involve evil aliens, monsters that symbolize the U.S.A. attacking poor Godzilla: Japan."

In the 1962 film *King Kong vs. Godzilla*, Kerr tells me, King Kong was a symbol of America, and the fighting between the monsters represented the conflict between the two countries. As recently as 1990—in *Godzilla vs. King Ghidora*—Caucasians from the future unleash a three-headed dragon in a nefarious bid to force Japan to buy foreign-made computers.

"To some Japanese, I'm certain, the *Enterprise* too is a metaphor for Japan: an isolated nation, fending for itself against a hostile universe. Inside the *Enterprise*, it's very comfortable and familiar. Outside, all is alien and unknown. That's how the Japanese view themselves in the world, and that's certainly what Godzilla was. But to answer your original question . . ."

"I forgot I had one."

"You asked what became of Godzilla. I'll tell you. As the Japanese film industry stagnated—along with everything else—Godzilla became a joke. He became so pathetic, so out of tune with even the Japanese audience, that today his only chance, his last hope in hell, is for foreigners to come along and produce the next great Godzilla movie. And that's exactly what's happening. The new Godzilla film is being made in America, by the same guys who did *Independence Day.*

"And that," Kerr concludes, laying another completed drawing on the floor by the space heater, "is the ultimate irony. The Japanese have even lost the ability to manage their own primal myth."

Kerr returns to his calligraphy, picking up steam. Deep in concentration, he draws increasingly fantastic kanji in blue ink flecked with gold. We spend long minutes watching the colors swirl together, making marbled patterns as luminous as abalone. Every so often he bends over the work with a paper towel,

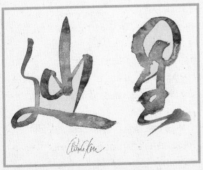

Hoshi Tandoru: Calligraphy by Alex Kerr.

drawing away the extra ink that has pooled around the elbow joints of the characters.

"People think it's all in the brush stroke, but it's all in the paper towel stroke." He winks. "Ancient paper towel technique, handed down from the Edo period."

At my suggestion, Alex executes the symbols for "star" (*hoshi*) and "trek" (*tadoru*; literally, "to arrive after a long journey"). The pairing pleases him so well that he executes an entire series, his arm flying without hesitation, his brush swollen with ink. The results are inspired; there is something otherworldly about these paintings. Like particle physicists plunging into the ecstasy of the atom, we lose ourselves in the quantum signature of the kanji.

MY FAIR WARRIOR

An Intrepid-class starship, the spermatozoon-shaped *Voyager* accommodates some 145 crew members. Compared to the *Enterprise* 1701-D, with its complement of more than fifteen hundred men, women, and children, Kathryn Janeway's ship seems cold and institutional. It looks like a Canton Road discotheque, hurled by a space-time glitch into the distant reaches of the Milky Way's Delta quadrant.

Kate Mulgrew, by contrast, owns an unpretentious home in Brentwood—the sort of sunny, picket-fence neighborhood you'd send your kids to for trick-or-treating. There's a white arched trellis, a bottlebrush tree, and orchids by the door. A Jeep Grand Cherokee (she drives herself to work at 6:30 every morning) sits in the two-car driveway, below a battered basketball hoop shared by her two adolescent sons. Bees buzz, and the aroma of barbecuing chicken wafts through the air. The place is vintage America, sweet and humid. It could've been lifted right out of a David Lynch film.

Mulgrew answers the door, wearing a white gossamer blouse over a black leotard. The instant we meet, I sense she's a force all her own. Janeway is stern, clipped, and conflicted; Mulgrew is casual, sensual, available. She and Janeway are on the same magnet, but they occupy different poles.

"Let's sit outside. It's such a lovely day." I follow her through the living room. The house is so comfortable looking, so informal, that I'm totally disarmed. I'm glad to see that the captain of *Voyager*—the warrior without a home—has such a cozy abode to come back to after a hard day's work.

Kate Mulgrew and Brannon Braga. (Photo by Ron Benbassat.)

Mulgrew reclines on the long green cushion of a poolside chaise, propped up on her elbow. Her feet are bare, her toes curled. It's been a tough season. First off, she was affronted by Paramount's decision to kill off Kes—an elf-like alien gal, played by Jennifer Lien, who'd been a *Voyager* regular for three years. Next, there was the matter of Kes's replacement: a Borgified vixen named Seven of Nine. Mulgrew has nothing against the new Borg character per se; it's the presentation she finds offensive. Seven of Nine will be played by Jeri Ryan, an actress built like a Hindu fertility goddess, and the costume they've stuck her in clings like sin.

"Janeway wouldn't allow it," Mulgrew declaims. "There's no way a captain in her position would let a woman dressed that way parade around her ship. What are they thinking? I've got a crew full of guys who haven't gotten laid for three years. They'd all be walking around with erections."

The table beside me holds a big tray of chocolate chip cookies and a pitcher of pink lemonade. Kate hands me a tall Mexican glass with an indigo rim. Ice clacks against the spout as she pours.

"Would you like some vodka in that?"

"I'm fine, thanks."

Her dog, Grace, nuzzles into my crotch, shedding dark brown hair on my Dockers. Mulgrew's own legs, stretching languidly from beneath a white skirt, are slim and fit. Her eyes are astonishing. She's got the vitality of a rock climber and a charged sensuality you don't see in Janeway. Most impressive, though, is her *directness*. She's a heartland farm gal, and the word *Hollywood* curdles in her mouth.

"I regret to this day that I raised my sons here." Mulgrew shakes her head. "It's not any place to live. It's an industry town. It's about being right, and about being rich and famous. And these things matter not to me, in the end. I grew up in the cornfields of Dubuque, Iowa," she says slowly. "and I'm the eldest of eight children, and I'm about as Irish Catholic as you're ever gonna get. And we are *absurd*, and *intense*. We believe in God, we believe in a lot of drinking, and we believe in a lot of sex. And great love. The dramas of our lives are the dramas of joined lives. Seldom is it the drama of terrific success—unless that success emanates from a *passion*."

I nod, dumbfounded. The most common complaint about Mulgrew—that she sounds like Katharine Hepburn on helium—evaporates when you hear her orate. She'd be deadly in sales.

"Los Angeles must seem like a purgatory to you."

"I'm biding my time. I have to be here for my work. And this is work I very much want to do."

Neither of us say it, but both of us know it: It's a wonder she got this job at all. Casting *Voyager*'s captain was a hellish saga, rife with pitfalls. For one thing, Rick Berman's enthusiasm (shared by co-creators Jeri Taylor and Michael Piller) for putting a woman in the "big chair" was not shared by Paramount. Hollywood execs are more conservative than Mormon lingerie, and straying from proven formulas fills them with dread.

Paramount would give it a shot, however, if the perfect actress were found. Here lay the second problem. Episodic television is a huge commitment of time and energy: sixty to seventy hours a week, with a few weeks of vacation every six months or so. Few actresses of credible captains' age (i.e., thirty-something on) were willing meet the demands of such a schedule—much less on a six-year contract.

Kate Mulgrew read for the part. So did Linda Hamilton, Susan Gibney, Lindsay Wagner, Kate Jackson, and a few dozen others. But the role was ultimately offered to Academy Award–winning actress Genevieve Bujold. Bujold had never done a television series before, but after much soul-searching, she assured Berman she could handle the strain.

She lasted two days.

Kate Mulgrew was called in for a second reading. Her first, given on a rainy summer day in New York City, had been abysmal; she'd left with a shrug and an apology. On her second try, though, she nailed the part down.

The whole thing smacks of fate. Mulgrew agrees; it was a turning point in her life.

"Let's just talk about it on the most spectacular level: I fell in love with Janeway." She pronounces the words almost breathlessly. "At my age, that's something. A lifetime, you search. I've played Hedda Gabler, and I've played Desdemona. In the theater, you find them. But in television and film it's very rare to encounter someone whom you really fall in love with. Least of all this captain of a starship! But I did. And it grows . . . and grows . . . and grows." She's like a little girl talking about her heroine—and the fact that she herself plays this heroine seems beside the point.

Kate peers over and refills my glass with lemonade. "Shall I bring out the vodka?"

"Really, it's a bit early in the day for me." Her intensity is like a kite, swooping in the air between us. I tug its string. "Do you dream about Janeway?"

"I dream about work," she admits. "About not getting a scene right. In all my dreams, I'm . . . scantily clad. It's so *obvious*! Am I 'clothing the character?' And the other night it was about eating the wrong chocolates!" She chuckles knowingly; I rack my brain for the symbolism.

"It's quite something, to be the Captain," Mulgrew allows. "Yes, I have anxiety about her. But I have much greater love than anxiety. I'm con-

STAR-STRUCK TREKKIE ASTRONAUT FOLLOWED HER IDOL

MARK CARO
Chicago Tribune, October 27, 1992

Mae Jemison received a hero's welcome in Chicago recently, and no wonder—the Morgan Park High School graduate became the first black woman in space last month.

The thirty-six-year-old astronaut's space shuttle flight inspired kids worldwide, but in a sense Jemison was just returning the favor: When she was growing up, she also was inspired by seeing a black woman in space—Lieutenant Uhura on *Star Trek*.

"I had always been interested in space flight and science and stars," said the sunny, down-to-earth Jemison. "What really happened with *Star Trek* is that it reinforced that. And it was wonderful to see her on board the ship because you never saw women and minorities in those situations."

What goes around comes around: The woman who recruited Jemison to be an astronaut was none other than Nichelle Nichols, who played Lieutenant Uhura before becoming involved with the space program. Jemison had already completed medical school and established herself as a researcher when she got the opportunity to make her dreams come true.

Still, she said, having a black woman in space shows society's progress. "We're starting to maybe try to get to that universe that so many of us Trekkies like to think about."

stantly looking for new ways to make her interesting. I drive home every night, asking myself: *Did you go to a different level today? Did you do your work?*"

Her devotion to Janeway, I'm beginning to see, borders on obsession. But I'm visiting Mulgrew at an awkward time, when circumstances have made her especially protective of her role. Jeri Ryan's

FROM "ASK CAMILLE,"

A WRITE-IN FORUM WITH

CAMILLE PAGLIA

Excerpted from the online magazine *Salon*,
December 1997 Web site:
askcamille@salonmagazine.com

Dearest Camille:

Knowing you're a staunch *Star Trek* fan, I wondered what your thoughts are concerning the current state of the franchise, particularly given *Voyager*'s recent ratings jump. While *Deep Space Nine* always struck me as a bit slow and dour, I'd hoped that *Voyager* would bring back some of the spark that *Next Generation* had at its peak. I love both the half-Klingon Torres (when the writers let her anger and humor show) and Capt. Janeway. And now that the mushy Kes has been replaced by Jeri Ryan's sexy, edgy Seven of Nine, I wanted to know: Do you think this show is finally poised to do the name *Star Trek* proud? And am I wrong for thinking the most interesting characters on the *Trek* series nowadays are the women?

—Spaced-out

Dear Spaced-out:

Yes, I adore *Star Trek* and consider it the most visionary exploration of our intergalactic future. The artful, visually elegant, psychologically intense TV series *The Next Generation* is my all-time favorite *Star Trek* spinoff. I'm afraid to say that I can't stand *Voyager*, with its cramped sets, dowdy costumes, ugly makeup, bad photography, and corny dialogue. I find Kate Mulgrew's stilted performance as Capt. Janeway utterly unbearable: She has all the forced, phony swagger of a ham amateur trying to play Shakespeare's transvestite Rosalind. . . .

However, when I saw this fall's sensational publicity campaign for Jeri Ryan's Seven of Nine (whose vampy, bust-revealing, silver-mauve body-suit provoked a prudish feminist backlash), I nearly passed out. My eyes popped out of my head: Never before have I more fully understood that piquant metaphor! Ryan is dynamite—lithe, sexy, and smart. And the entire creative team that designed her costume and produced those gorgeous, high-porn PR photos (which blanketed newspaper TV supplements) deserves the golden apple of Aphrodite.

—Camille Paglia

arrival on *Voyager* has been a hard pill to swallow. The spectacular young actress has taken the show by storm; she's been featured on the cover of a dozen magazines and is broadly credited with 'saving' the show. While Mulgrew can't complain about *Voyager*'s ratings rise —or the fact that 'Seven' gives Janeway the best foil she's ever had— the fact that Ryan receives exclusive credit for these things drives her to distraction.

"It's as if the producers have suddenly understood my capacity as an actress," she says, "but they couldn't see it without, as you say, the 'foil' of this other character." Mulgrew draws a breath, runs a hand through her hair. "But make no mistake: I was coming. I feel a new confidence, which really takes wing in my scenes with Jeri. But all that happened toward the end of the third season; well before she came aboard."

Imagine, Mulgrew suggests, that *Future Perfect* flops. A few months later, some kid waltzes in and writes more or less the same book, which leaps to the top of the bestseller list. How would I feel?

"But I'm wise," she allows. "And I have a very rich and rewarding personal life. And it's a good job; I'm not about to cut off my nose to spite my face. I like Jeri Ryan, and I'm grateful for the fact that she's enhanced the show. But it's hard to read the reviews and not feel sad."

It's clear that the role sustains her. But how does she sustain the role? What sources does Mulgrew draw from when Janeway is commanding the bridge? "I grew up on the Greeks," she tells me, "and I've read the lives of the great saints and mystics." But her guiding light is Mother Columba, a spiritual mentor Mulgrew first met under tragic circumstances, at the age of thirteen.

Kate's sister Tessie had died of a brain tumor. It was an agonizing decline that spanned three years, and left the Mulgrew clan fractured. Her mother—who had earlier pulled the children out of church—returned to God.

Mother Columba was the abbess of Our Lady of the Mississippi, a Trappistine convent in Dubuque. "My mother would spend weeks down there," Mulgrew recalls. "My curiosity was piqued, and I went to see her, too. Over the years, she's become a solace for me. The last time I visited, we spoke about Hollywood. Could my spiritual life survive here? Suddenly, as we were discussing God and love and sex and Hollywood, I realized: She's a bit like Janeway, Columba. No *earthier* woman ever lived; no woman more in touch with the very journey I've been describing.

"But the journey was deeper for her. She could *exalt* it. So when I left Dubuque, I thought, 'This is going to be a good secret. I'll take it back to *Voyager*. And I will try to work our dynamic into the show somehow.'"

There's a mild irony here. In the 24th century, according to Rodden-berry, organized religion will have vanished, as least on Earth. Kathryn Janeway would no more pour her heart out to a Trappistine abbess than Mr. Spock would consult a Hassidic rabbi.

"How, exactly, has Mother Columba's influence shown up in Janeway?"

Mulgrew leans back on the chaise and draws her knees up to her chest. "I think Janeway is very good. She has a noble heart. But what I find most compelling about her is her *brokenness*. That's the delicious part. She's always arguing, right? The minute she makes a strike for nobility, she herself is stricken by the horrible reality that she's just a human being—a woman, desperately lonely, scared, and overwhelmed with responsibility. But in the next breath—the deeper breath, after she recollects herself—she knows she can do it. Because it's the deeper commitment."

"It's a pity," I say, refilling our glasses, "that 'Gene's Vision' doesn't permit you to program Mother Columba on the holodeck."

"But that's *my* issue, not Janeway's. Janeway is a notorious scientist, not known for her love of God."

It was Kate Mulgrew's mother who suggested that Janeway would seek out her peers, and consult historical figures for guidance. She would go to the old masters: people who had cultivated their creativity with a great depth of soul. *Voyager*'s producers took this note, suggesting an ongoing relationship with the great artist and inventor Leonardo da Vinci. But what about Mulgrew herself? Which historical figures would she long to break bread with?

"Jesus Christ," the actress answers without pause. "And Mary Magdalene with him. All spiritual figures, because that's my whole thing in life. Thérèse of Lisieux, and Saint Augustine, to enrich the conversation. And I would put Eleanora Duse, the great Italian actress, in there as well . . ."

The pool filter gurgles, and the phone chirps unanswered. We're both lost in thought. Who would *I* materialize on the holodeck? It's a challenging question, like being asked to name five historical figures you'd invite to a dinner party. I'd download Mark Twain, of course. And Scheherazade, definitely. Alexander Calder, perhaps, and Ursula K. LeGuin. But I'd probably spend most of my time hanging out with Louis Armstrong.

Mulgrew asks about my *Star Trek* encounters. I describe a few of the things I've seen: the Sapporo *Torrekki* party, the Klingon wedding, Hungarian kids drafting *Voyager*-inspired starships. But what does she, the woman charged with carrying the mythos forward, make of all this? Does the global fascination with *Star Trek* spring from wander-lust—a primal longing to explore the stars—or, as Vonnegut suggested, the more prosaic dream of a warm, supportive family?

Mulgrew listens carefully, her tourmaline eyes unblinking. "Mr. Vonnegut's point is well taken," she says. "It *is* a family drama. But would it be a drama of such compelling proportions if we were not lost in space in the 24th century? I don't think so. It also comes from an unbelievably exciting extension of the imagination that can put us into the future—with hope and with curiosity. That's the glue. That's the attraction. It triggers everything that's exciting about human nature." She frowns. "But I frankly do not understand the global proportions. I don't *get* the phenomenal aspect of it, because I'm so subjectively involved. And we don't hear about all that in Hollywood. We've been low man on the totem pole around here."

"I guess that's why Paramount brought in a Borg babe with big tits. They're looking for something that will sell the show to their assumed audience: boys between the ages of eighteen and thirty."

She offers a pained smile. "If that's their main thing, all I can say to you is, *Why did they hire a female captain in the first place?* A middle-aged female captain is not going to appeal to their demographic! A man would; or I might, as a first officer. So they're going to have to readjust their thinking a little . . . along with me. I can bend a little bit; they've got to bend a little bit. They have to understand that it's *adult* women and men who find this captain appealing. And girls, all over the world.

"As for young boys, between eighteen and thirty—" her voice tightens with conviction. "They want a good story more than anybody else. They need the mythology more than any other faction or demographic group. They don't need any more tits and ass than they already see in every hour of their day." Mulgrew shakes her head. "Maybe I'm wrong. I hope I'm not wrong." She sighs and reaches for the pitcher. "Are you ready for some vodka?"

"Aw, what the hell."

Kate skips into the house, returning with a bottle of Absolut. She pours my drink—one part lemonade, one part vodka—and does herself the same turn. We toast to Janeway and the success of *Voyager*. "Where were we?" she asks.

"I'm admiring your house. All the flowers. Why aren't there flowers on *Voyager*'s main bridge?

"There are flowers in my ready room, always. And in my quarters.

Which we never see, because Janeway doesn't sleep. She doesn't sleep, and she doesn't eat. Have your ever seen her eat? She never eats!"

That's not all she doesn't do. "Sooo . . . what about Janeway's sexuality?"

"Ahhh." Her whole body shifts forward, catlike. "This is a *problem*," she admits. "Because Kate Mulgrew's sexuality is high. And *deep*. What I'm going to say to you may sound a bit bottled up, but it's not. I've thought about this very long and very hard: *Janeway wouldn't risk it*. She loves the crew too much. I love the ship too much. I simply couldn't jeopardize it." When she speaks as the captain, her voice changes; she radiates command. But a moment later she's the Irish tigress, growling and licking her paws. "I'm sorely tempted . . ."

"And if you gave in to that temptation?"

"I would say Chakotay would be my target. We have an allegiance that is not shared by the others, with the possible exception of Tuvok— and that dynamic is not *visceral* enough for Janeway. There's touch involved with Chakotay. There are male eyes looking at me. There's a warmth and a quickness that happens between us, because it happens between Robert [Beltran] and Kate.

"But my feeling is that if I were to have an affair with him—or anybody, for that matter—I couldn't run *Voyager*. Under the best of circumstances, it would affect my command. And these are not the best of circumstances. If I start sleeping with somebody, and I'm dealing with some horrible alien species, my focus is going to be off. Trying to focus when you're in love takes the discipline of twenty-five Green Berets in the trenches."

"Sometimes it makes work easier; it opens up the world."

"I would like to have a relationship with Chakotay," Mulgrew pronounces, "unsurpassed on prime-time television. One of depth, integrity, complexity, nuance, suggestion. Let it be ripe with tension. But let us not drop trou."

"Eh?"

"Trousers. That's not going to happen until the end. Even then, I think it should be left to the imagination of the viewers."*

"But Kirk, Picard, Sisko—all the other captains have gotten . . ."

"Yes, but they're *hombres*, Jeff. Their stakes are lower than mine. And what's good for the goose is not always good for the gander. When a

---

* The studio seems to agree. A scene written into a fourth-season *Voyager* episode, calling for a long and passionate kiss between Janeway and Chakotay, was violently opposed by Brannon Braga—although Mulgrew wanted to play it through.

woman makes love, it's not the same. I've made love enough in my life to tell you. And the effect it has on me when, indeed, I make love . . ." Her nostrils flare. "*Everything* is bigger for the woman."

"That won't change by the 24th century?"

"I hope not! It's what makes the match between us so splendid. That's why men throw their hearts and their lives away for a great woman. That's what they admire more than anything: the beauty of her sex. The responsibility. The depths of it. It's *deep*."

Wow. I sit back, speechless. Jane Jetson meets Gloria Swanson; this is more than I bargained for.

"More vodka?"

"Please."

———

When I ask Mulgrew if there's a story she'd personally like to see on the show, her answer throws me for a loop.

"I'd do an episode in which we see how *funny* the captain really is. I'd put her up against a whole bunch of weird enemies. And I'd have her just run wild, disarming them at every turn—with jokes, and with stories. It would be a whole different take on Janeway. Big! Wild! And very funny."

There are precedents in the *Star Trek* universe, of course. The original series used humor to great advantage, as did TNG. One particular *Deep Space Nine* episode—"Our Man Bashir," a shameless James Bond parody—was hilarious, a tour de force. But it's unlikely that Paramount will take such liberties with *Voyager*. They've chosen a different course: bigger explosions, deadlier space battles, and the centerfold sexuality of Jeri Ryan. The imagined ambrosia, once again, for the Turborg-and-testosterone set.

It is here, after a few long drinks, that Mulgrew asks *me* a question. It's the one I've been dreading. How, in my opinion, does *Voyager* compare with *The Next Generation*?

I answer as tactfully as I can. *The Next Generation* could be downright fabulous; when it was, there was nothing to equal it. And Patrick Stewart, by anyone's lights, was a tough act to follow. But even *The Next Generation*, I remind her, took years to catch on. *Voyager* may come of age as well; it could happen the very next season.

Mulgrew sympathizes with the irritation I felt when the show's brightest arena for conflict—the friction between *Voyager*'s Starfleet officers and the Maquis resistance fighters they took aboard in the

Now, *Voyager*

BERNARD WELT
Mythomania, May 1995

Beneath all the phasers, transporter beams, and dilithium-powered warp drives, every *Star Trek* show so far has essentially been about running away from home. And if it is Peter Pan who captains the Lost Boys in Never-Neverland and fights the pirates, it is Wendy who leads the children back to the security of their home.

So we can easily tell where [*Star Trek: Voyager*] is headed, with its themes of abandonment and loss. After many close calls with temporal disturbances and wormholes, encounters with alien races and internal dissension, Captain Janeway will one day discover that she has only to click her heels three times and repeat "There's no place like home" to return to our cozy little corner of the galaxy.

The parallel to Dorothy Gale's marvelous adventure is in places too exact to be entirely coincidental. After all, the captain and her crew are snatched up from familiar surroundings by the galactic equivalent of a tornado; while Neelix, the first really beastly alien to be featured on a *Star Trek* series, is clearly a Cowardly Lion; and the holographic Doctor, like Data, is a Tin Man in search of a heart.

What is really of interest, though, is that Captain Janeway inspires the viewer not only because she is something new, but because she is something very ancient, of Dorothy and Wendy's line. The male hero may go far afield to find the patriarchal god—to challenge him, replace him, or make atonement to him. Jim Kirk and Jean-Luc Picard knew him as a sky god, to be found only where no one has gone before. But the female hero brings her brood home.

pilot—was flattened. The rebellious Tom Paris, the half-Klingon B'Elanna Torres, the Native American Chakotay—all were emasculated, and turned into vanilla Starfleet apologists. Nor has the arrival of Seven of Nine improved their standing. Some of the peripheral characters (like Harry Kim, Neelix, and even the marvelous holographic doctor) have been herded even further into the background.

Mulgrew, however—who felt severely underused the first few seasons—is finally getting fed.

"It's an entirely different feast than I had expected," she admits. "This was not my dream menu; but it's every bit as nourishing. And that's because the producers are seeing something that's far more compelling to them than 'Mother Earth,' or the 'nurturing captain,' which had a milquetoasty effect."

"And what might that be?"

"It's the element of flinting; it's what happens between myself and Jeri Ryan. Because our characters are contentious; they're full of dynamite, that someone could put a spark to at any moment. And there's an androgynous quality in Jeri that highlights my extreme, passionate femininity. That's something that the most passionate of the men—Bob Picardo, who plays the holographic doctor—can't do, because he's a hologram. And they didn't allow it between Chakotay and Janeway."

Still, anyone who encounters Mulgrew personally realizes she could be better used. Her Irish passion and intensity, direct as a lighthouse beam when you sit beside her, read like comic-book antics on the small screen. Here, I realize, lies the irony of Mulgrew's success. The world may be ready for a female starship captain, but the concept is still wobbly. *Star Trek*'s writers—mainly a bunch of guys in their thirties—haven't figured out how to make the character breathe. And Mulgrew wants it all: philosophy, spirituality, courage. She wants *depth*. She wants her love for Janeway to rattle on the screen like a shaman's drum, inspiring everyone who sees her.

The sun hangs low, glowing through the trees that give her modest yard an air of lush Mediterranean privacy. "It's frustrating," she says softly, "because I probably care more than the other two captains *ever* cared. And yet I'm struggling for the venue that they were given." There's a brief pause, then Mulgrew sits up. Her face brightens.

"But now that they see this change, they're going, 'Oh, yes! Let's do this, and let's do that!' They put stuff in my mouth now that comes very naturally. And if something comes out that I like, I get to keep it; whether it's in the script or not." A beat. "Small things, of course. But the point is, they're sensing a new confidence. The thing that was missing from Janeway in the first few seasons, that's there now, is that I *own* her. And I have no fear."

We've been talking for hours. The bottle of Absolut sits empty, beside the ravaged cookies. I brush the dog hair off my legs and prepare to leave. We walk back through the house.

The living room is a gauntlet of distractions. Every wall and table is laden with mementos from Mulgrew's personal and professional life. It's a potpourri of imagery and memorabilia, from paintings by her sister-in-law to Tom Thumb's 1855 wedding shirt (an heirloom from her great-grandmother, who worked with Thumb in the circus). There's a satinwood carving of the Balinese god of wisdom, a photograph of Mulgrew with Hillary Clinton, and a Hirschfeld sketch of the *Voyager* crew. At my request, Kate gives me the full tour. Hardly a room in the house (except for her sons' lairs) lacks some homage to her alter ego. The guest bathroom is virtually a shrine, with a dozen of Janeway's magazine covers—from *TV Guide* to *Working Mother*—framed over the vanity.

Mulgrew's expecting guests, and has yet to marinate the chicken. We make a final detour into the dining room. "I want to show you one more thing," she says.

On a varnished wooden shelf, overlooking the luxurious table, is a framed portrait of Captain Kathryn Janeway.

I've seen lots of publicity shots, but this one is different. It's a three-quarters profile. Janeway's eyes look into the lower distance; her left hand curls under her chin. Unlike Rodin's *Thinker*, who seems anchored to the Earth, this figure is more melancholy and ephemeral. She is a woman on an aerie, gazing down from an inaccessible height. It's pensive, vulnerable, and soft, a side of the captain we've never truly seen.

Mulgrew stands before it, arms crossed, her eyes mirroring the portrait's complexity. I look from one to the other and realize: *This is not a portrait of Janeway. It's a photo of Kate Mulgrew.*

"That's my favorite picture of her," Mulgrew says at last. "That's the way I see her."

AWAY MISSION IX: DO ALIENS HAVE BUDDHA NATURE?

It began with a rumor, as so many things do.

I first heard it in 1996, while writing about the making of *First Contact* for *Details* magazine. Five or six years ago, the *Los Angeles Times Magazine* had reportedly published a photograph showing the Dalai Lama on the set of the *Enterprise*, posing with actor Brent Spiner in full Data garb.

The Dalai Lama a Trekker? Astounding, but possibly true. I already knew that the sixty-two-year-old Tibetan Buddhist monk (who fled his homeland in 1959, after the Chinese occupation) takes an active interest in particle physics. I was aware that he'd met with neurosurgeons, mathematicians, and astronomers, exploring the tantalizing territory where Eastern mysticism meets Western science. Most telling of all, I knew that, as a boy the Dalai Lama had owned a telescope that he trained on the citizens of Lhasa—far below his perch atop the vast Potala Palace.

According to the beliefs of Tibetan Buddhism, the Dalai Lama is the human incarnation of Chenrezig: the bodhisattva of compassion, whose thousand arms and eyes tend to the suffering of sentient beings everywhere. Strictly interpreted, a bodhisattva is a person who has attained the enlightened state of a Buddha, and can thus redeem his or her chips for everlasting bliss in nirvana. But bodhisattvas don't retire. They choose instead to be reborn over and over and over again, lifetime after lifetime, until all sentient beings win freedom from suffering.

Such beings could be called the Buddhist answer to "heroes." An interesting concept—since the traditional Western model of the muscled, macho hero is long in the tooth. Far more appealing is the selfless and creative person who can attain spectacular results without relying on intimidation or violence. Rigoberta Manchu and Aung Sang Suu Kyi are prime examples of such figures, as were Martin Luther King, Jr. Caesar Chavez, and Gandhi. But are such enlightened beings limited to the world of politics and civil rights? What about other extraordinary individuals, who relieve suffering through less conventional means?

It has long amused me to think of Jean-Luc Picard as a sort of 24th-century bodhisattva; a hybrid, perhaps, of Ponderosa-style heroes and the Dalai Lama himself. Both the captain of the *Enterprise* and the Tibetan monk are committed to nonviolence; both are passionate negotiators. And both men are revered by millions as spiritual guides and larger-than-life examples of the best that humanity can strive for.

I searched in vain for the photograph. Though my contacts at Paramount confirmed its existence, no one could remember exactly when, or even where, it had appeared. Several maddening months went by before a sympathetic *Voyager* staffer unearthed the studio's copy of the original slide and sent it to me by FedEx.

It was not quite as advertised, but it was close. The snapshot was taken in 1990 or '91, when His Holiness and his retinue had toured the western United States. In the picture, nearly two dozen monks from the Namgyal Monastery in McLeod Ganj, India (where the Dalai Lama now lives) are crowded onto the *Enterprise*'s transporter pad, surrounding the pale-faced Data. The Dalai Lama himself is not present, but many of his most important attendants—including his ritual master, Tenzin Dakpa Tashi—are. His Holiness, I deduced, might also be a fan, even if his hectic schedule had made a visit to the set impossible.

Twenty to beam up: Data and the Namgyal monks on the *Enterprise* transporter.

It was a leg to stand on. I sent a fax to the Dalai Lama's office, requesting an interview. In late January—while I was visiting Arthur C. Clarke in Sri Lanka—a reply arrived. My audience was approved, and scheduled for February 15.

————

Ten hours by overnight train, on the Jammu Mail from Delhi to Pathankot; three more by taxi to Dharamsala, through the greenery of Punjab. From there it's a stomach-churning ride up switchback roads to McLeod Ganj, a former British hill station more than a mile above the Indian plains. The snowy peaks of the Dhauladhar Range rise above the town like frosted biscuits, Hokusai waves, chipped Baccarat bowls.

McLeod Ganj is a world apart from the truck-breath, deaf-making diesel realm of New Delhi. There are birds tweeting, kids laughing, and the percussive splash of slop buckets emptying from overhead windows. Along muddy thoroughfares, stray cows and squatting vegetable wallahs face each other in a delicate truce. Eight-year-old monks cluster around the doors of darkened video theaters, gawking at the latest Jackie Chan and Jean-Claude van Damme movies. Scores of shops sell prayer flags and curios, earrings and anklets, Nivea cream and Halls mentholyptus lozenges.

A sense of expectation hangs in the air. The Dalai Lama's annual teaching will begin in two weeks, and the population of foreign visitors is swelling steadily. Soon, thousands of curiosity seekers and Buddhist devotees will swarm through the narrow streets.

For the time being, though, things are calm. In the evening, savvy travelers head for the Green Hotel, where an expatriate chef prepares Sicilian cuisine. Strolling in, I hear a loud conversation: a half-dozen people are arguing about Area 51, the top-secret military facility where research on captured UFOs has allegedly taken place. As I approach their table, I'm greeted by two American monks: Thupten, a baby-faced, dirigible-sized former Navy man, and his rail-thin companion, Tenzin, a former aide to General Colin Powell. Both monks are huge *Star Trek* fans. We spend the evening wolfing down lasagna, rehashing favorite TNG episodes, and debating whether or not Tribbles have Buddha nature.

My interview with the Dalai Lama is scheduled for the next afternoon. At lunchtime I stop by the office of the Tibetan Womens'

Congress to print out my questions. Afterward I hike to a nearby waterfall, several kilometers up a packed dirt road. It's good to be away from the hubbub of town, in a place where the sky is not subdivided by power lines and the hills rise up in an unbroken wave of whale blue shale. A dozen monks are washing their clothes in the river; the yellow and vermilion of their robes is handsomely photogenic against the stones. And I think to myself: *Having an audience with the Dalai Lama and asking him about* Star Trek *is like meeting the Buddha and asking him to recommend a good Indian restaurant.*

A fifteen-minute walk down the main drag leads to the Namgyal complex, which shelters the residence of His Holiness. After much paperwork and an intimate body search, I'm escorted to the house itself. It is pale yellow, almost institutional in architecture; a far cry from the Potala Palace. Inside, the air is chilly. A potbellied stove in the waiting room radiates no heat. The walls are cluttered with medals, citations, and honorary degrees. I snoop around for a glimpse of the Nobel Peace Prize, awarded to the Dalai Lama in 1989 for his (so far futile) efforts to wrest Tibetan autonomy from the occupying Chinese.

Despite his many honors, Tenzin Gyatso—the fourteenth Dalai Lama—is a man without airs. He describes himself as a "simple Buddhist monk," whose most cherished wish is to live a life of retreat and meditation. That's not going to happen. As the most eloquent and charismatic spokesman for the Tibetan diaspora, he is continually besieged by requests for audiences and interviews, while his responsibilities as a spiritual leader occupy the remainder of his time.

Ten minutes later I'm led through French doors and into the audience room. Here it is warmer, and there are couches arrayed beneath a large altar. I sit down, setting my notebook on a low table. Then I rise abruptly, for His Holiness is being escorted into the room.

The Dalai Lama appears fit and alert. His eyes are welcoming, curious, and brightly amused. It's been perhaps a week since he last shaved his head, and the stubble on his scalp shows less gray than I would have thought. At sixty-two, he appears ageless. Though he tends to stoop—out of humility, I suppose—he is tall and big-boned, born in the rough-and-tumble landscape of northeastern Tibet.

His Holiness, the XIV Dalai Lama, in Dharamsala. (Photo by Brent Stirton.)

But this is merely his outward appearance. Far more

profound is the effect of his personality. The cynical tongue is stilled: here is the Loveliest Man in the World. His humility, wisdom, and kindness illuminate the room like halogen bulbs. Offering him the traditional greeting of a *kata*—a white silk scarf—I nearly giggle with pleasure. It is difficult to overstate how *safe* I feel. No one's gonna get you while you're in this presence: not the Chinese, or the Martians, or the IRS.

His Holiness clearly remembers using his telescope as a boy. He recalls turning it away from the streets of Lhasa, and directing its lens toward the Sun (with a proper filter, he assures me) and Moon. This was in the 1940s. By the time men walked on the Moon, he was already in exile. Even so, he followed the lunar landings on All-India Radio.

"Some of our Tibetan scholars," the Dalai Lama exclaims, "still do not believe it happened!" From the Moon's appearance in the Project Apollo photographs, the scholars were convinced that the astronauts had actually landed atop Mount Meru, the physical and spiritual center of Buddhist cosmology.

He dismissed such claims. The Dalai Lama's interest in modern astronomy had flowered in the early 1960s. "I owned at least ten books about the Moon, Sun and stars," he says. "At that time, I even remembered all the distances to the different planets. Since then I have forgotten!" He laughs loudly. "So, you see, I was fully convinced of the scientific explanation about cosmology."

Still, he continued to draw on Tibet's time-honored sources. Buddhist scriptures, His Holiness tells me, speak of limitless worlds, of endless galaxies and parallel universes. These are not necessarily visible to our "gross senses," but may be perceived only through "subtle mind": a skill requiring years of practice in the art of meditation.

"Different scriptures," he says, "offer different explanations about the universe. This opens up our minds to many possibilities; not just the scientific."

I ask the Dalai Lama if moving toward the stars—to "seek out new life and new civilizations"—is humanity's destiny. He raises his eyebrows.

"I don't know," he replies. "I don't think that it's humanity's destiny. No harm, to try to reach those areas and settle—but it is quite certain that the whole world cannot shift there. In any case, our planet, this planet, will always be humanity's home."

"What does Tibetan Buddhism say about the possibility of life on other worlds?"

LAZYBONES (EL PEREZOSO)

Pablo Neruda
(translated by Alastair Reid)

They will continue wandering,
these things of steel among the stars,
and worn-out men will still go up,
to brutalize the placid moon.
There, they will found their
  pharmacies.

In this time of the swollen grape,
the wine begins to come to life
between the sea and the mountain
  ranges.

In Chile now, cherries are dancing,
the dark mysterious girls are singing,
and in guitars, water is shining.

The sun is touching every door
and making wonder of the wheat.

The first wine is pink in colour,
is sweet with the sweetness of a child,
the second wine is able-bodied,
strong like the voice of a sailor,
the third wine is topaz, is
a poppy and a fire in one.

My house has both the sea and the
  earth,
my woman has great eyes
the colour of wild hazelnut,
when night comes down, the sea
puts on a dress of white and green,
and later the moon in the spindrift
  foam
dreams like a sea-green girl.

I have no wish to change my planet.

"Sentient forms of life—similar to human beings—do exist on other planets," the Dalai Lama replies. "Not necessarily in our solar system, or even in our universe, but beyond."

"Do you *believe* this," I ask, "or do you *know* this?"

"Believe," he answers without hesitation. "So far, I haven't met any person who recalls a previous life from another galaxy." Still, he insists, such beings doubtless exist—probably with five sense organs and emotional capabilities similar to our own. All will be capable of suffering and compassion; all will be responsive to kindness or cruelty.

"According to both Western cosmology and Tibetan Buddhism," I say, "everything in the universe was created from the same microcosmic particles. So would extraterrestrials be subject to the laws of karma and reincarnation?"

"Yes! Yes! Maybe, I think, they will have a different form. But generally speaking, the same laws. Perhaps," he adds thoughtfully, "some differences in dealing with anger, and other negative emotions. But basically, the same."

But our meetings with these ETs, the Dalai Lama warns, must be motivated by good intentions. "Do we find a new neighbor? Make a new friend? Then, positive!" he declares. "But find a new neighbor, create problems and fight—then, more suffering! If our planet is not a stable, compassionate world, even if we meet someone out there, it will only create an additional enemy. If we use the same intentions as we do here—conquer, exploit—well, they're sentient beings, too! They also have ideas that are selfish! They will retaliate!

But if we cultivate a nonviolent approach and visit with a warm heart—good!" He leans forward, slapping me powerfully on the knee.

"If Your Holiness were given the opportunity to orbit the Earth in the space shuttle," I inquire, "would you accept?"

There is a moment's silence. The Dalai Lama stares at me with wide eyes before replying. "If very safe—then I will go!" He laughs uproariously and wipes his eyes on the sleeve of his robe.

"Is this a dream of yours? To view the Earth from orbit?"

"Interesting . . ." He nods, considering the question seriously. "But not *essential*. Still much work to be done here, on this Earth. Until there is no poverty, no illness. Once everything is okay on this planet—no further problems—then we'll need a holiday!"

I steel myself, and ask the Dalai Lama about *Star Trek*. Has His Holiness ever watched the show on Indian television? Indeed he has, but only the original series. He recalls with hilarity the "man with the big ears": Spock.

The previous day, I tell him, I'd met with Tenzin Dakpa Tashi, the ritual master who appears in the snapshot taken while the Namgyal monks were touring Paramount Pictures. Tashi had proposed that the people who write *Star Trek*—Brannon Braga and Ron Moore, for example—might unconsciously be anticipating *Shambhala*: a peaceful, ideal realm that, according to Buddhist texts, will emerge on Earth several centuries in the future. He'd raised a compelling point. The defining features of Roddenberry's world—goodwill among all beings, a peaceful planet, and the ability to explore the galaxy with our best foot forward—are very similar to Tashi's description of a mythical Buddhist utopia. Yet another example, perhaps, of Gene's Vision touching a chord in the collective unconscious.

"Your Holiness," I ask, "Do you believe that our space-faring future, as portrayed in the *Star Trek* programs, may be a vision of Shambhala?"

He ponders the question for a moment. Then he crouches back in his chair and mimes aiming a phaser at me. "Even in the future, many unique weapons!" The Dalai Lama grins impishly. "So not much different than now, I think!"

Our allotted time has ended, but His Holiness seems to be enjoying our chat. Having the ear of the Dalai Lama is a rare occurrence in my life, so I pose a few more questions. Inspired by the slide of the Namgyal monks surrounding Data, I ask about artificial intelligence.

The British mathematician and logician Alan Turing, I explain, developed a famous test to determine whether or not a computer could be considered conscious. In his "Turing Test," a computer and a human subject are concealed in separate rooms. An interrogator asks questions of both via a terminal, not knowing which is which. If the questioner cannot tell, from the replies, which respondent is human and which is a machine, the computer has "passed."

I ask if the Dalai Lama has a similar test; one which would enable him to decide to his own satisfaction whether or not a machine or robot possessed consciousness.

"If a machine *acts* like a sentient being," he replies, "I think that it should be considered a sentient being. A new kind of sentient being." Words are not enough; in the Buddhist belief system, the force generated by one's actions—karma—is crucial. Still, His Holiness says, Buddhist scriptures speak of different ways of taking birth in this world. The traditional way is through the womb, but other means are also possible. These might be through chemical or even electrical processes. If conscious computers are developed, they will deserve the same respect we give to sentient beings.

Star Trek, of course, assumes a very cozy relationship between humans and technology. Machines are our constant companions. From quick spanks at communicator badges to full-body sizzles beneath the transporter beam, there's rarely a scene that doesn't include a little dance between the characters and their props. Does His Holiness find this an alarming vision? Is it possible, on general principle, for reliance upon technology to exceed healthy limits?

The Dalai Lama leans forward, regarding me mischievously. "If a machine is ever created that can instantly make a good heart, a warm heart," he pronounces, "without any need for meditation or practice..." He falls back in his chair, laughing. "Then I will immediately tell our Chinese brothers and sisters 'Please! You buy this!' "

I had expected the Dalai Lama to come down on one side or another of these issues. But the common thread in his responses, I'm discovering, is the expansive view that technology itself is neither good nor evil. Even his reply to my comments about the Internet, and the plague of information addiction that seems to be sweeping the globe, surprises me.

"One aspect of buddha-hood," he reminds me, "is *omniscience*. So, once again, the gathering of information is neither good nor bad. In this case—and in all cases!—everything depends upon intention! It is always a matter of motivation, and result. So long as no harm to others, then I think, okay!"

The final question on my notepad is so absurd that I'm worried it might offend him. So far, though, my venerable host has shown only the best humor. I take the plunge.

"You've been quoted as saying," I begin, "that, depending on the view of the Tibetan people, you may be 'the last Dalai Lama.' Here's a twist on that issue. Through the science of cloning, it may be possible—in the near future—to take some DNA from Your Holiness, and use it to create potentially endless reproductions of yourself. If this were done, you could *literally* be the last Dalai Lama—for centuries to come! What do you think of that?"

The monk and his attendants laugh so loudly that the needles on my tape recorder leap off the scale. "You can reproduce my physical body," the Dalai Lama quips at last. "But mind?" He taps his skull, the mythic repository of countless lifetimes. "I don't think so!"

———

That evening I return to the Green Hotel for dinner. Thupten and Tenzin are waiting; they listen attentively as I describe my interview, amazed by the sensible replies I received to some admittedly silly questions. When I get to the part about the aliens, though—and the Dalai's Lama statement that they will probably have similar senses and be capable of both suffering and compassion—Thupten eyes me dubiously.

"Is that so?" He plunges a fork into a head-sized wedge of lemon cheesecake. "Did you ask about the Borg?"

DEFINITELY NOT SWEDISH

It's late June, *First Contact*'s final week of production. Los Angeles is an oven; desiccated jacaranda leaves litter the streets like grotesque health food chips. Heat rises from the asphalt in carpet-thick waves, and the air smells of tacos.

Braga, Moore, and I trot to Stage 29 to watch Frakes shoot the eagerly awaited "blow job" scene. The notorious pas de deux between Data (Brent Spiner) and the Borg queen (Alice Krige) comes midway through the film—a point where the bad guys are winning and the home team's prospects seem bleak indeed.

The sets look terrific. *The Enterprise* has been boarded, captured, and transformed into a nefarious Borg hive. Main engineering is a festering techno-jungle, with pipes and catheters dangling like vines above the warp core; I half expect a Borgified Tarzan to come swinging down. Cyborg drones lurk in sparking niches, their waspy uniforms blinking like radar detectors. And dear old Data, lashed to an electrified autopsy table, is the horizontal prisoner of the bald and lascivious Borg queen.

```
Data: Who are you?

Borg queen: I am the Borg.
```

Data: That is a contradiction. The Borg have a collective consciousness. There are no individuals.

Borg queen: I am the beginning, the end, the one who is many. I am the Borg.

Grips creep like pill bugs around the set, following the camera as it tracks Queenie's circuit around the prone android. Frakes is on the edge of his seat, grinning like Bluebeard. I'm right behind him, barely daring to breathe. It's not just me; the scene has everyone in its spell. When Frakes cries "Cut!" a pneumatic exhalation escapes from the spectators and crew.

Moore nudges me with his shoulder. "When we wrote this scene," he whispers, "I visualized it being far more private, somehow. There were Borg working in the shadows; I envisioned them more in the background than they are in this shot. I also imagined a moist, slimy feel—kind of organic. The Borg queen was just a head, floating up above. Now its clicks onto a body." He pauses. "But it's become difficult to remember my original images. I'm always having to reset my mind."

Frakes calls for silence, and the cameras roll again:

Data: Forgive me . . . but the Borg do not evolve, they conquer.

Borg queen: By assimilating other beings into our Collective, we are bringing them closer to perfection.

Data: Somehow I question your motives.

Borg queen: That is because you have not been properly . . . stimulated yet.

Cut. Braga's hands grip the back of Frakes's chair. He gestures toward Spiner. "Brent is acting the scene to perfection. He always gives you something more. And Alice Krige is *perfect.* She finds a weakness, a desire, and exploits it. I've never said this . . . but I've always dug her. Ever since *Ghost Story*—the creepy eroticism that she had."

"I like the way she just *watches* him," Moore adds. "It's both actors. It's their chemistry. She's completely in control. Data is definitely the guy squirming beneath the microscope."

"It's very sadomasochistic," I agree. "And very erotic."

"The hallmarks of *Star Trek*," deadpans Moore.

"It's a sexually charged scene, but what's fun is that it's *subtle*." Braga leans toward my ear. "The Borg queen strips the artificial flesh off of Data's arm and grafts, in its place, a postage stamp–sized square of organic skin: *real* skin. She bends over and blows on it—*and it gets goose pimples.*"

I can already see the MPA rating: PG-13 for violence, intense situations, and oral sex between androids. "Will they shoot the goose bumps today?" I can't imagine how they'll manage it in this heat.

"No, that's VFX: visual effects. Those, along with the other opticals, are done at Industrial Light & Magic, in Marin County."

Moore's still focused on the scene in progress. He reaches out, framing the set with splayed hands. "We'll start with this big, spectacular reveal while Krige is talking. First you'll just see a head—and then her whole body. From the body, it'll go into this scene, and get tighter and tighter—all the way down to Data's skin and the Borg queen's lips. You'll have a nice sense of being drawn into something."

"It's an incredibly sexual moment as you see Data react." Brannon's foot is tapping; he's more animated than I've seen him since his party. "That's what's great about this genre. We can do sex in little, metaphorical ways that are much more sexy than if she actually pulled down his pants and whipped his android dick out. You know what I'm saying?"

I think I do: the joys of consummating Gene's Vision are where you find them.

But the scene, really, is about much more than sex—although neither Braga nor Moore, incredibly enough, seem to acknowledge this. What I'm watching, deliciously executed by Krige and Spiner, is a mask dance, a tango between the bright and dark forks along humanity's path. On one side there's Data, an android so advanced that he owns a cat. On the other there's the Borg queen, the deadly seductress, half vixen, half distributor cap.

It's the very conundrum that Gates McFadden described during our late-night rendezvous on the Vulcan landing set. Technology has become, and will remain, as indispensable to our society as fire. But will it be our dominatrix or our pal? Will it elevate us toward the stars or cuff us down with false promises? This is the real metaphor of *First Contact*, from beginning to end.

"Whose idea was this scene, anyway?"

Moore frowns, concentrating. "I seem to remember that Rick Berman had the image of the blow job. Of the prickly, goose bump hairs. We came in with the idea of the queen and the grafted organic skin."

The scene will take all day to shoot. We relax against a Turbolift door, watching the grips and gaffers change the lighting. A dozen extras in rubber Borg suits cluster in front of a fan, trying desperately to cool off. Makeup was at 3:30 A.M.; they've been wearing these body condoms for eleven straight hours.

"This film will come out after *Independence Day*," I remark. "The hype for that movie is everywhere. You think *First Contact* can compete?"

BETTER THAN A GROUCHO MARX DISGUISE

BY TOM FARRE, KAREN FRANSE, IAN G. JACOBS, AND HILLARY RETTIG

VARBusiness on TechWeb/February 1, 1997

Rockwell International, the $10 billion defense contractor in Cedar Rapids, Iowa, is converting at least some of its operations to civilian commerce. It's targeting the business market with the newly-released "Trekker 2020," a compact, ruggedized, wearable, speech-recognition-enabled, eyeball-monitor-equipped Pentium computer.

The Trekker makes the user look like a version of the Borg, the aliens from the latest *Star Trek* movie. Judging from the huge crowd waiting to demo one at a recent trade show, "Resistance is futile."

"Absolutely," says Moore. "All those films—*ID4, Mars Attacks, Starship Troopers*—are throwbacks to the 1950s: the paranoia of invasion. Which is fine. It's a fun genre. But *First Contact* is something else. It's a film that says, 'Our destiny is Out There, and it is a *good* thing.' It's a positive message."

"*Star Trek* is really much more about narrative and the characters. This is a lame analogy," Braga admits, "but *Independence Day*'s like a great roller-coaster ride. Whereas *First Contact* is like going on Pirates of the Caribbean. There's a lot more to take in." The bottom line, he concludes, is that *First Contact* is the better movie. There's every reason to believe it will cross over into the non-Trekker audience, and skyrocket past the magical $100 million mark.

Alice Krige stops by to say hello. She's sweetly serene, still embodying the Borg queen's sultry calm. Moore introduces us. I return her smile as best I can. Claws and hooks bite into her naked rubber scalp, and thick blue veins pulse beneath the latex. Her appearance is chilling, yet undeniably arousing.

Braga compliments Krige on her performance and assures her that the tension is building beautifully. "I'm so glad," she croons, "that we have the luxury of doing these scenes in chronological order."

When she walks off, we notice her feet: The Borg queen is wearing pink bunny rabbit slippers.

———

Spiner and Krige finesse their remaining scenes. They're consummate professionals. Watching them work is like listening to a great classical guitarist: you can relax completely, lose yourself in the mastery of the craft. Still, their dance has an aura of melancholy. This is, after all, the last day of primary shooting. Though a few scattered retakes may later be necessary, this marks the formal end of *First Contact*'s production.

Brannon must be reading my mind. "I can't believe it's over," he says. Ron nods silently. "We weren't nearly as involved in the filming of *Generations*," Braga explains. "We were much more hands-ons with this one."

"Do you normally spend a lot of time on the *Voyager* sets as well?"

"Sometimes." He taps his fingers on a backlit engineering schematic. "But I often forget it's just a television show. I become so much a part of this universe that I find myself immersed in heated philosophical debates about time travel and aliens, and I have to stop myself and say, '*Wait*! What I'm talking about isn't even *real*!'"

Moore grins; he could be an Eagle Scout on a Paramount tour. "There is nothing quite as cool," he declares, "as writing this stuff down and then *seeing* it. Something that you've created in your little office. You hack away at your computer, and then you come here and visit the starship *Enterprise*." His eyes dart around in fascination. "That's the best part of my job: I get to stand on the *Enterprise*."

"Mine, too," I reply.

"When it's all done, and the burden is off . . . this is the best time." Braga gazes across the set, the warp core throbbing in his glasses. "In the end, when Ron and I sit down in that movie theater, we're just like everybody else. We're there to watch the movie, and see it all come to life."

Moore and Braga are called off to a production meeting, and depart with cursory waves. I should leave now as well. My chaperones have vanished, and I've got a plane to catch. But I linger a while longer, unable to pull myself away.

There are corners of space-time we will visit only once: places where fantasy and reality commingle, and life takes on a dreamlike aspect.

Though the fleeting nature of these events is what makes them so intense, knowing this fact makes little difference. We can't bear to see such moments end.

Standing on the Borgified *Enterprise*, surrounded by this convincing but temporary world, I recall a ritual I witnessed at a San Francisco museum years ago. After months of painstaking work, Tibetan monks were completing a six-foot-wide sand mandala in the museum's atrium. They had placed countless particles of colored sand in an ancient pattern, creating a circular tapestry of exquisite detail. More than a mere picture, this was a sacred residence; a powerful deity named Kalachakra dwelt in its center. Adept meditation would cause the finished mandala to blossom into Kalachakra's palace: a Buddhist paradise with jeweled gates opening to the four directions.

Mandalas like these are exercises not in visual art, but in the practice of self-realization. The perfect world they depict is neither illusory nor theoretical; it is our own Earth, transformed by wisdom and compassion.

But a sand mandala, beautiful as it may be, is nothing more than a vehicle. When the rituals attending its creation are complete, the design is swept away. The grains of sand are gathered up and spilled into the sea.

Likewise, the *Enterprise* 1701-E will not exist much longer. The alchemical spells that transformed paint, plywood, and Plexiglas into a Sovereign-class starship will be broken, and the coach will be a pumpkin again. *First Contact's* intricate sets will be dismantled, hammered apart, and recycled. Divorced from any earthly setting, existing only on celluloid and magnetic tape, the scenes and images I've witnessed these past weeks—Captain Picard's victory over the Borg, Cochrane's historic flight, humanity's invitation to the stars—will cross the world in big flat cans. They will flicker on screens from Kansas City to Kashi. From there, they will travel to a deeper place still. Sooner or later, the world they envision may bloom.

———————

My pilgrimage to *Star Trek's* foundry, with its thousand-watt lights and Mylar stars, has been a passage to Oz. But my visa has expired, and the Munchkins are looking at me funny. It's time to click my heels.

I exit the stage, pushing through the heavy metal door into blinding sunlight, back into the open-air grill of Los Angeles. Clouds wilt in the sky, and the air tastes like mercury. In the distance I hear gunshots, and the pneumatic chop of helicopter blades. I climb into my rented Grand Am, feel under the seat for my machete, and drive back to the 20th century.

HOLD THE CHICKEN

Opening night of *First Contact* at the Grand Lake Theatre is completely sold out. At 8:45, manager Roger Brown paces near the ticket booth, staring at the ticket holders massed against the plate glass doors like Mongol hordes.

Oakland's Grand Lake is one of the most beautiful cinemas on the West Coast. Built as a combination vaudeville and movie house, it opened in 1926 with *The First Year*—the screen version of John Golden's successful stage play—preceded by *Felix the Cat in Blunderland*. Above the marquee, a three-story-high roof sign, sizzling with incandescent fireworks, throws multicolored reflections onto the waters of Lake Merritt. Now the anchor of a five-theater multiplex, the main auditorium still seats 875, making it one of the biggest first-run houses in North America. There's even a Wurlitzer organ, trotted out for special occasions.

"This is our first sellout," Brown says, "since *Jurassic Park*. It's especially amazing because the movie's spread so thin—it's playing in at least six other theaters, in the area."

"Four thousand theaters nationwide," I volunteer.

"*What?* That's insane . . ."

A gaunt young man with a shaggy red mustache, Brown looks thrilled and vaguely nauseated. He's terrified that the late show will be oversold. He miscalculated for the seven o'clock, and had to turn away more than forty ticket holders; the 9:30 screening, meanwhile, sold out well in advance. Since fire regulations in California movie theaters prohibit standing room, everyone who can't find a seat will have to go home.

That will include me.

This was more than bad planning. I was the victim of my own spite. The truth of the matter is that I have no business being in Oakland at all. I was certain I'd spend this evening in Hollywood. Last spring, during an unguarded moment, Brannon Braga had handed me a fabulous invitation. On the opening night of *Generations*, he told me, Ron Moore and he had hired a stretch limousine and cruised greater Los Angeles, ducking into theaters and drinking in audience reactions. On Friday, November 22, they would perform the same rite for *First Contact*. Would I like to join them?

For six months I'd banked on the event. There could be no better way to experience the premiere. The chemistry between the two writers, as they lapped up their richly deserved kudos, would be priceless.

While I was booking my ticket to Burbank in early November, I'd faced a dilemma. Brannon might have pre-opening night plans—some kind of cast or studio party. I didn't want to crowd him. Should I arrive on Thursday evening, or on Friday? I phoned his office to find out which he'd prefer. The next morning, his secretary returned my call. Brannon was terribly sorry, he said, but Rick Berman had just asked Brannon and Ron to join him in *his* limousine. It was out of the question for them to refuse . . .

I set down the receiver in a state of shock, my gleeful anticipation shattered. Angry and disappointed, I decided to shun opening night altogether. Fuck 'em! I washed my hands of it, making a date with my girlfriend instead. At 7:30 on the dot, I arrived at her house for an evening of onion-smothered chicken and sleaze-hall blues. It didn't work. I got so mournful and distracted so fast that she heaved her dinner out of the oven, shrouded it in foil, and shoved me toward the door.

"You've got to be there," she said. "The chicken can wait."

At 9:15 the vomitory doors burst open, and the first wave of dazed-looking humanity breaks from the theater. I accost a couple leaving the show. "So whad'ya think?"

"Awesome," the woman beams. "Almost as good as *The Wrath of Khan*..."

"Two thumbs up?"

Her partner laughs. "I don't have *enough* thumbs."

As the 7 o'clock crowd flows out, Brown supplies an interesting factoid. The economics of the film industry are constructed, he says, so that it's in a studio's best interest to have a big opening weekend. Paramount will take home 90 percent of opening week sales, 80 percent of the second week, and 70 percent of the third. After that the split falls off to a steady 60/40. All the hype and promotional expenses surrounding these openings suddenly makes sense.

With ten minutes until show time, I move outside to canvas the crowd. Darrin Laurelsson, a powerfully built black man wearing a thick velvet cloak, is among the first in line. He's been waiting since 5:00. A Trekker all his life, he arrived at opening night with a group of thirty-six friends.

"We all grew up together," Laurelsson explains. "A lot of us were Trek babies."

"How so?"

"Our mothers let dinner burn because they were watching *Star Trek*."

Farther back I run into Todd Baeson—the only fan in a Starfleet uniform. I glance at his collar, noting the modest pair of pips.

"Just a lieutenant?"

"Well, I give myself one for every opening night. I started with *Generations*..."

There's a flurry behind us as a few moviegoers demand to know who and what I am. "I'm one of you," I explain and turn back to Baeson. "You have a favorite episode?"

"Definitely. 'Arena,' from the original series. The one where Kirk is stranded on a planet with that giant, lizard-headed Gorn, and has to make a weapon from whatever stuff is lying on the..."

" '*An incredible fortune in stones*,' " I interrupt, quoting directly from the episode. " '*Yet I would trade them all for a hand phaser, or a good solid club...*' "

There's a stunned silence. A bushy-haired, cigar-smoking kid behind us—think Kramer—gapes at me. "You're not one of us," he says, tossing his mane. "You're *waaay* more obsessed."

By now the line stretches around the block, a frenetic millipede whose jaws gnaw at the ticket window. Suffering from a sudden attack of demophobia, I run back into the lobby.

The ticket ripper nudges Brown's arm. "You ready?"

"In a second." Brown turns to me. "You'll have to get out of the way."

"Where?" I still don't have a ticket.

"Uh, dunno . . ."

I gesture with my head to the theater. "How about in there?"

He winces with bottled chagrin, but nods. "Go on."

I race into the auditorium. It is empty and silent: the eye of the cyclone. Popcorn, cups, and Hot Tamales are strewn about the floor; a lost neck warmer lies in the aisle. I stare about in awe. This chaotic, littered theater, with its domed ceiling, neoclassical golden urns, and acres of brocaded velvet, will soon be a virtual starship itself—transporting a crew of 875 to whatever destination the boys in the Hart Building have charted for them. I find a seat, kick aside an empty carton of Junior Mints, and steel myself for the deluge.

Roger drops the ropes, and the masses pour in. There is a scramble for the choicest seats and a feeding frenzy for the second best, followed by a flurry of Brownian motion. Within fifteen minutes the crowd has sieved down, and every seat in the house is filled. There is something familiar about the settling-in process; it's like one of those plastic puzzles where you have to tilt and shake a bunch of tiny metal balls into the appropriate holes.

I look toward the front of the theater. Something's afoot . . . could it be? *Yes!* There is an enormous cheer as the mighty Wurlitzer rears up, lofted upon its hydraulic dais, before the electrified crowd. Chinese and Mexicans, Hmong and African Americans, Bangalorian nerds and transplanted New York Jews, slackers with nose rings, homeboys in Nikes, women with kohl-blackened eyes, fat kids up to their elbows in real buttered popcorn, all of Oakland has come together to welcome this newest member of the *Star Trek* family, this $40 million baby that Ron and Brannon have been burping all summer.

My rods and cones sit up. There is a lull in the collective din and a suddenly perceptible drop in the light level. Then sheer pandemonium—for the music abruptly begins.

You've never heard Jerry Goldsmith's *Star Trek: The Next Generation* theme until you've heard it played on a wind-powered Wurlitzer in the Grand Lake Theatre. The audacious strains penetrate every corner of the hall, alive with the adenoidal nostalgia of the silent-film era. The wacky use of 1920s technology to introduce a 24th-century space saga in a 1990s movie theater is too poignant to bear. I find myself in tears.

It's a strange experience, watching a movie that one has seen being made—like eating in a glitzy restaurant after spending a few months in the kitchen. A seemingly impossible transformation occurs between the raw ingredients and finished product. All the stems and gristle have been trimmed away; whole scenes that Braga and Moore agonized over are gone, consigned to the cutting room floor. Still—despite my potentially intrusive insider's view—I effortlessly surrender to the story. I forget about the tacked-up cardboard, the giant Ritter fans, the masking tape marks on the deck of the main bridge. The whole is greater than the sum of its parts. *First Contact* barrels along with relentless energy, a pan-galactic feast. *They done good*, I think to myself, listening to the audience cheer in all the right places.

When it's all over I remain in my seat, watching the house empty. The racial panoply of Oakland is the world in microcosm, and as I study people's faces, I realize that the space brats have done it again. The eighth film in the *Star Trek* canon will amaze Trekkers all over the planet. From Westminister to Ouagadougou, the myth will endure. There is literally no end in sight.

I grab my jacket and move outside, the last one to leave the theater. Just overhead, the thousand bulbs of the Grand Lake's immense roof sign blink out. The show is over; my chicken awaits.

Stepping from beneath the darkened marquee, I stare up at the sky. It is startling, after this long journey into deep space, to see the actual stars.

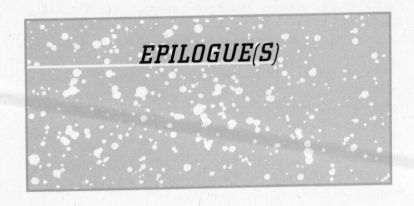

EPILOGUE(S)

I. The People's Republic of Borgistan

First Contact grossed over $95 million in U.S. theater receipts. The fact that it was the highest-grossing *Star Trek* movie in history is moderately satisfying to Brannon Braga. Still, a year after he and Ron Moore locked the script in Moore's Hart Building office, Braga paces his living room with a restless stride.

"It still irks me that it didn't cross the $100 million mark domestically." He slaps a Marlboro Light out of a tight new pack. "If it tops that, it's a certified smash hit."

"Did the movie do what you hoped it would?"

"Did it break out of the genre? No. Was it the next *Independence Day*? No. But hey—it's a *Star Trek* movie."

And hey—a good *Star Trek* movie is good enough for Paramount. The studio immediately began budgeting for the sequel. In June of 1997, *Daily Variety* had reported that Patrick Stewart had been offered $12 million—more than twice his fee for *First Contact*—to star in the ninth *Trek* film, *Insurrection*. Jonathan Frakes would again direct.

Braga turned down Berman's offer to write the screenplay. With Jeri Taylor on the verge of retirement, he's slated to take the helm as *Star Trek: Voyager*'s executive producer. It's an overwhelming job, and he's already in training. During my visit he's working days, nights, and weekends, rewriting scripts for the show's fourth season. He screens some dailies for me on his home television. They're awesome. Adding actress Jeri Ryan as Seven of Nine was a stroke of genius. She's totally hypnotic, a master of the cool and deadly regard—when I can tear my eyes off her latex.

"The breasts are a bit of a problem," Braga confirms. "They aren't really that big, but the costume is highly reflective. And the lighting comes too much from above. So it's become like 'Russ Meyer in Space' at this point. We're trying to fix that, because our intention was not to have that 3-D effect."

The intention was to deliver to viewers what *Voyager* initially promised: a strong Borg presence on the series. And it may have worked. The show's ratings seem to be climbing. Even the media, which was writing *Voyager*'s obituary in 1996, has praised the new season's opening episodes.

"1997 has been a very important year," says Braga. "We're getting ten times as much fan mail, and an embarrassing amount of publicity. The general feeling is that *Voyager* is a different show. It's leaner, meaner, and more action-oriented, with a lot more sex appeal."

I wonder if he, Rick Berman, and Jeri Taylor haven't tapped into a deeper vein as well. The Borg may be to the 1990s what the Klingons were to the 1960s: a reflection of America's political antipodes. When the original *Star Trek* introduced Klingons, they were transparent reflections of the Soviet menace: gruff, imperialistic, and ruthless. The Borg, on the other hand, seem to express our fears of a more contemporary juggernaut: China.

"That's interesting," Braga nods. "The Borg, to me, represent the antithesis of the American obsession with the individual. We're obsessed with the rights of the individual, and cultivating individualistic children. The Borg are the ultimate threat to such sensibilities. You lose all individuality, and are assimilated into a big hive mind."

But such subtleties might tend to get buried, at least at first, beneath critical evaluation of Ryan's spectacular hardware.

Braga bristles. "Needless to say, we were immediately accused of stooping to the lowest common denominator: putting tits and ass on the show. But our idea was to add a great Borg character. Does it hurt that she's a babe? I don't think so. The two things *Voyager* needed at the beginning of this new season were a new character to spice things up—

to add tension and interest—and a little sexuality. We saw hundreds of actresses. It took a long time; it's rare to find a beautiful woman who can act. But we finally lucked out, and found Jeri Ryan. And now that they've seen her perform, Americans seems to have embraced her."

Indeed they have. To paraphrase P. T. Barnum: No one ever went broke underestimating the horniness of the 18-to-30 male demographic group. But I don't underestimate Ryan, either; she'll appeal to hip, tough chicks—the Xena, Madonna, and Camille Paglia set—as well. My personal prediction is that Seven of Nine will become the most popular character on any *Star Trek* show since the original series . . . since Spock himself.

And who knows? Sophisticated Chinese might one day adopt the brilliant, conflicted Seven of Nine as their own role model—just as the Japanese have adopted Data.

Now *that* would be a cultural revolution.

II. Roddenberry's Ashes

On a warm spring afternoon in 1997, several tablespoons of Gene Roddenberry's ashes were fired into orbit aboard a Pegasus rocket.

The Great Bird's ashes were in good company. A dash of Timothy Leary also made the trip, as did the the residue of twenty-two other individuals and a host of science experiments. The families of the deceased, including Gene's widow, Majel Barrett-Roddenberry, paid $4,800 each for shipping and handling.

The cylindrical can containing these ashes, which were packed into individual tubes the size of Ashton cigars, will circle Earth for six years. When the satellite's orbit decays, the bright signature of a shooting star will etch the night sky. The spacecraft, and everything on it, will be incinerated down to the atomic level, becoming part and parcel of the atmosphere.

For LSD guru Leary, the send-off seems somehow appropriate. He'd have relished the notion that everyone on Earth would, at some point, inhale a minor dose of him.

As for Gene—well, I think we should have waited. Roddenberry's ashes don't belong in a shallow orbit. They should be tucked into the armature of some interstellar probe, along with half-a-dozen digitally encoded episodes from the four *Star Trek* series. Someday, a zillion years from now, human (or humanoid) space-farers will catch up with the probe, and discover the tiny shrine. By then, of course, Rodden-berry's dreams will have hopefully come true—and our progeny will know exactly who to thank.

III. Breakfast on Mars

Friday, July 4, 1997: The sun rises over Ares Vallis on Mars at 2:00 P.M., Pacific time.

At the same moment, a tribute to *Star Trek* creator Gene Rodden-berry begins in the packed auditorium of the Pasadena Civic Center. The homage is part of Planetfest '97, a three-day Mars-watching event sponsored by the Planetary Society.

It's their third such shindig. The first was held in 1981, with a live display of the images from *Voyager 2*'s Saturn flyby. Planetfest '89 came next, when the same spacecraft whizzed past Neptune.

Despite the success of the two previous fests, no one expected such a massive turnout this time. The scheduled speakers—science fiction writers, astronauts, and members of the Mars team—are as thrilling to this assembly as movie stars. Exhibitors run the gamut, from the University of Arizona (whose team designed *Pathfinder*'s 3-D imaging camera) to Space Camp, California. Michael and Denise Okuda are on hand, signing their *Star Trek Encyclopedia*; the Meade Telescope Company is raffling off a ten-inch reflector. Merchants in modular booths hawk everything from Mars globes to *Space Odyssey* screen savers.

It's one-quarter science fair, three-quarters religious revival. If you were to ask any of the more than seven thousand attendees what the message was, each one would tell you the same thing: *It's time to go back*. Go back where? *Out there*.

After a two-decade hiatus, that journey is again underway. One hundred fifty million miles from Pasadena, the first rays of morning sunshine strike the solar panels of the *Mars Pathfinder*. Silently, instantly, the charging of the spacecraft's solar batteries begins.

Society president Bruce Murray, a Caltech professor of planetary science and geology, is the first at the main stage podium. The movement toward racial diversity in space exploration, he declares reverently, all started with Gene Roddenberry's conviction that people of all races would join in the journey to the stars. Next up is former astronaut Buzz Aldrin, the second man to walk on the Moon. With his crimson

Edwin "Buzz" Aldrin,
Merlin of moonwalkers.

suit, planetary tie, and piercing blue eyes, Aldrin—who'd earlier evoked moans of rapture with his elaborate scheme to place tourist hotels in translunar orbit—looks like a modern-day Merlin. He, too, has high praise for Roddenberry, who "bridged the gap" between our abilities and our destiny. "A *whole* people," Aldrin concludes, "must have the ability to nurture the Earth—and the pride to go to Mars."

Indeed, the very motto of Planetfest '97 is "Earth Invades Mars." The gag notwithstanding, I think I hear a note of resignation in the slogan. All hope of finding intelligent life on the red planet, hostile or friendly, is well and truly gone. But if we don't like the news from Mars (as radio journalist Scoop Nisker would say), we'll have to go out and make some of our own.

An hour after the Martian sunrise, *Pathfinder*'s camera scans the heavens in search of the distant sun. Once the lens is accurately oriented, the space probe's high-gain communications antenna is deployed. It pans across the brick-hued sky, pointing at last to Earth.

A few seconds later, the onboard computer phones home.

Back at the convention center, *Voyager* cast member Tim Russ takes the microphone. "I'm not a Vulcan," Russ announces, "but I play one on TV . . ." The old saw draws megayuks from the many *Trek* fans scattered throughout the auditorium. Russ pronounces a few words of gratitude to Gene Roddenberry, to whom he owes his job. He then conveys his admiration for *Pathfinder*, which has made it to Mars without the benefit of *Voyager*'s warp drive.

"Probably just as well." He shrugs. "There's always something going wrong with our ship anyway."

In the beat between Russ's joke and the audience reaction, the screen behind him flares to life. A video camera mounted in JPL's Space Flight Operations Facility (SFOF) broadcasts a live feed of the celebration in progress at mission control. Flight System Manager Brian Muirhead bearhugs Project Manager Tony Spear; they're surrounded by a dozen other people who look like they've just dropped Ecstasy. In a dry, nasal twang—the official accent of all space jockeys, regardless of hair length—Robin Vaughn, a member of the navigation team, proclaims "nominal" results. Every aspect of the landing, she announces, has met or exceeded expectations. Several packets of technospeak follow, each greeted by cheers from the assembled neogeeks.

I turn to JPL engineer Steve Matousek, who is sitting beside me in the hushed auditorium, for a translation.

"The first data just came in from *Pathfinder*" he whispers. "First of all, it landed right-side up. The spacecraft is resting flat; there was only a 30 percent chance of that." Nearby spectators get wind that Matousek knows what's up, and glom on to our conversation. "The antenna found the Earth with no problem, all the spacecraft's systems are functioning . . ." People two rows up are starting to turn around. ". . . and signal strength is running within one-tenth of a decibel. It's *fantastic*." He shakes his head; by now there are thirty people hanging on his every word. "It's unreal. Perfect. Almost too good to be true."

At precisely 4:28 P.M., the first live pictures from Mars in twenty-one years reach Earth. The photographs are received at SFOF, and fed in real time to the video projector at Planetfest '97. One by one they appear on the enormous screen. Each new image is met with wild cheers. "Twist and Shout" plays somewhere in the background, probably over at mission control.

It's like a giant orgasm after years of foreplay. For the next few days, the longing that brought everyone together in this room will be satisfied.

The black-and-white pictures themselves are astonishing. Ares Vallis appears to be a bone-dry plain, strewn with very big rocks. Soft hills rise in the distance. The scene is uncannily familiar; it could be a campsite in South Dakota's Badlands.

I nudge Matousek. "Is that a calculator in the sand?"

"It does look a little too much," he observes warily, "like the Mars yard . . ."

Earlier in the day I'd heard that Richard Hoagland—a vocal proponent of the "Face on Mars," who also believes that NASA is suppressing images of ancient structures on the Moon—had stationed himself outside the JPL pressroom to promote his various obsessions. Today's events, I realize, demonstrate how unlikely such theories are. Never has information so exotic, or potentially risky, been more cheerfully exposed. *Pathfinder*'s images are appearing before us at the same moment they are seen by Project Manager Tony Spear, Vice President Al Gore, and Jay Leno. If the camera was to reveal a spired skyline—or even a tree—no one on Earth could cover it up. The information would be global coin within twenty-four hours.

Each new photo of the Martian landscape draws shouts and whistles from the thousands of people jammed into the auditorium. There's an adrenalized sense of history-in-the-making, and a surging sense of pride in America's legendary ability (so baffling to my Bangalorian architect friend) to make things work. What makes it infinitely more dramatic is the fact that Mars, its stark lifelessness notwithstanding, looks so much like Earth. The mood in the auditorium is one of giddy reunion, as if we've suddenly discovered a distant sibling. You can feel the brainwaves pulsing through the room: *We can go to Mars*, everyone is thinking. *It belongs to us.*

And the individual being honored at this precise moment is Gene Roddenberry. Not Clinton, Bush, or Reagan; not Tony Spear, or even the Planetary Society's co-founder, the late Carl Sagan. The tribute overlapping this moment is dedicated to the man who created *Star Trek,* and kept the dream of space exploration alive.

Shit, I'm thinking. *Maybe he was a genius, after all.*

APPENDIX

PRIME DIRECTIVE:

THIRTY-ONE WORLD WIDE WEB SITES FOR YOUR CYBER-TREKKING PLEASURE

COMPLIED BY LEWIS WARD & JEFF GREENWALD

[Key: ST = Star Trek, TOS = The Original Series, TNG = The Next Generation]

1) **Starfleet International**
http://www.sfi.org/
Truly a World Wide Web site, it offers both depth and style.

2) **The Klingon Language Institute**
http://www.kli.org/
Shakespeare's *Macbeth* in Klingon? Sheer originality makes this a must-see.

3) **Star Trek Nexus**
http://members.aol.com/treknexus/
Ease of use and depth of content make this an exceptional site.

4) **Star Trek: Continuum**
http://www.startrek.com/default.asp
The official Paramount site offers a wealth of interactivity and info.

5) **Star Trek: WWW**
http://www.stwww.com/
An index to other sites, this is a fantastic resource for any fan.

6) **Main Engineering**
http://mainengineering.simplenet.com/
Has a slick layout, games, and current info.

7) **Holodeck 3**
http://www.holodeck3.com/
Features cool graphics, interactivity, and an extensive database.

8) **Warp Drive, When?**
http://www.lerc.nasa.gov/WWW/PAO/warp.htm
NASA is taking a look at the science fact of interstellar travel.

9) **Star Trek Universe**
http://startrek.beyoung.com/
Lots of interesting info and loads of cool audio files.

10) **Star Trek: The Next Generation**
http://www.ugcs.caltech.edu/st-tng/
If TNG is your bag, this site covers all the bases.

11) **Klingon Imperial Diplomatic Corps**
http://www.klingon.org/
If you thought Klingon culture was an oxymoron, this site might change your mind.

12) **Das Star Trek Universum**
http://aia.wu-wien.ac.at/Startrek/titelseite.html
A large German site with lots of info and pictures.

13) **The Borg Collective**
http://members.aol.com/borgqueenn/thecollective.html
A creative site loaded with graphics and info.

14) **Star Trek Italian Club**
http://www.stic.it
Italian site with a great layout and current info.

15) **Mania.com's Jeff Greenwald Interview**
http://www.mania.com/tv/features/jeffgreenwald.html
A detailed article about *Future Perfect*'s author by ace Mania reporter Michelle Green.

16) **Civilian Astronaut Corps**
http://www.mayflowerrocket.com/
This group wants to start sending tourists into space before the year 2000.

17) **Klingon Warrior Society**
http://ourworld.compuserve.com/homepages/Klingon/
More than just blood and guts, this site also features art and technology.

18) **Guide to Animated Star Trek**
http://www1.ridgecrest.ca.us/~curtdan/TREK/TAS.cgi?FILE=Main
A beautifully rich site devoted to the animated series.

19) **Starbase 17**
http://www.starbase17.com/
An exceptional site with info about everything but TOS.

20) **The Ferengi Cultural Hub**
http://freenet.buffalo.edu/~bj803/ferengi.html
A well-designed, extensive overview of the Ferengi race.

21) **Planet Star Trek Quiz**
http://www.usaweekend.com/98_issues/980712/980712planet_trek_quiz.html
Jeff Greenwald's *USA Today Star Trek* quiz, based on this very book!

22) **Borg Institute of Technology**
http://grove.ufl.edu/~locutus/Bit/bit.html
The off-beat humor alone makes it worth visiting.

23) **Starbase Kobe**
http://www.hi-ho.or.jp/sbko-hq/indexE.html
A Japanese site featuring links and current *Star Trek* news.

24) **Base Estelar Cervantes**
http://www.geocities.com/Area51/Dunes/9501/
A well-designed site for Spanish speakers in the Americas.

25) **Vulcan Information Centre**
http://www.ludwig.ucl.ac.uk/st/StarTrek/Vulcan/Vulcan.html
This British site, though visually a bit dull, offers extensive records about our pointy-eared alien cousins.

26) "Science Friday" Star Trek Dialogue
http://www.sciencefriday.com/pages/1998/Jul/hour2_072498.html
Authors Jeff Greenwald and Lawrence Krauss *(The Physics of Star Trek)* mix it up in this lively NPR interview (RealAudio available).

27) Recursos Star Trek en España
http://bbs.seker.es/~alvy/trek.es.html
A fun Spanish site with lots of current info.

28) Locutus' Assimilation Ring
http://www.geocities.com/Area51/Vault/7279/Ring.html
If you have a *Star Trek* page already, this claims to be the biggest web ring on the net.

29) Khemorex Klinzhai!
http://www.khemorex-klinzhai.de/
The German-based Klingon fan club.

30) The United Federation of Trek Sites
http://www.netten.net/~campbell/ufts/
A web ring with a positive, inclusive editorial bent.

31) The "I Hate Star Trek" Page
http://members.tripod.com/~Desslok/dietrek/trkstink.htm
True love shines through the rage.

ACKNOWLEDGMENTS

Though friends and Trekkers on five continents contributed to this book, there were a handful of people whose generosity and hospitality made *Future Perfect* possible. I'd first like to thank Rick Berman, for allowing me unusually broad access to the *First Contact* sound stages; Jeri Taylor, for her wit, warmth, and candor; and Ron and Ruby Moore, for some good conversation and great champagne. Brannon Braga, sinner and saint, supported and inspired this project from its inception. His insights proved indispensible, while his friendship and generosity made my visits to Hollywood a pleasure. Thank you, bro'.

Also at Paramount Pictures, I'm deeply grateful to Michael O'Halloran and the lovely and enterprising Karen Regan. Sincere thanks as well to Ira Steven Behr, Scherry Braga, Winrich Kolbe, Lolita Fatjo, Michael Gerbosi, Bob Gillan, Elliott Marks, Deborah McCrea, Joe Menosky, Wendy Neuss, Michael Okuda, Sandra Sena, Rick Sternbach, Eric Stillwell, Kristin Torgen, Michael Westmore, Alex Worman, and the indomitible Herman Zimmerman.

Jonathan Frakes is one helluva guy, and I thank him most sincerely for making me feel welcome on his set. Other *Star Trek* cast members who generously contributed their time to this book include Robert Beltran, Roxann Biggs-Dawson, Michael Dorn, Alice Krige, Jennifer

Lien, Gates McFadden, Kate Mulgrew, Leonard Nimoy, Tim Russ, and Patrick Stewart.

The initial inspiration for this book came from my good friend Brian O'Donoghue, during a conversation at his Rip O'Roaring Kennel in Alaska. Rob Brezsny, Dan Clurman, and Karen Finley sat down with me early on, and helped plot out some initial strategies. Many friends provided aid and insight: Brady Kahn, Joe Kane, Mary Roach, Angelika Sinner, Richard Kohn, Robin Daugherty, Jeanne Meyers, Debra Pughe, Scoop Nisker, David Rubien, Diane Summers, Leslie Roberts, Bob Attiya, Mike Rosell, Diana Wong, Alix Pitcher, Bonnie Zane, Nick Gregory, Kate Wrightson, Anne Cushman, Jen "The Eskimo" Frame, Roxy Lippel, John Krich, Ada Mei, Bob Cowart, Amy Johns, Tim Chambers, and Imke Beator. Kiloquads of thanks to Mimi and Peter Buckley, who opened their home and their hearts to a very frazzled space jockey.

Among the individuals who eased my way at home and abroad, I gratefully acknowledge Mary Anderson-Harris of Creation Entertainment, Chris Kreski, David Jacobson, Torsten Frantz, Jens Schafer, Andreas Duck, Astrid Jekat, Ralf Gebhart, Lawrence Schoen, Alberto Lisiero, Steven G. Brant, Allan Michand of the Grand Lake Theater, and to Sanjib Bhandari, Ruhee, Sanita, Sabina, and Nirja of the K@mandu Cyber Café. Portions of this book appeared previously in *Details, Wired, Wired UK, Salon,* and *American Way.* For help with those pieces I thank Tim Moss, John Battelle, Gary Kamiya, David Talbott, Scott Rosenberg, and Dana Joseph-Williams.

Many thanks to my agent, Joe "Ursa Major" Spieler, and to my tough-love editor, the brilliant—and heroically patient—Wendy Wolf.

Lastly, I owe an incalculable debt to my three terrific assistants. Lewis Ward served as my Emmisary to the Internet, making contacts and setting up meetings throughout Europe and Asia. He also collected many of the book's sidebars and assembled the appendix of *Star Trek* Web sites. Maia Hansen, starship trooper, brought her sly scrutiny to bear on the manuscript during its final stages. Though I was waxing Borgish by that point, her humor and optimism never flagged.

But my ultimate expression of gratitude goes to Lynn Rapoport, who spent a full year transcribing often incomprehensible interviews, reviewing my notes, and copyediting each new draft. Her radiant energy propelled *Future Perfect* from take-off to splashdown. Lynn: you're a star.

PERMISSIONS

Grateful acknowledgment is made for permission to reprint the following copyrighted works:

"To Boldly Go—Away" by Jennifer Weber, *The Sacramento Bee*, March 15, 1996. Copyright, The Sacramento Bee, 1996.

Excerpts from "The Science of *Star Trek*" by David Allen Batchelor. © 1993 by David Allen Batchelor.

Excerpts from *The Dilbert Future* by Scott Adams. Copyright © 1997 by United Media, Inc. Reprinted by permission of HarperCollins Publishers, Inc.

"Donde Muy Pocos Latinos Han Ido" by Frank del Olmo, *Los Angeles Times*, March 19, 1995. Copyright, 1995, Los Angeles Times. Reprinted by permission.

Excerpt from "Is *Star Trek* in Need of Affirmative Action?" by Leah Garchik, *San Francisco Chronicle*. © San Francisco Chronicle. Reprinted by permission.

"British Customs Officials Consider Mr. Spock Dolls to Be Illegal Aliens" by Dana Milbank, *The Wall Street Journal*, August 2, 1994. Reprinted by permission of The Wall Street Journal. © 1994 Dow Jones & Company, Inc. All rights reserved worldwide.

Excerpt from "Beam Me Up, Gorby!" by Leonard Nimoy. Appeared in *USA Today*, November 29, 1991. By permission of the author.

Excerpt from "Holograms Turn Traditional Candy Into Edible Art" by Laurie Ann Peach. Appeared in *Christian Science Monitor*, April 29, 1997. By permission of the author.

Excerpt from "When Aliens Start to Look a Lot Like Us" by Jon Pareles, *The New York Times*, May 26, 1996. Copyright © 1996 by The New Times Co. Reprinted by permission.

Letter from Gene Roddenberry to Arthur C. Clarke. © Estate of Eugene W. Roddenberry. Reprinted with permission. All rights reserved.

Excerpt from "Everybody's a Critic" by Lewis Ward, *The San Francisco Bay Guardian*. By permission of the author.

Poem from *Cat's Cradle* by Kurt Vonnegut, Jr. Copyright © 1963 by Kurt Vonnegut, Jr. Used by permission of Delacorte Press/Seymour Lawrence, a division of Bantam Doubleday Dell Publishing Group, Inc.

"Translating the Bible into Suitable Klingon Stirs Cosmic Debate" by Carrie Dolan, *The Wall Street Journal,* June 13, 1994. Reprinted by permission of The Wall Street Journal. © 1994 Dow Jones & Company, Inc. All rights reserved worldwide.

Correspondence from Marina Bailey to Jeff Greenwald. By permission of Marina Bailey.

"Star-Struck Trekkie Astronaut Followed Her Idol" by Mark Caro, *Chicago Tribune,* October 27, 1992. © Copyright Chicago Tribune Company. All rights reserved. Used with permission.

Excerpt from "Ask Camille," *Salon* online magazine. By permission of Camille Paglia.

Excerpt from "Now, Voyager" from *Mythomania: Fantasies, Fables, and Sheer Lies in Contemporary American Popular Art* by Bernard Welt (Art issues Press, 1996). © 1996 The Foundation for Advanced Critical Studies, Inc. Reprinted by permission.

"Lazybones (El Perezoso)" from *Selected Poems* by Pablo Neruda, translated by Alastair Reid. By permission of Jonathan Cape.

INDEX

W

X

Z

FOR THE BEST IN PAPERBACKS, LOOK FOR THE

In every corner of the world, on every subject under the sun, Penguin represents quality and variety—the very best in publishing today.

For complete information about books available from Penguin—including Puffins, Penguin Classics, and Arkana—and how to order them, write to us at the appropriate address below. Please note that for copyright reasons the selection of books varies from country to country.

In the United Kingdom: Please write to *Dept. EP, Penguin Books Ltd, Bath Road, Harmondsworth, West Drayton, Middlesex UB7 0DA.*

In the United States: Please write to *Penguin Putnam Inc., P.O. Box 12289 Dept. B, Newark, New Jersey 07101-5289* or call 1-800-788-6262.

In Canada: Please write to *Penguin Books Canada Ltd, 10 Alcorn Avenue, Suite 300, Toronto, Ontario M4V 3B2.*

In Australia: Please write to *Penguin Books Australia Ltd, P.O. Box 257, Ringwood, Victoria 3134.*

In New Zealand: Please write to *Penguin Books (NZ) Ltd, Private Bag 102902, North Shore Mail Centre, Auckland 10.*

In India: Please write to *Penguin Books India Pvt Ltd, 11 Panchsheel Shopping Centre, Panchsheel Park, New Delhi 110 017.*

In the Netherlands: Please write to *Penguin Books Netherlands bv, Postbus 3507, NL-1001 AH Amsterdam.*

In Germany: Please write to *Penguin Books Deutschland GmbH, Metzlerstrasse 26, 60594 Frankfurt am Main.*

In Spain: Please write to *Penguin Books S. A., Bravo Murillo 19, 1° B, 28015 Madrid.*

In Italy: Please write to *Penguin Italia s.r.l., Via Benedetto Croce 2, 20094 Corsico, Milano.*

In France: Please write to *Penguin France, Le Carré Wilson, 62 rue Benjamin Baillaud, 31500 Toulouse.*

In Japan: Please write to *Penguin Books Japan Ltd, Kaneko Building, 2-3-25 Koraku, Bunkyo-Ku, Tokyo 112.*

In South Africa: Please write to *Penguin Books South Africa (Pty) Ltd, Private Bag X14, Parkview, 2122 Johannesburg.*